2285 £6.95

Dependency Theory

Dependency Theory

A Critical Reassessment

Edited by
Dudley Seers

Frances Pinter (Publishers) Ltd., London

© Dudley Seers 1981

First published in Great Britain in 1981 by
Frances Pinter (Publishers) Limited
5 Dryden Street. London WC2E 9NW

reprinted 1983

ISBN 0 903804 84 0
ISBN 0 86187 327 0 (paperback)

Typeset by Donald Typesetting, Bristol
Printed and Bound by Short Run Press Ltd., Exeter.

Contents

List of Tables

Diagram

Notes on Contributors

Dudley Seers (editor) is a Professorial Fellow and former Director of the Institute of Development Studies at the University of Sussex. His previous appointments have included Director-General of the Economic Planning Staff, Ministry of Overseas Development and Senior Lecturer in Economic Statistics, University of Oxford. He has worked as consultant to several overseas governments, the World Bank, the OECD and United Nations regional commissions, and also been President of the European Association of Development Institutes. He is the author or editor of several books in the area of development studies.

Manfred Bienefeld is a Fellow of the Institute of Development Studies at the University of Sussex. He has worked in Tanzania and Portugal, and has published on various aspects of development and on British economic history. He is currently working on industrialisation strategies.

Rita Cruise O'Brien is a part-time Fellow of the Institute of Development Studies at the University of Sussex. She has worked and published numerous articles on international communication problems, and has a book on the subject forthcoming. Other publications include *White Society in Black Africa* (1972) and *The Political Economy of Underdevelopment* (1980). She is currently working on specialised information.

Zofia Dobrska is Professor at the University of Warsaw. She has taught and conducted research at universities in Tanzania and Zaire. She specialises in the theory of economic development, especially strategies of industrialisation and the choice of techniques.

David Evans is a Fellow of the Institute of Development Studies at the University of Sussex. He is currently working on issues in international political economy. His earlier work was on income distribution and the Australian tariff.

Zdzisaw Fiejka is Associate Professor and chief of the section on the economics of developing countries in the Institute of World Economy in Warsaw. He is also a part-time lecturer at the University of Warsaw. He previously served for many years with the United Nations, dealing with problems of industrialisation, employment and industrial aspects of international relations.

Geoff Lamb is at present with the Development Research Centre of the World Bank. He has worked in the Caribbean, East Africa and South Asia. He is a political scientist, currently working on development politics, institutional processes and the State.

Jan J. Milewski is at the University of Warsaw. He has worked in Nigeria, including as a member of the 1979 ILO mission on basic needs. He specialises in the modern economic history of West Africa.

Gabriel Palma is Senior Lecturer in Quantitative Economics at the North East London Polytechnic. He has taught and conducted research at universities in Chile and England, and was a member of the Executive Committee of the Chilean National Planning Office (1971-2). He has published on socialism in Chile and on dependency and development.

Luc Soete is a joint Fellow of the Institute of Development Studies and the Science Policy Research Unit at the University of Sussex. He is an economist with particular interest in industrial economics and industrial innovation. He is currently working on the international diffusion of technology.

Preface

Contacts between the Institute of Development Studies (IDS) at the University of Sussex and Polish social scientists have been growing. Discussions were held on various occasions between Richard Jolly, Director of IDS, and myself, on the one hand, and Zofa Dobrska, Zygmunt Pioro, Bogodar Winid and Piotr Zeydler-Zborowski of the University of Warsaw, on the other, about the possibility of a small and intimate conference that would enable us to get to know each other's approaches better. This eventually took place in October 1979 at Ojrzanow, outside Warsaw, thanks to the hospitality of the University of Warsaw, and in particular of the Director, Professor Zygmunt Pioro, and other colleagues from that University's Institute of Geography of Developing Countries. Colleagues from other parts of the University and from the State Commission of Planning took part, enlarging the scope of the discussion.

The following attended, apart from those whose papers are reproduced in this volume:*

> Iza Budzynska
> Jan Kieniewicz
> Marja-Liisa Kiljunen (IDS)
> Jan Kulig
> Marian Ostrowski
> Marian Paszynski
> Zygmunt Pioro
> Piotr Zeydler-Zborowski

Everyone took part in an individual capacity and the papers commit nobody but the authors.

It is impossible to give even a short summary of the long discussions held in Ojrzanow, but the papers presented here, which cover the core of the discussion, were revised subsequently. For reasons independent of the editor, not all papers prepared for the conference could be reproduced in this volume.

The topic chosen for the conference was dependency in general, but the organisers decided not to impose any specific approach on the participants. The idea was to arrange a meeting of the people working in two cooperating institutes and to give them a chance to present views arising from their own research on a question of common interest, rather than any specific subject within the field. So the volume shows a variety of approaches. Of course, it should not be considered representative of either 'British' or

---

* It may have looked like an Anglo-Polish symposium, but I was the only British subject present — IDS Fellows come from all over the world.

'Polish' schools or approaches to dependency theory. In both countries there are many other scholars working in this subject.

I would like to thank Lyn Gorman for copy-editing this volume, and members of the secretarial staff at IDS who worked on the typescript.

Dudley Seers

INTRODUCTION

Dudley Seers

The theory of dependency, or *dependencia*, has still scarcely made much impression on the social scientists of Europe or North America. This reflects our parochialism. The referencing of our professional papers reveals that not many of us even glance at journals and books published overseas. Our isolation has been somewhat mitigated by the growth since the war of centres of regional and development studies, and by increasing numbers of academic exchanges and international conferences, especially those of the professional associations. But few economists of 'the North' could even today give an authoritative assessment of the work of Raúl Prebisch, say, nor are our sociologists and political scientists much better informed about their counterparts in Brazil or Mexico. It is hard to resist the conclusion that most of us just do not care, assuming tacitly that nothing of intellectual significance is produced in the backward continents, a hangover from the colonial period.

That must be one explanation for the widespread ignorance about this Latin American school (apart of course from specialists on Latin America, mostly historians). Another is that much of the published work is naturally in Spanish. When dependency is discussed here, it is often in terms of the work of André Gunder Frank, who is not a Latin American at all, nor a representative member of the school; indeed, he disowns it himself. But he is the one writer broadly in this tradition who has had much work published in English.

This neglect of dependency theories became still less defensible after the publication of a special number of *Social and Economic Studies* in 1973 (Vol. 22, No. 1) edited by Norman Girvan, consisting of a symposium of important papers from the school, translated from the Spanish. Still, this periodical is published by the University of the West Indies, so I doubt whether many social scientists elsewhere ever saw it.

The loss is not only ours but also that of our students and policymakers, and thus the people of our countries. To justify that statement, which may seem surprising, let me go back to the context in which dependency theory emerged.

It is very much a product of a particular place and particular historical period.[1] Since the war, Latin Americans have come to see themselves as 'underdeveloped', which naturally carries implications for economic ideology. These were worked out during the 1950s in the Economic

Commission for Latin America (ECLA), led by Raúl Prebisch: the central theme there, at that time, was a fore-runner of 'dependency' theory, 'structuralism'. This was a response to the 'monetarism' of neo-classical economists which had become manifest in policies the International Monetary Fund was requiring many Latin American governments to follow.

The basic argument of the structuralists was that neither inflation nor related foreign exchange shortages were primarily due to the 'irresponsibility' of individual Finance Ministers (an explanation which is difficult to reconcile with the coincidence of the simultaneous acceleration of price rises in many different countries). They were attributable basically to supply inelasticities, in the face of widespread political pressures for development. Then the ability of those with strong bargaining power (especially monopolistic manufacturers and trade unions) to protect their real incomes propagated the primary inflation.

In an economy with deep structural problems of this kind, reflecting factor immobility, limits on the quantity of money do not bring inflation to a halt, except in a very long period and at the cost of a fall in the real incomes of those who are unorganised and a rise in unemployment to levels which are politically unacceptable. It is astonishing to see European economists groping their way to similar conclusions in the 1980s, as if their Latin American colleagues had not developed a critique of monetarism, especially the policies of the International Monetary Fund, two decades earlier.[2]

One of the tenets of the structuralist school was that the underdevelopment of Latin America was due to its reliance on exports of primary products, which were subject to terms of trade that both fluctuated in the short term and deteriorated in the long (the Prebisch-Singer thesis[3]). This was a major justification for import substitution behind tariff walls, which would, it was expected, reduce the dependence of Latin America on foreign manufactures, and thus on the industrial countries, especially the United States.

But while these policies reduced the imports of certain finished goods, such as consumer durables, they required increased imports of capital equipment, intermediate products, raw materials and fuel. They also mean greater reliance on the transnational corporations (TNCs), which provided much of the technology and capital, and indeed were a necessary source for filling the 'gap' that Prebisch showed existed between anticipated foreign exchange supplies and those needed to maintain a satisfactory pace of growth. At the same time, the priority for industrialisation led to increased imports of foods.

The realisation that import substitution created new, and possibly more dangerous, forms of dependence converted the ECLA 'structuralists' into 'dependency' theorists. They did not abandon the earlier theories but changed the emphasis and added other features. They drew on another insight of Prebisch's, that the world consisted of a 'core' of dominant nations and a 'periphery' of dependent ones. Dependence theory was also reinforced, as Gabriel Palma points out, in a review of the theories and their origins with which the book starts,[4] by the spread of Marxist critiques of imperialism.

Palma brings out the variety in the school ranging from those whose approach is basically neo-Marxist to writers who are more conventional.[5] There is, however, a common core, an emphasis on external influences that distort the process of development. Study of these influences leads to a historical approach, refreshingly unusual in the development profession. Another characteristic of writers in this broad area is that they stress political and cultural influences as well as economic. (It is an interesting anomaly that many Latin Americans who point to the dangers of cultural dependence do so by drawing on Marxism, a basically European doctrine.)

No European can fail to hear some echoes in dependency theory of our own problems. While structural rigidities are not the same as in Latin America, they are conspicuous here too — especially in countries geographically on the periphery of Europe, such as Ireland, Portugal, Spain, Yugoslavia, Greece and Turkey, but also, to some extent, Finland, Britain and Italy. Such rigidities have been evidenced, as in Latin America — though not quite so dramatically — by chronic inflation and persistent payments deficits. Moreover, these countries are increasingly dependent on the core of Europe, and all, even the most advanced, have been heavily penetrated by foreign-based TNCs.

Yet, despite the relevance of dependency theories to European problems, they have made little headway in our universities. There are other reasons, apart from our parochialism and the linguistic weaknesses already mentioned. First, an explicitly interdisciplinary school does not fit readily into the typical unidisciplinary syllabi and research programmes. Perhaps more important, its style runs counter to prevailing academic fashions. An economist, in particular, who picks up a book by a dependency theorist is likely to notice the lack of algebra. (This might even lead him to put it down straight away!) The fashionable models are mathematical, and to the greatest extent possible, quantifiable. This is understandable. It would be very convenient if only social problems could be reduced to algebraic functions: the solutions would then be straightforward. In any case, quasi-mathematical theories are easier to teach, and the student's grasp of them easier to examine: a degree in economics now guarantees a certain capacity to manipulate complicated functions, which may have something to do with 'intelligence'. (It also suggests a trained capacity for irrelevance!)

Many of the propositions of dependency theory cannot easily be cast in mathematical terms, still less are they readily quantifiable. The theory is in large part about hierarchies, institutions and attitudes. (Perhaps the most important factors, in international relations especially, are the least quantifiable.) Thus dependency theory appears to the mainstream economist (and to some extent to the traditional practitioners of other disciplines) to lack 'rigour'. It affronts the aspirations of economists to be genuine 'scientists' like their colleagues in the physical sciences. Even those who are sympathetic to the school try to reformulate and test its propositions in terms of growth rates, coefficients of concentration of income, etc., as if these were crucial variables.

Having said all that, one must admit that a great deal of writing in the dependency field is indeed of rather low professional quality.[6] The exemption properly claimed from mathematical formulation because of the qualitative and complex nature of the theory, reflecting the real world, is often taken as a licence to make speculative generalisations without any empirical base (even when some such base could well be constructed). 'Rigour' truly understood does not require the application of mathematics where it is inappropriate. Quite the contrary! But it does demand a degree of care in formulating propositions as precisely as possible (a point made by David Evans), in searching for verifiable forms, and in dealing fairly with the evidence – not, as is the shocking habit of ideologically-committed social scientists of all schools, picking out whatever evidence fits one's theories and ignoring the rest. (Almost *any* theory can be 'verified' in that way!)

Still, this book is not just another condescending European dismissal of dependency theory. It is written by people who, while they are critical of certain aspects of writings in the dependency tradition, sympathise with the general approach, value the insights it has provided, and believe it is worth much more serious study than it has received so far. We, especially Manfred Bienefeld and David Evans, point out that while the school has not yet provided answers which are as correctly framed or as universally applicable as the theorists concerned may think, it raises the right questions – much more relevant ones than those derived from neo-classical economics. Our purpose is not to praise dependency theory, but not to bury it either, rather to raise constructive criticisms that might lead to its improvement and greater acceptability.

It certainly needs developing. On the face of it, the highly dependent newly industrialising countries (NICs) like Singapore, South Korea or Brazil, should not have grown so fast for so long. They are, especially to those dependency theorists who have stressed the limits to capitalist development in the periphery, an abomination. Yet they can no longer be treated as a temporary, limited exception.[7] Manfred Bienefeld deals with this awkward question. His conclusion is that, while this experience may have overthrown some of the more simplistic formulations of dependence, the core of the theory is still intact. The success of the NICs, he argues, is due to a number of particular conditions. They have attracted foreign direct investment and loan capital at a time when United States productivity growth has been slow. He stresses the political repression which is a common feature of NIC governments, and raises questions about how adequately they represent the long-term 'national interest'.

Geoff Lamb also discusses initially the claims of neo-classical economists that NICs provide paradigms for countries starting to become industrialised. Here he uses the examples of Sri Lanka and Trinidad which have explicitly modelled their development strategies on Singapore and Puerto Rico respectively. He argues for more attention to social classes than is customary in the work of dependency theorists: what finally limits the usefulness of the NICs as a model for Sri Lanka and Trinidad is that the latter lack an indigenous capitalist class. But while the growth of the NICs is a challenge to at least the more catastrophic versions of dependency theory, they do not quite fit the Marxist theory of imperialism either, with its emphasis on common interests between the native capitalists and not only the 'patriotic intelligentsia' but also the working class and the broad peasant masses.

Jan Milewski's case study of Nigeria is more agnostic on the question of the damage done by dependence on the world capitalist economy. He shows that the roots go back some way in history, long before the colonial period and the TNCs. Capitalism has become accepted in Nigeria and a local capitalist class has emerged too; whether real economic independence can be built on it remains to be seen.

David Evans views the fundamental question at the international level as not one of periphery versus core, but of labour against capital, and in particular stresses the problems raised for the working class, especially that part of it which enjoys economic privileges. This distances him both from those whose main interest is in the capacity of the state (rather than class alliance) to reduce dependence incrementally (Prebisch, Cardoso, Sunkel, *et al.*), and those who advocate semi-autarkic solutions which he sees as facile (Frank and Amin).

My own paper poses the question: why have governments which have tried to 'delink' from the world economy been on the whole so unsuccessful — that of Allende in Chile, for example, the Portuguese Revolutionary Government, the Manley regime in Jamaica? What repercussions might be feared by a government attempting such a strategy? I argue that the body of dependency theory contains far more of relevance than neo-classical economics, but that — inconveniently for theorists of any kind, especially those of an ideological bent — characteristics such as a country's population, resource base, location, also affect the degree and nature of its dependence, as does the quality of political leadership.

Zdzisław Fiejka asks a complementary question: what hinders *international* action to redeploy industrial production towards the periphery, as part of a New International Economic Order? He discusses the opposition of the governments of capitalist countries (stressing the diversity of their interests) and the failure to use machinery created for consultation about sectoral problems. This analysis points to the increasing role of non-governmental bodies, the staffs of international agencies and the TNCs, but emphasises the lack of success so far in making the objectives of the latter consistent with broader social needs (which neo-classical economists would expect not to be a serious problem, provided monopolistic tendencies were restricted).

One of the problems about 'dependency' is that it is a portmanteau concept. The remaining papers deal with particular types of it. Rita Cruise O'Brien's paper discusses a dimension of dependency which has been rather neglected. Although much has been written about social and cultural domination of the South by the North through the media, little attention has been paid to unequal access to specialised information. But she argues for some caution in developing countries towards rather excessive claims for new technological systems, especially 'informatics', which could accentuate their dualism.

Zofia Dobrska also raises some questions about modern technology. She criticises both TNC spokesmen and socialist theorists (an unlikely alliance!) for their uncritical acceptance of this, especially in view of the current shortage of capital. Moreover, socialists should see that appropriate technology is consistent with socialist ideas. Although the search for appropriate technology is far from straightforward, there are some options.

Luc Soete's paper, also on technological dependence, is written from a rather different position. He criticises the whole concept of technological dependence with an original argument that indigenous scientific capacity is not nearly as important as the school assumes (otherwise Britain would dominate Japan and West Germany!). The very sales of technology by the main innovators undermine their position. This is supported by evidence that (like the success of the NICs) has to be assimilated somehow by dependency theorists.

A reader will see mirrored in this book the central division in the dependency school itself. While Palma calls, as Cardoso and Sunkel do, for detailed studies of specific situations before postulating models, most of the authors, following Baran, perhaps, rather than Frank, would be interested in whether an existing general theory, Marxism, developed in and for Western Europe, needs adapting to fit the realities of the Third World and if so how. Perhaps in the end the difference might not be so great as it seems, because those of us who are empirically minded would accept Manfred Bienefeld's point that we inevitably approach research with *some* framework, even if we are not aware of it. Theories however, to be relevant, will inevitably embody empirical content, and this had better be made explicit and verified, objectively, by specific case studies, rather than simply intuitively assumed.

All the essays in this book do, in fact, combine the theoretical and empirical, though with a mix that varies somewhat from author to author. I hope that readers in Western and Eastern Europe will find it helps them understand the dependency school's strengths and weaknesses, and that our Latin American colleagues will be able to make some use of this contribution to the debate they so fruitfully initiated.

Notes

1. Although people from other continents have also contributed a good deal, especially the Egyptian Samir Amin (who wrote in French).
2. A seminal work was Osvaldo Sunkel, 'La inflacion chilena: un enfoque heterodoxo', *El Trimestre Economico*, Vol XXV, No. 4, 1958, also published in English in *International Economic Papers* (London), No. 10, 1960. See also Baer and Kerstenetsky (eds.), *Inflation and Growth in Latin America*, Irwin, 1964, for a debate on IMF 'conditionality' in the context of Latin America in the early 1960s.
3. An authoritative review of the statistical sources and economic contributions on this issue by John Spraos (*Economic Journal*, March 1980) comes to the tentative conclusion that, over the seven decades to 1939, the evidence does not contradict the thesis, though the series chosen by its protagonists did exaggerate the deterioration. If the period is extended up to the 1970s, the deterioration is open to doubt, even if petroleum is excluded.
4. A revised and extended version of his paper, 'Dependency: A Formal Theory of Underdevelopment or a Methodology for the Analysis of Concrete Situations of Underdevelopment?', *World Development*, Vol. 6, No. 7/8, 1978, pp. 881-924.
5. Another review of the main writers, which concentrates on tests made of the school's propositions, can be found in Steven Jackson, Bruce Russell, Duncan Snidal and David Sylvan, 'An Assessment of Empirical Research on Dependencia', *Latin American Research Review*, Vol XIV, No. 3, 1979.
6. One example, out of hundreds that could be quoted (and this comes from a book with many useful insights):

   In this way and given the economic superiority of foreign capital and the enormous political forces of the hegemonic centre, inside each one of the dependent countries structurally founded relations are being generated between the national bourgeoisie of the hegemonic centre, in such a way that the system of internal domination shows the loss of identity of the national monopolistic bourgeoisie, whose interests are becoming identified to a growing extent with the interests of big international capital.

   Sergio Ramos Cordova, *Chile: Una Economia de Transicion?*, (Prize Essay), Casa de las Americas, Havana, 1972, p. 85. Extract translated by Dudley Seers.
7. It is the continued fast pace of Brazilian economic growth that has recently somewhat discredited dependency theory in Latin America itself, although only the most simplistic, catastrophic versions of the theory have really been overthrown. After all, Latin America still shows dependent relationships in many fields that shape its development (or lack of development), in some respects more so than ever.

1 DEPENDENCY AND DEVELOPMENT: A CRITICAL OVERVIEW[1]

Gabriel Palma

May one talk of a 'theory of dependency'? If so, what general implications does it have for contemporary development strategy? Do we find under the 'dependency' label theories of such a diverse nature that it would be more appropriate to speak of a 'school of dependency'? Is it even correct to describe as theories the different approaches within that school? And if so, what general implications might each one have for contemporary development strategy?

Some writers within the dependency school argue that it is misleading to look at dependency as a formal theory, and that no *general* implications for development can be abstracted from its analyses. Some of those who argue that there is such a theory flatly assert that it leads inescapably to the conclusion that development is impossible within the world capitalist system, thus making development strategies irrelevant, at least within that system. Others, on the other hand, who speak in terms of a theory of dependency, argue that it *can* be operationalised into a practical development strategy for dependent countries.

If the problem of extracting direct lessons from the dependency analyses is a difficult one, it is no less difficult to survey what has been a diffuse and at times contradictory movement, inextricably a part of the recent history of Latin America itself, of individual nations, and of the post-war development of international capitalism, and drawing its inspiration from such diverse intellectual traditions as the long and involved Marxist debate concerning the development of capitalism in backward nations, and the post-1948 ECLA critique of the conventional theory of international trade and economic development.

The complex roots of the dependency analyses and the variety of intellectual traditions on which they draw make any attempt at a comprehensive survey difficult. The difficulty is further compounded by the fact that in one way or another the dependency perspective has so dominated work in the social sciences in Latin America and elsewhere in recent years that it would be literally impossible to review the overwhelming mass of writing that has appeared, aimed at either supporting or refuting its major theses, or simply reflecting its sudden ascendancy in academic and institutional circles hitherto relatively closed to radical critiques of current orthodoxy. Added to this is the fact that in one way or another those who have contributed to the dependency school have been directly and actively involved in the major political struggles and controversies of post-war Latin America.

Not only has this left an indelible mark on their own work, but it has often led their opponents to cloud the issues by carrying the debate to purely ideological terrain, thus adding to the confusion surrounding the dependency analysis itself by promoting an increasingly sterile discussion with little thorough consideration of its theoretical and historical roots.

I believe that previous surveys of dependency writings have in particular failed to clarify sufficiently its roots in the tradition of Marxist thought on the development of capitalism in backward nations, thus giving rise to a great deal of misunderstanding. I have therefore attempted particularly to place it within this tradition. Marxism is a highly complex subject, and its contribution to the analysis of capitalist development in backward nations is no less so. At the same time, it is precisely in this area of Marxist thought that we find the widest divergencies between the writings of Marx and Engels and those of many contemporary Marxists. Without doubt, the attitude of some Marxist writers today that capitalist industrialisation in the periphery is no longer feasible goes against the spirit and the letter of Marx's writings. Nevertheless, as a general rule, we do not find in them an effort to explain these divergencies; but on the contrary, their writings give the impression that Marxist interest in the problems of capitalist development in peripheral countries and areas of the world only began in 1957, with the publication of Baran's *The Political Economy of Growth*.

In this context, what is important, as Sutcliffe has argued, is to ask whether the differences are attributable to changes in 'circumstance or diagnosis' (1972 a, p. 180). That is to say whether capitalism has been transformed in such a way that the industrialisation of the periphery cannot take place within the capitalist system, or whether it is that Marx's analysis is itself over-optimistic regarding the possibilities of industrialisation in the backward areas of the world.

I distinguish three principal phases in the development of Marxist thought concerning the problems of capitalist development in backward countries and areas of the world. The first, essentially that of Marx and Engels, analyses capitalism as an historically progressive system, which will be transmitted from the advanced countries (through colonialism, free trade, etc.) and which will spread through the backward nations by a continual process of destruction and replacement of pre-capitalist structures. As a result of this process a series of new capitalist societies would arise, whose development would be similar, in the post-colonial period, to that of the advanced countries themselves; this, then, would be followed by the development of the series of contradictions proper to the capitalist system, which would tend to lead them to a higher stage of development.

The second approach to the development of capitalism in backward nations, found primarily in the writings of the so-called 'classics of imperialism', concerns itself, first, with the peculiarities of the development of Russian capitalism, and afterwards with that of other backward areas of the world in the 'monopolistic' phase of the world capitalist system. As regards the development of Russian capitalism, its historically progressive character is stressed, but this development is no longer analysed simply as a process of destruction and replacement of its pre-capitalist structures, but as a far more complex process of interplay between internal and external structures. These analyses stress the difficulties resulting from 'late' industrialisation, the ambiguous role of foreign capital (from Western Europe), and the great capacity for survival of pre-capitalist structures. As regards capitalist development in other backward areas of the world, we may distinguish two major historical stages in the analyses of the 'classics of imperialism'. The first is characterised by its analysis (following Marx) of capitalist development in the colonies as historically progressive, but (qualifying Marx's analysis) limited by the new imperatives of the advanced economies in their monopoly phase. Faced with these imperatives the advanced nations were, in the view of these writers, succeeding in restricting modern industrialisation in the colonies. Nevertheless, they stress that once the colonial bonds are broken modern industrialisation could eventually take place. Thus the capitalist development of backward nations would take on a similar character to that of the advanced nations. At the same time they insisted that this process of post-colonial industrialisation would in no way be free from political and economic difficulties and contradictions; on the contrary, the emerging national bourgeoisie would face the difficult, but by no means impossible, task of developing their own bourgeois revolutions, and the no less difficult but equally possible task of 'late' industrialisation.

It was only in the twenties that a second approach began to emerge as emphasis was placed on a different set of difficulties (particularly of a political nature) hindering the process of post-colonial industrialisation.

The third approach was first developed at the end of the fifties, and 'took off' with the publication of the already mentioned work of Baran; it is characterised by the acceptance, almost as an axiomatic truth, of the argument that no Third World country can now expect to break out of a state of economic dependency and advance to an economic position beside the major capitalist industrial powers. This is a very important proposition since it not only establishes the extent to which capitalism remains historically progressive in the modern world, but also thereby defines the economic background to political action. Yet, too often, the question is ill-defined; it is not self-evident; its intellectual origins are obscure; and its actual foundations are in need of a fuller analysis. It is in this third phase that the analyses of the dependency school emerge.

I complement this analysis with a discussion of the other major source of inspiration behind dependency, the ECLA (United Nations Economic Commission for Latin America) school and the attempts to reformulate its thinking which followed the apparent failure of ECLA-inspired policies of import-substituting industrialisation.

I distinguish three approaches within the dependency school, and conclude that the most successful analyses are those which resist the temptation to build a formal theory, and focus on 'concrete situations of dependency'. I have stressed that the contribution of dependency has been up to now more a critique of development strategies in general than an attempt to make practical contributions to them.

Marx and Engles on the development of capitalism in backward nations

It is not easy to analyse Marx's and Engels' approach to the development of capitalism in the backward regions of the world, as their remarks on the subject are scattered throughout their respective works. In Marx's case, although the analysis of the capitalist mode of production in *Capital* is of profound and systematic brilliance, his specific references to the concrete forms in which this mode of production is developed in backward regions are not found there, but in various of his other works. Of relevance among his political writings is the *Communist Manifesto* (1848); among his theoretical writings, the preface of *A Contribution to the Critique of Political Economy* (1859); among his correspondence, that with his contacts among the Russian left; and among his articles to newspapers, those in the *New York Daily Tribune* between 1853 and 1859. Unfortunately, his concrete references are almost all concerned with India and China, with only superficial references made to Latin America. This is unfortunate not only because we are ourselves interested in Latin America, but more significantly because the subcontinent would have provided Marx with a backward region already developing in a way which would be typical of post-colonial societies in later years, with the exception of those of European settlement. While formally free, the countries of Latin America were economically backward and dependent.

In a letter written in the closing years of his life, Marx stressed that in *Capital* he had studied only the genesis of capitalism in Western Europe (Marx, 1877, p.253). Nevertheless, it is from that same work that we can deduce with clarity his analysis of the tendencies which would guide the expansion of the capitalist economies towards the backward regions of the world. The most relevant chapters are those concerning primary accumulation (1867, Ch.XXIV) and foreign trade (1894, Ch.XIV).

The central element behind the need of the advanced capitalist economies to expand is the need to develop an effective means of countering the tendency for the rate of profit to fall; such expansion makes it possible to expand the scale of production, to lower the costs of raw materials and of the products needed to maintain and reproduce the labour force at home (making it possible to keep wages low), and thus to increase the surplus by helping to preserve the low organic composition of capital. Furthermore, for a period the capitalist in an advanced country can gain a higher rate of profits by selling 'in competition with commodity producers in other countries with lesser facilities for production . . . in the same way that a manufacturer exploits a new invention before it has become general' (1894, Section 5).[2]

Nevertheless, Marx did not confine himself to the analysis of the driving forces which lead to the expansion of capitalism. In his analysis of the effect of this upon the backward regions, following the Hegelian tradition, *he distinguishes between the subjective motivations for this expansion and its objective historical results*. On the one hand, he condemns this expansion as the most brutalising and dehumanising that history has ever known, but, on the other, he argues that it is necessary if the backward societies are to develop. Only capitalism, he argues, can provide the necessary economic and technological infrastructure which will enable society to allow for the free development of every member according to his capacity; and capitalism can only develop in them through its penetration and imposition from abroad. Only on the basis of this dialectical understanding of capitalism can we understand the famous affirmation in the preface to the first edition of *Capital* that 'the backward country suffers not only from the development of capitalist production, but also from the incompleteness of that development' (1867, p.xiv).

In general terms we may say that *it is analytically convenient* to distinguish two intimately connected levels in Marx's analysis of the development of capitalism in backward nations. One relates to the *necessity* (both political and economic) of capitalism as an essential step towards higher forms of development of productive forces, the other to the *possibility and viability* (both political and economic) of its development. These two levels of analysis are present in the Marxist tradition with differing degrees of emphasis. In Marx's writings on the subject the central concern is with the necessity for capitalist development, with its feasibility taken completely for granted. In the present day however the emphasis is placed more on the second level of analysis, that of the feasibility of capitalist development in the periphery.[3]

As regards the first aspect, the necessity of capitalist development, Marx states very clearly, at least until the important change which comes towards the end of his life, that socialism can only be attained through capitalist development, and that this will not be produced in the backward regions of the world by the development of their own productive forces, as was the case in Western Europe, but by the impact upon them of the capitalism of Western Europe itself.

Marx is overtly hostile to the modes of production in existence in non-European societies, chiefly on the grounds of their unchanging nature, which he saw as a drag on the process of history, and thus a serious threat to socialism. This led him, while condemning the brutality and hypocrisy of colonialism, to regard it as historically necessary.

Initially, in the *Communist Manifesto* Marx and Engels appear to refer to the backward nations *en masse* as 'barbarians', 'semi-barbarians', 'nations of peasants', and 'the East', in a manner which contrasts strikingly with their meticulous study of European society and history, and is particularly unsatisfactory in a work which makes the strongest possible claim to be based upon a universally applicable scientific interpretation of history. However, eleven years later, in the preface to *A Contribution to the Critique of Political Economy*, Marx made a more serious attempt to relate the socio-economic conditions of the non-European world to his general theory of history, but he did so elliptically, and in a way that has bedevilled Marxism ever since. Discussing the stages of economic development, he strongly brings out the dialectical tensions inherent in every period, saying, in a passage that has become classic:

> No social order ever disappears before all the productive forces for which there is room in it have been developed; and new, higher relations of production never appear before the material conditions of their existence have matured in the womb of the old society (1859, p.21).

Proceeding to analyse the four modes of production, Asiatic, Ancient, Feudal and Capitalist, he leaves the Asiatic mode in a form which is difficult to understand. There is a clear perception of a kind of continuity (its movement produced by the development of contradictions) between the Ancient, Feudal, Capitalist and Socialist modes of production, but the Asiatic mode is left disconnected, as if it had neither past nor future.[4]

If Marx never directly discusses this problem he does so indirectly, stressing time and again that it should not be forgotten that the horizon of his work on the discussion of historical development is essentially European. In a letter written to a Russian Socialist journal in 1877 he warns his readers not to

> metamorphose (his) historical sketch of the genesis of capital in Western Europe into a historical-philosophical theory of the general path every people is fated to tread, whatever the historical circumstances in which it finds itself,

and goes on to criticise any approach which seeks to understand history 'by using as one's master-key a general historical-philosophical theory, the supreme virtue of which consists in being supra-historical'.

The problem of the Asiatic mode of production is not merely the academic one of establishing how far Marx's theory of history is consistent and universal; it is that as it does not possess a dialectic of internal development *it can only evolve through the penetration of European capitalism*. For this reason Marx analyses European expansion in India as brutal, but 'a necessary step towards Socialism' (1853). Such an expansion would have a destabilising and disintegrating effect on the Asiatic mode of production, re-stabilising and re-integrating such societies in a capitalist mode of development which would bring with it the development of productive forces and generate an internal dynamic which would lead such societies towards higher stages of development.

It is essential to note here that Marx makes no distinction between endogenous capitalist development (such as occurred in Western Europe) and that which is introduced from outside. Irrespective of its origins, capitalism once implanted in a society will develop in a certain way. If one of its central characteristics is to develop both objective wealth and poverty, this would exist within each society, rather than between societies.

Only fleetingly in the case of China and with much greater clarity, towards the end of his life, in the case of Russia, does Marx recognise the possibility that different traditional structures could be capable of serving as a starting-point for movement towards more advanced stages of development; in the first case he speaks ironically of the possibility of a bourgeois revolution, in the second of a socialist revolution.

In February 1850 there was a wave of agrarian unrest in China, and Marx wrote:

> when our European reactionaries, on their next flight through Asia will have finally reached the Chinese Wall, the gates that lead to the seat of primeval reaction and conservatism — who knows, perhaps they will read the following inscription on the Wall: 'République Chinoise — Liberté, Egalité, Fraternité! (quoted in Averini, 1976, p.251).

Regarding the Russian case, in reply to a letter from the Russian Marxist, Vera Sassoulitch, in February 1881 (to which we shall return later) Marx stresses the possibility that the particular traditional agrarian structures of Russia could serve as a starting-point for socialist development. He reaffirms this point of view together with Engels, in the preface to a new Russian edition of the *Communist Manifesto* in 1882.[5]

Passing now to the analysis of Marx's attitude regarding the possibility of capitalist development in the non-European world, it must be stated that Marx leaves no room for misinterpretation; the dynamism and capacity for expansion of the youthful capitalism of his period would be reproduced in any society which it penetrated; furthermore, he seemed to expect a proliferation of autonomous capitalist societies, fundamentally similar to those in Western Europe. There are three particular excerpts which have become obligatory points of reference, and to which we need refer only briefly. In the *Communist Manifesto* Marx and Engels argue that the development of capitalism in Western Europe will 'compel all nations, on point of extinction, to adopt the bourgeois mode of production'. Five years later, in his article on the *Future Results of British Rule in India* (1853), Marx argues that English imperialism will not be able to avoid the industrialisation of India: 'when you have once introduced machinery into the locomotion of a country which possess iron and coals *you are unable* to withhold it from its fabrications' (the emphasis is mine). Finally, fourteen years later, in the preface to the first edition of *Capital* we find this famous statement: 'the country that is more developed industrially only shows, to the less developed, the image of its own future'.

We may then conclude, with Kiernan, that 'so far as can be seen, what he (Marx) had in mind was not a further spread of Western imperialism, but a proliferation of autonomous capitalism, such as he expected in India and did witness in North. America' (1967, p.183). As was stated in the introduction, there is no question that the attitude of some Marxist writers today that capitalist industrialisation in the periphery is no longer feasible goes against the spirit and the letter of Marx's writings. Throughout the analysis I shall attempt to establish whether the divergencies are attribu-table to changes in circumstance or diagnosis.

From Marx and Engels to the 'classics of imperialism'

If Hilferding (1910) had already provided an important Marxist study of imperialism, it is in Luxemburg (1913), Bukharin (1915) and Lenin (1916) that we find the most important contributions from the period in which capitalism was moving through its monopoly phase. I shall refer only briefly to the works of Luxemburg and Bukharin; as regards Lenin's work, I shall concentrate on those aspects which are most relevant to the issues under discussion.

Rosa Luxemburg's *The Accumulation of Capital* (1913) was the first Marxist analysis of the world capitalist economy in the light of the three concerns outlined earlier in this paper, and remains among the most com-plete; it is certainly the only one of the classic writings on imperialism which sets out to provide a systematic analysis of the effect which imper-ialism would have on the backward countries. Unfortunately, the rigour, profundity and creativity of the analysis are limited by the fact that, following the Marxist tradition of the period, she underestimates both the increase in real wages which takes place as capitalism develops in the advanced countries, and the internal inducement to invest provided by technological progress. Consequently she overplays and misunderstands the role of the periphery in the process of accumulation of capital in the developed countries, for these two factors have played a vital role in rescu-ing capitalism from the difficulties and contradictions which it creates for itself. Thus the periphery has played a role both qualitatively different and quantitatively less important than that which her analysis depicts.[6]

Nikolai Ivanovitch Bukharin contributed to the analysis of imperialism principally in his works of 1915 and 1926. In the first he analyses the two most important tendencies in the world economy of the time, tendencies which were made manifest jointly and in contradiction to each other. These were the rapid process of internationalisation of economic life (the integra-tion of the different national economies into a world economy) and the process of 'nationalisation' of capital (the withdrawing of the interests of the national bourgeoisies within their respective frontiers). The most interesting feature of the second work is its polemic against Luxemburg's *The Accumulation of Capital*. From the point of view of our interest, it is unfortunate that although Bukharin stresses continually throughout the course of his work that imperialism is a phenomenon which connects the advanced and the backward economies, and criticises Luxemburg's view on the subject, in no part of his work does he analyse in concrete terms the effect of imperialism upon the backward countries.[7]

When one is analysing Lenin's work it is particularly important to bear in mind (as with the work of any political leader who is not writing for purely academic reasons, but with specific and concrete political ends in view), the political context in which the works were written. In fact it is necessary not only to consider the usual problems concerning the separation of 'history' and 'concept', 'theory' and 'practice', and the 'role' of ideology, but also to be aware that the relative emphases in these works are frequently functions of tactical moves related to factional disputes.[8] Furthermore, in the case of Lenin's *Imperialism, The Highest Stage of Capitalism* (1916) he himself was careful to point out that he wrote it 'with an eye to the Tsarist censorship . . . with extreme caution, by hints, in an allegorical language' (1916, p.1). The political situation within which and as a contribution to which Lenin wrote his analysis of imperialism was characterised by the outbreak of World War I and the subsequent collapse of the Second International.

Within a week of Austria's declaration of war on Serbia on 28 July 1914, the whole of Europe was at war. Lenin himself arrived in Switzerland on 5 September after a long odyssey, and set himself up in Berne. He was faced with a difficult double task: firstly, to explain to the international socialist movement the nature of the forces which had unleashed the war, and secondly, to account for the position adopted by the working class parties of the advanced capitalist countries (which had led to the collapse of the Second International). If for the first of these tasks he could avail himself of the analysis provided by Marx of the tendencies of capitalist development, and the later contributions of Marxists such as Hilferding, for the second he could draw on no previous analyses. Traditional Marxist analysis could not be applied simply and directly to explain why the proletariat of the advanced capitalist countries in general, and the social-democratic parties of the left in particular, had placed themselves alongside their respective bourgeoisies and against one another when the war broke out.[9]

It was no easy task to explain the capacity, unforeseen by Marx, of capitalism to extend to important sectors of the working classes some of the benefits of its development; nor was it simple to derive the relevant political conclusions. This would in fact be the most important contribution of *Imperialism, The Highest Stage of Capitalism*, and would make it Lenin's most important theoretical work, just as the *Development of Capitalism in Russia* (1899) is his most important study of the development of capitalism in a backward nation, and is in my view the pioneering classic of dependency studies.

To prepare himself for his difficult task Lenin re-read Marx and Hegel with great care, and produced his *Philosophical Notebook* (1915) as a result. In it he stresses the necessity to understand Hegel's logic (and to give due importance to the subjective element of the dialectic) in order to understand the development of capitalism in advanced countries. After this, now settled in Zurich, he wrote, between January and July 1916, his own study of imperialism, emphasising in the 1917 preface to the Russian edition and the 1920 prefaces to the French and German editions the dual political purpose I have mentioned above. He thus makes it clear that his purpose in writing the work is different from that of Bukharin or Luxemburg.[10]

For analytical purposes we may distinguish three major themes in Lenin's work.[11] The first is the description of the most important political and economic changes in the advanced countries of the capitalist system, the second, the analysis of the changes in international relations which had resulted, and particularly the role played by international capital, and the third, the discussion of the future tendencies of the capitalist system in its monopoly or imperialist phase, and above all the effect these would have on its historical progressiveness. There is no systematic analysis of the effect that this phase of the development of capitalism will have on the backward regions of the world (the third concern to which I referred earlier). However, as we shall see later, it is possible to deduce from the analysis of the development of capitalism in the advanced countries in the system an implicit account of the effects it will tend to have in those backward regions. Nevertheless, in order to understand this implicit account it is necessary to go back seventeen years to the *Development of Capitalism in Russia*, which is intimately connected with the analysis in the later work.[12]

Lenin's 'Development of Capitalism in Russia'

Within the Marxist tradition it is in Lenin's work that we find the first systematic attempt to provide a concrete analysis of the development of capitalism in a backward nation. In his analysis he

> formulated with simplicity what would be the core of the dependency analyses: the forms of articulation between the two parts of a single mode of production, and the subordination of one mode of production to another (Cardoso, 1974a, p.325).

In this work then, we find a detailed and profound study of the forms in which developing capitalism in Russia is articulated both to the economies of Western Europe and to the other existing modes of production in Russia itself. That is to say, the way in which Russia — its classes, state and economy — is articulated to the corresponding elements in the countries of Western Europe. The essay was written as part of a profound controversy in Russia itself regarding the necessity and the feasibility of capitalist development there. Discussion of this is particularly relevant, as it was in the context of an identical controversy in Latin America in the 1950s and 1960s that the contribution to dependency studies was made.

Given that Russia was the first backward country in which Marxism developed, it is not surprising that it should have been the setting for the first Marxist debates regarding the feasibility of capitalist development, and as I have stated, Lenin's *Development of Capitalism in Russia* was part of this debate and of his constant polemic with the Narodniks.[13]

The central argument of the Narodniks was that capitalist development was not necessary for the attainment of socialism in Russia, and that from an economic point of view it was by no means clear that capitalism was a viable system for a backward country such as Russia. They laid great stress upon the problems created by 'late' entry into the process of capitalist industrialisation. They were convinced that the Russian peasant commune[14] with its system of communal ownership was essentially socialist, and capable of forming the basis of a future socialist order; hence Russia might indeed lead the rest of Europe on the road to socialism.

From what Marx and Engels had written before they became interested in the Russian case it is possible to deduce *a priori* their disagreement with the Narodniks. It was a central point of their analysis that the peasantry, fundamentally on account of its feudal origins, was a backward element in European society in relation to the capitalist bourgeoisie and, *a fortiori*, in relation to the proletariat. Wherever capitalism was advanced, the peasantry was a decadent class.[15] On this account, it is placed in the *Communist Manifesto* alongside a number of petty bourgeois groups, as Marx and Engels speak of 'the small manufacturers, the shopkeepers, the artisan and the peasant ...'. Only when the bourgeoisie and the proletariat, together or apart, are incapable of carrying out the bourgeois revolution and the overthrow of feudalism would it be permissible to support the peasantry and its political organisations, let alone to fight for its interest in individual ownership of the land.

At the end of the 1860s, attracted by the development of the left in Russia, Marx and Engels learnt Russian and threw themselves into the current debates there. In 1875 Engels was stressing the necessity for capitalist development, though less as a necessity of an absolute nature than as a result of the fact that the Russian system of communal property was already decadent. For this reason it was impossible to 'leap over' the capitalist stage through the transformation of the communal institutions of the feudal past into the fundamental bases of the socialist future. On the other hand, he argued, the triumph of the socialist revolution in the advanced capitalist countries would help Russia itself to advance rapidly towards socialism (see Carr, Vol.2, 1966, p.385).

Two years later Marx entered the debate with the letter discussed above. In it he expresses a position similar to that of Engels, arguing that the possibility that a different transition to socialism might take place in Russia no longer appeared to exist:

If Russia continues on the path which she has been following since 1861 (the emancipation of the serfs) she will be deprived of the finest chance ever offered by history to a nation of avoiding all the ups and downs of the capitalist order.

In the following year a group of young Narodniks led by Plekhanov broke with the rest and headed for Switzerland; their differences were both political and theoretical, in that they opposed the use of terrorism and embraced the spirit and letter of the *Communist Manifesto*. Nevertheless, they came to adopt positions 'more Marxist than those of Marx himself', and in 1881 Vera Sassoulitch wrote to Marx seeking a clarification of his views regarding the peasant commune. After composing three long drafts, which are among his papers, he contented himself with a brief response. His analysis of *Capital*, he stated, was based upon conditions in Western Europe, where communal property had long since disappeared; this analysis was by no means mechanically applicable to Russia, where such forms of property still survived in peasant communes. Nevertheless, for these to serve as a starting-point for a 'socialist regeneration of Russia' they would require a series of conditions which allowed them to develop freely. Nowhere in his reply does Marx express any doubt that capitalist development is possible in Russia; his argument is that perhaps given the specificity of the Russian situation the price of capitalist development in human terms would be too high for it to be counted as a progressive development.[16]

Regarding the other facet of the controversy with the Narodniks, that of the possibility of capitalist development in Russia, it is in the writings of the Narodniks that it is first suggested that capitalism may not be viable in a backward nation. Thus the Narodnik writer Vorontsov argued that 'the more belated is the process of industrialization, the more difficult it is to carry it on along the capitalist lines' (quoted in Walicki, 1969, p.121). For the Narodniks, furthermore, 'backwardness provided an advantage in that the technological benefits of modern capitalism could be used, while its structure is rejected' (Sutcliffe, 1974a, p.182).

For these reasons then, for the Narodniks it was not only possible but economically imperative to escape from the capitalist stage and move directly towards socialism. This same position will be found, as we shall see, in the 1960s in Latin America in the writings of one group of dependency writers.

In the last decade of the nineteenth century, along with the first industrial strikes in Russia, there appeared a number of Marxist groups, while the Narodniks, caught in the blind alley of terrorism, were beginning to lose influence. One of these was the 'League of Struggle for the Liberation of the Working Class', which appeared in Petrograd in 1895; among its members was a disciple of Plekhanov, who wrote successively under the pseudonyms of 'Petrov', 'Frei' and 'Lenin', the latter after 1902. The young

Lenin entered vigorously into the debate with the Narodniks, writing his major contribution towards it, the *Development of Capitalism in Russia*, between 1896 and 1899.

Lenin agreed with the Narodniks only in one respect — that capitalism was a brutalising and degrading economic system. Nevertheless, like Marx, he distinguished clearly between this aspect of capitalism and the historical role which it played in Russia:

> Recognition of the progressiveness of capitalism is quite compatible . . . with the full recognition of its negative and dark sides . . . with the full recognition of the profound and all around social contradictions which are inevitably inherent in capitalism, and which reveal the historically transient nature of this economic regime. *It is the Narodniks who exert every effort to show that an admission of the historically progressive nature of capitalism means an apology for capitalism . . . .* The progressive historical role of capitalism may be summed up in two brief propositions: increase in the productive forces of social labour, and the socialization of that labour (1899, pp.602-3). (The emphasis is mine.)

Their differences were not only at a theoretical level however; for Lenin the Narodniks were in error over basic matters of fact. Lenin shows, after a long and detailed study of the labour market in Russia, that capitalism was already developing rapidly, and that it should already be considered as essentially a capitalist country, although 'very backward as compared with other capitalist countries in her economic development' (1899, p.507).

Furthermore, regarding the 'obstacles' to the development of capitalism in Russia identified by the Narodniks, such as unemployment and under-employment, he states that these are the *characteristics* of capitalist development, and that the Narodniks are guilty of transforming 'the basic conditions for the development of capitalism into proof that capitalism is impossible' (1899, pp.589-90).

For Lenin what was indispensable was the profound study of why the development of capitalism in Russia, while rapid in relation to development in the pre-capitalist period, was slow in comparison to the development of other capitalist nations. It is in his approach to this question that, in my opinion, we find his most important contribution to the study of the development of capitalism in backward nations.

His analysis of the slowness of capitalist development in Russia (which some dependency writers would still insist on describing as 'the development of Russian underdevelopment') has three inter-related themes: (i) the weakness of the Russian bourgeoisie as an agent for the furthering of capitalist development; (ii) the effect of competition from Western Europe in slowing the growth of modern industry in Russia; and (iii) the great and unexpected capacity for survival of the traditional structures of Russian society.

Regarding the weakness of the Russian bourgeoisie, Lenin was taking up a theme already discussed by the Russian left.[17] The interesting feature of his analysis is that he relates this weakness to the ambiguous role played by foreign capital (from Western Europe) in the development of Russian capitalism. On the one hand, it accelerates the process of industrialisation, while, on the other, it lies behind the weak and dependent nature of the small Russian bourgeoisie.

In what he says in relation to the second factor which explains the slower pace of Russian capitalist development, Lenin stresses that as Russia was industrialising 'late' the development of its modern industry had to compete not only with the production of traditional industry (as the first countries to industrialise had had to do) but also with the far more efficient industrial production of advanced countries within the capitalist system.

Finally, Lenin places great emphasis and explanatory value upon the great capacity for survival of traditional structures in Russia:

> In no single capitalist country has there been such an abundant survival of ancient institutions that are incompatible with capitalism, producers who (quoting Marx) 'suffer not only from the development of capitalist production, but also from the incompleteness of that development' (1899, p.607).

An important aspect of Lenin's analysis of the survival of traditional structures (and one that is particularly relevant to the present situation in backward nations) is his treatment of the interconnections which develop between the different modes of production which existed in Russia: 'the facts utterly refute the view widespread here in Russia that "factory" and "handicraft" industry are isolated from one another. On the contrary, such a division is purely artificial' (1899, p.547). Lenin's view of capitalist development in Russia can be summarised as follows: (i) in conformity with the central tradition of classical Marxist analysis he sees it as politically necessary and economically feasible; (ii) through a concrete analysis he shows that its development is fully underway; (iii) the development of capitalism in backward nations is seen for the first time not simply as a process of destruction and replacement of pre-capitalist structures, but as a more complex process of interplay between internal and external structures; in this interplay, the traditional structures play an important role, and their replacement will be slower and more difficult than previously supposed; and (iv) despite the complexity of Russian capitalist development, both it and the bourgeois revolution which would accompany it would eventually develop and become relatively similar to that of Western Europe. (The development of capitalism in Russia would therefore be a kind of 'slow-motion replay' of the same development in Western Europe.)

I shall now examine the relationship between this analysis of Russian capitalism and Lenin's theory of imperialism.

The later development of Lenin's thought regarding the development of capitalism in backward nations

The two historical events which had a profound influence upon the future development of Lenin's thought in all its aspects were the revolution of 1905 and the collapse of the Second International. If the second of these showed that it was by no means clear that the development of capitalism led necessarily and 'inevitably' to socialism, the first had shown the concrete possibility of interrupting capitalist development, avoiding its potential risks, and transferring to the proletariat the task of completing the democratic-bourgeois revolution.

The collapse of the Second International showed that as it developed, capitalism also created an unforeseen capacity to assimilate important sectors of the proletariat, and that therefore the development of its internal contradictions would take a more complex path than had hitherto been realised.

Marx had emphasised that capitalist development was condemned by its own nature to resolve its difficulties and contradictions through transformations which would necessarily lead to the creation of others even greater. Nevertheless, there seemed to be one aspect of capitalist development which at least in the medium term was acting in the opposite direction: rising real wages. These, essentially a result of the organisation and struggle of the working class, played a crucial role in the development of capitalism, both from the point of view of its political stability, and of the increase in effective demand, so essential for the realisation of surplus value.

In explaining both this capacity of capitalism to increase real wages much more than had been foreseen, and the political effect which it had upon the working class in the advanced capitalist countries, Lenin placed great emphasis upon the 'superprofits of imperialist exploitation' (1916, p.9). Not long afterwards, Henry Ford, following the analysis already proposed by Hobson (1902, 1911), stated:

> If we can distribute high wages, then that money is going to be spent and it will serve to make storekeepers and distributors and manufacturers in other lines more prosperous and this prosperity will be reflected in our sales. Country-wide high wages spell country-wide prosperity (1922, p.124).

Kalecki (1933, 1934, 1935) and Keynes (1936) would later incorporate this insight into a new theoretical conceptualisation of the development of capitalism; two years later, Harold Macmillan would refer as follows to the enormous political importance of extending to the working class some of the material benefits of capitalist development:

> Democracy can live only so long as it is able to cope satisfactorily with the problems of social life. While it is able to deal with these problems,

and secure for its people the satisfaction of their reasonable demands, it will retain the vigorous support sufficient for its defence (1938, p.375; quoted in Kay, 1975, p.174).

In this context it is important to recall that although Marx's expectations regarding the standard of living of the working class under capitalism are not entirely clear, it seems evident that he did not expect an increase of the magnitude which eventually occurred. It emerged later that capitalism was going to provide rising real wages at a rate relatively similar to the rhythm of its development but only after a considerable 'time-lag' (see Hicks, 1969, pp.148-59). In 1923, in what would be his last article, Lenin wrote:

> but the Western European countries are not completing this development (towards socialism) as we previously expected they would. They are completing it not through a steady 'maturing' of socialism, but through the exploitation of some states by others (quoted in Foster-Carter, 1974, p.67).

The train of history was not going to drop its passengers off at the station of their choice, socialism, unless they took charge of it at an earlier stage. The contribution of the events of 1905 in Russia was precisely that it showed that it was possible, though by no means necessarily economically feasible.

From 1905 onwards, first in Trotsky and Parvus and later in Lenin, there began a change of position regarding the necessity of continuing with capitalist development. As we saw earlier, Marx had stated that no social order would disappear before having developed all the productive forces it could contain, and that higher relationships of production would not appear until the old order had run its full course. The events of 1905 showed both the limitations of the development of capitalism in Russia and the concrete possibility of interrupting it, transferring to the proletariat the task of completing the democratic-bourgeois revolution. Nevertheless, Engels had argued that for this to happen there would have to be a revolution in Western Europe. Russia could play the role of the weakest link in the capitalist chain, and with the help of more developed socialist societies could follow the path towards socialism more rapidly. Therefore, the socialist revolution could begin in a country such as Russia, but it could not be completed there.[18]

However, the events of 1905 not only showed Lenin and the Bolsheviks the path to follow; they also showed Nicolas II and his brilliant Minister, Stolypin, the need to embark upon a rapid process of social, economic and political restructuring if revolution was to be avoided. Of the transformations which they initiated Lenin said: 'our reactionaries are distinguished by the extreme clarity of their class consciousness. They know very well what they want, where they are going, and on what forces they can count' (quoted in Conquest, 1972, p.61).

By this time Lenin's attitude towards the necessity for capitalist development was different than it had been in 1899. Should the policies of
Stolypin succeed, and Russia enter definitively onto the capitalist path,
the revolution would have to be postponed for a long time. As early as
1908 Lenin saw the dangers of Stolypin's policies:

> The Stolypin constitution and the Stolypin agrarian policy mark a new
> phase in the breakdown of the old semi-patriarchal and semi-feudal
> system of Tsarism, a new movement towards its transformation into a
> middle-class monarchy . . . . It would be empty and stupid democratic
> (sic) phrase-mongering to say that the success of such a policy is 'impos-
> sible' in Russia. It is possible! If Stolypin's policy continues, Russia's
> agrarian structure will become completely bourgeois (quoted in Laclau,
> 1972, p.69, my translation).

The events of the subsequent period, which ended with the assumption
of power by the Bolsheviks in October 1917, are the subject of one of the
great controversies of modern history. On the one hand, the policies
initiated by Stolypin showed clearly that Lenin's analysis of the potential
of capitalist development was correct; during that period Russia enjoyed a
considerable industrial boom; and by 1917 the peasants were owners of
more than three-quarters of Russian farmland. Perhaps it was factors such
as these which led Lenin to conclude a lecture given in Zurich on 9 January
1917, only months before he was to come to power, with the words 'we
of the old generation will perhaps not live to see the decisive battles of our
own revolution' (1917, p.158, my translation).[19] But, on the other hand,
it was precisely that industrial boom which strengthened the left in general
and the Bolsheviks in particular. As the Mensheviks exercised political
control over the older proletariat, the Bolsheviks needed a new proletariat
to strengthen them — the industrial boom supplied them with it.

This already lengthy analysis can be pursued no further here. I have
tried to extract from it its most important contributions to the debate
which would later develop concerning the development of capitalism in
other backward nations.

Russia then had a series of characteristics in common with countries
which would later attempt capitalist development, such as those related
to 'late' industrialisation, and to the leading role played by foreign capitalism and technology, and those linked to the emergence of a social class
structure somewhat different from that resulting from capitalist development in Western Europe, and more complex in its composition, with a
relatively weak and dependent bourgeoisie, a small but strong proletariat,
and a relatively large 'sub-proletariat' which is its potential ally.[20]

Equally however, there are also significant differences: Russia was never
the colony of a Western European power; late industrialisation is not always
the same if it occurs at different stages of development of the world
capitalist system; and as Lenin demonstrates brilliantly for the Russian

case, the particular features of the development of capitalism in any backward region will depend significantly on the characteristics of the pre-capitalist mode of production. In the case of Latin America for example, if there were countries (such as Brazil, Mexico, Chile and Argentina) which were attempting to industrialise in the same period as industrialisation was taking place in Russia, the social formations of those countries, inherited from Portuguese and Spanish colonisation, were very different from those of Russia itself.[21] In any case, while it is clear that the analyses of Lenin and his contemporaries cannot be applied mechanically to the development of capitalism in other periods and in other backward regions of the world, it remains true that in Lenin's analysis especially we find the essential road to follow; this is the study of the concrete forms of articulation between the capitalist sectors of the backward nations and the advanced nations in the system, and of the concrete forms taken by the subordination of pre-capitalist forms of production to the former, and to the rest of the system. It is essentially the study of the dynamic of the backward nations as a synthesis of the general determinants of the capitalist system (external factors) and the specific determinants of each (internal factors).

But if neither Lenin, Bukharin nor Luxemburg studied the concrete development of capitalism in other backward regions of the world, it is possible to derive from their analyses of imperialism the 'general determinants of the capitalist system' or the 'external factors' as they are generally labelled, which those regions will confront in their attempts to pursue capitalist development. These are essentially the driving forces which impelled the advanced capitalist countries towards the domination and control of the backward regions of the world: the specific determinants, or 'internal factors' as they are generally called, will depend upon the characteristics of the particular backward societies.

The driving forces behind the economic expansion of the advanced capitalist countries are identified, with differences of emphasis in each analysis, in the financial and in the productive spheres. The two are intimately connected, and are the result of a single process of transformation in the advanced capitalist countries. The financial driving forces are related to the need to find new opportunities for investment, due to the fact that their own economies are incapable of generating them at the same rate as they generate capital; those of the productive sphere are related to the necessity of ensuring a supply of raw materials, and continued markets for manufactured products. Thus it is that Bukharin and Preobrazhensky define imperialism as 'the policy of conquest which financial capital pursues in the struggle for markets, for the sources of raw material, and for places in which capital can be invested' (1919, p.155).

The result of this would be a tendency towards a greater integration of the world economy, a considerable degree of capital movement, and an international division of labour which would restrict the growth of backward economies to the production of mineral and agricultural primary products. For these primary products to be supplied cheaply, the labour force in the backward countries would have to be kept at subsistence level.

As a result of the effects of the expansion of the advanced capitalist economies as they enter the monopoly phase of their development, the economies of the backward countries will tend to be characterised by increasing indebtedness and by a productive structure which leads them to consume what they do not produce, and to produce what they do not consume. The fundamental characteristics of the development of such economies will obviously depend upon the particular characteristics of the export sectors they develop, and the terms on which they exchange products and obtain capital.

If these relationships were shaped within a colonial context, they would clearly be unequal, and therefore for the colonial nation the possibilities of development would be very restricted. If they were shaped within a post-colonial context, the possibilities of development would depend upon the capacity of the national bourgeoisies and other dominant groups to establish a more favourable relationship with the advanced countries in the system, or upon their capacity to transform the economic structure of their respective countries, in an effort to develop through a different type of integration into the world economy.

We may summarise the classical writers' conception of what capitalist development in the backward regions of the world would tend to be as follows: imperialism would tend to hinder industrial development, but once the colonial bonds had been broken the backward countries would be able to develop their economies in a different way, and eventually to industrialise. This industrialisation, given its 'late' start and probably with the presence of foreign capital and technology, would face problems and contradictions, but as in the Russian case, these would not be insuperable. In the words of Rosa Luxemburg:

> the imperialist phase of capital accumulation . . . comprises the industrialisation, and capitalist emancipation of the hinterland . . . (bourgeois) revolution is an essential for the process of capitalist emancipation. The backward communities must shed their obsolete political organisations, and create a modern State machinery adapted to the purpose of capitalist production (quoted in O'Brien, 1975, p.16).

This description of the role of capitalism in the colonies clearly differs from that of Marx and Engels, as it refers to different stages of capitalist development in the advanced countries. Discussing their writings, I showed how for them the Asiatic mode of production was characterised by its lack of internal tensions, which bestowed upon it an unchanging nature. The penetration of capitalism from abroad would therefore perform the task of 'awakening' them. It follows directly that the concrete forms which the process would adopt would necessarily depend upon the type of capitalism involved.

Marx expected that the process which began with the development of railways in India would necessarily end with the placing of that country on the path towards industrialisation. For the classical writers on imperialism, on the other hand, while capitalism continued to be progressive in the backward nations of the world, it was precisely its progressiveness which would create contradictions with the needs of monopoly capitalism in the advanced countries; within a colonial context the imperialist countries can and will hinder the industrialisation of the colonies. Once the colonial bonds are broken the incipient national bourgeoisies can proceed with the development which was hindered by the colonial bonds, completing the bourgeois revolution and attempting to industrialise. These writers did not of course mean to suggest in any way that such attempts at post-colonial industrialisation would be free of problems and contradictions: they felt that, as in the Russian case, such countries would be able to overcome such problems and industrialise. Should that prove to be the case, there would appear in the post-colonial period new capitalist societies relatively similar to those in Western Europe (as in the United States and her regions of European settlement).

Nevertheless, the political independence of the backward nations has not been followed by development, contrary to the expectations of the authors I have been discussing. Even more, *in the case of Latin America it is precisely in the post-colonial period* that the development of individual nations (with the due economic and political variations) has taken upon itself the articulation with the advanced capitalist countries which the classical writers on imperialism noted in the colonies – the growth of their productive sectors concentrated on primary products, whether mineral or agricultural; the limited degree of industrialisation; and financial dependence.

From imperialism to dependency

Only around 1920 did a new vision of capitalist development in the backward nations begin to be developed within Marxist thought (see Lenin, 1920). It would be formulated explicitly at the Sixth Congress of the Communist International (the Comintern) in 1928. This approach differs from that which preceded it in that in its analysis it gives more importance to the role played by the traditional dominant classes of the backward countries (generally termed oligarchies). The power of these élites was seen to be in contradiction with the transformations of internal structures which would necessarily be brought about by capitalist development in general and industrialisation in particular (the 'bourgeois revolution'). There would therefore exist objective conditions for alliances between these groups and imperialism, destined to avoid such transformations.

In the 1928 Congress then, Kusinen introduced new 'Theses on the Revolutionary Movement in Colonial and Semicolonial Countries' (Degras,

1960, pp.526-48). In them he argues that

> the progressive consequences of capitalism, on the contrary, are not to be seen there (despite the increase in foreign investment). When the dominant imperialist power needs social support in the colonies it makes an alliance first and foremost with the dominant classes of the old pre-capitalist system, the feudal-type commercial and moneylending bourgeoisie (sic), against the majority of the people.

In my opinion this Congress may be considered the turning point in the Marxist approach to the concrete possibilities of the historical progressiveness of capitalism in backward countries. From this point onwards, the emphasis will be placed not only on the obstacles which imperialism can and does impose on the process of industrialisation during the colonial period (obstacles which could be overcome once the colonial bonds had been broken), nor simply on the obstacles to any process of industrialisation which starts late (the technological gap, the ambiguous role of foreign capital, and so on), which could be overcome, as had been demonstrated during the Stolypin period in Russia; now the historical progressiveness of capitalism in the backward regions of the world — in the colonial *and* post-colonial periods — is analysed as being limited by the previously mentioned alliance between imperialism and traditional élites, the so-called 'feudal-imperialist alliance'.

As the process of industrialisation in the backward countries was seen in contradiction not only with imperialism, but also with some internally dominant groups, the ability of the incipient national bourgeoisies to develop it in the post-colonial phase would depend upon their political capacity to assert themselves over that alliance, and to impede the adoption of such policies as, for example, those of free trade which it sought to impose.

This double contradiction in capitalist development in Latin America (particularly in the process of industrialisation) which would tend to be transformed into a single contradiction through the alliance of the groups in question, figures prominently in the political and economic analysis of large sectors of the Latin American left (including the Communist parties of the sub-continent), right into the 1960s.[22] Furthermore, it seems to have had an influence (albeit naturally an unacknowledged one) upon the ECLA analysis of the obstacles facing Latin American development, as we shall see later; the attempt to go beyond the terms of this analysis would be the common starting-point of the different approaches that I shall distinguish within the dependency school.

On this analysis then, the major enemy was identified as imperialism (in one way or another the omnipresent explanation of every social and ideological process that occurred), and the principal target in the struggle was unmistakable: North American imperialism. The allied camp, on the same analysis, was also clear: everyone, minus those internal groups allied with that imperialism (and in particular those groups linked to the traditional export sector). Thus the anti-imperialist struggle was at the same time the struggle for industrialisation. The local state and national bourgeoisie appears as the potential agent for the development of the capitalist economy, which in turn was looked upon as a necessary stage. The popular fronts would draw on this analysis both of the historical role which capitalism should play in Latin America, and of the obstacles which it would find in its path.

This simple analysis of Latin American capitalist development would be maintained by the majority of Latin American left-wing groups until the time of the Cuban Revolution (1959). The discrepancies which originally existed between the guerrilla movement and the old Cuban Communist Party (the Partido Socialista Popular) regarding the character which that revolution should assume are well known, with the former arguing for an immediate transition to socialism,[23] the latter for the process previously analysed, which was traditionally sought in Latin America.

The Second Declaration of Havana (1962) and the declarations and resolutions of the first conference of OLAS (the Latin American Solidarity Organisation) of 1967 left no doubt regarding the path which was chosen: the democratic and anti-imperialist revolution which the continent required could only take a socialist form:

> The so-called Latin American bourgeoisie, because of its origins and because of its economic connections and even kinship-links with landowners, forms a part of the oligarchies which rule our America and is in consequence incapable of acting independently . . . . It would be absurd to suppose that . . . the so-called Latin American bourgeoisie is capable of developing a political line independent . . . of imperialism, in defence of the interest and aspiration of the nation. The contradiction within which it is objectively trapped is, by its nature, inescapable (quoted in Booth, 1975, pp.65-6).

It is precisely within this framework, and with the explicit motive of developing theoretically and documenting empirically this new form of analysis of the Latin American revolution that Frank enters the scene, initially with his article in the *Monthly Review* (1966) and later in a more elaborated form in his well-known study of the development (or underdevelopment) of Chile and Brazil (1967).

In this way Frank was to initiate one of the most important lines of analysis within the dependency school. At the same time, both within and outside ECLA,[24] there began the development of the other two major approaches which I shall distinguish in this type of analysis of Latin American development.

The dependency analysis

The general field of study of the dependency analyses is the development of peripheral capitalism. Its most important characteristic is its attempt to analyse it from the point of view of the interplay between internal and external structures. Nevertheless, we find this interplay analysed in different ways.

The majority of the survey articles which have been written regarding these analyses tend to distinguish between three major approaches within them. The first is that of those who do not accept the possibility of capitalist development in the periphery, but only of the 'development of underdevelopment'; the second, of those who concentrate upon the obstacles which confront capitalist development in those countries (particularly market constrictions); and the third, of those who accept the possibility of capitalist development in the periphery, placing the emphasis upon the subservient forms which it adopts with respect to capitalism of the centre.

While I accept that this classification is adequate from a certain perspective, I feel that on a more profound analysis it is less than satisfactory. In my opinion, the differences which divide dependency analyses go further than discrepancies regarding simply the possibility of development within a capitalist context in the backward areas of the world.

For my part (and with the necessary degree of simplification which every classification of intellectual tendencies entails) I shall distinguish three major approaches — not mutually exclusive from the point of view of intellectual history — in dependency analyses. The first is that begun by Frank and continued by the 'CESO School' (CESO being the Centro de Estudios Sociales of the Universidad de Chile), and in particular by dos Santos, Marini, Caputo and Pizarro, with contributions by Hinkelammert, of CEREN (Centro de Estudios de la Realidad Nacional of the Universidad Catolica de Chile). Its essential characteristic is that it attempts to construct a 'theory of underdevelopment' in which the dependent character of the peripheral economies is the hub on which the whole analysis of under-development turns: the dependent character of these economies would trace certain processes causally linked to its underdevelopment. The second approach, found principally in Sunkel and Furtado, is that characterised by the attempt to reformulate the ECLA analyses of development from the perspective of a critique of the obstacles to 'national development'. This attempt at reformulation is not a simple process of adding new elements (both political and social) which were lacking in the ECLA analysis, but a thoroughgoing attempt to proceed beyond that analysis, adopting an increasingly different perspective. Finally, I distinguish that approach which deliberately attempts not to develop a mechanico-formal theory of dependency, by concentrating its analysis on what have been called 'concrete situations of dependency'. In the words of Cardoso:

The question which we should ask ourselves is why, it being obvious that the capitalist economy tends towards a growing internationalization, that societies are divided into antagonistic classes, and that the particular is to a certain extent conditioned by the general, with these premises we have not gone beyond the partial — and therefore abstract in the Marxist sense[25] — characterization of the Latin American situation and historical process (Cardoso, 1974, pp.326, 327).

What would be needed therefore is the study of the concrete forms in which dependent relationships develop; that is to say, the specific forms in which the economies and politics of peripheral nations are articulated with those of the advanced nations.

It is not that this approach does not recognise the need for a theory of capitalist development in the different parts of the periphery, but that (in part as a reaction to the excessive theorising in a vacuum characteristic of other analyses of dependency) it places greater emphasis upon the analysis of concrete situations. The theoretical reasoning which can be developed at present concerning capitalist development in backward nations is strictly limited by the lack of case studies; the need at the moment is for 'analytic' rather than 'synthetic' work.

That is, without a considerable number of concrete studies any new theory which may be elaborated concerning capitalist development in the periphery will necessarily fall into the trap of the 'dialectic of thought', which consists of the working out upon itself of an abstract dialectic, starting from previously constructed concepts.

Dependency as a theory of underdevelopment. There is no doubt that the 'father' of this approach is Paul Baran. His principal contribution to the general literature on development (Baran 1957) continues the central line of Marxist thought regarding the contradictory character of the needs of imperialism and the process of industrialisation and general economic development of the backward nations.[26] Thus he affirms at the outset that 'what is decisive is that economic development in underdeveloped countries is profoundly inimical to the dominant interests in the advanced capitalist countries' (1957, p.28).

To avoid such development the advanced nations will form alliances with pre-capitalistic domestic élites (who will also be adversely affected by the transformations of capitalist development), intended to inhibit such transformations. In this way the advanced nations would have easy access to domestic resources and thus be able to maintain traditional modes of surplus extraction. Within this context the possibilities of economic growth in dependent countries would be extremely limited; the surplus they generated would be expropriated in large part by foreign capital, and otherwise squandered on luxury consumption by traditional élites. Furthermore, not only would resources destined for investment thereby be drastically reduced, but so would their internal multiplying effect, as capital goods would have to be purchased abroad. This process would necessarily lead to economic stagnation, and the only way out would be political.

Starting out with this analysis Frank attempts to develop the thesis that the only political solution is a revolution of an immediately socialist character; for within the context of the capitalist system there could be no alternative to underdevelopment (Frank, 1967).

For the purpose of this analysis we may distinguish three levels in Frank's 'model of underdevelopment'. The first is that in which he attempts to demonstrate that areas in the periphery have been incorporated into the world economy since the early stages of their colonial periods. The second is that in which he attempts to show that such incorporation into the world economy has transformed the countries in question immediately and necessarily into capitalist economies. Finally, there is a third level, in which Frank tries to prove that the integration of these supposedly capitalist economies into the world economy is necessarily achieved through an interminable metropolis–satellite chain, in which the surplus generated at each stage is successively drawn off towards the centre. On account of this he develops a subsidiary thesis:

> If it is satellite status which generates underdevelopment, then a weaker or lesser degree of metropolis–satellite relations may generate less deep structural underdevelopment and/or allow for more possibility of local development (Frank, 1967, p.11).

But as the weakening of the satellite–metropolis network can, according to Frank, *only take place* for reasons external to the satellite economies, of a necessarily transient nature, it follows that there is no real possibility of sustained development within the system.[27] According to this analysis, the only alternative becomes that of breaking completely with the metropolis–satellite network through socialist revolution or continuing to 'underdevelop' within it.

In my opinion, the value of Frank's analysis is his critique of the supposedly dual structure of peripheral societies.[28] Frank shows clearly that the different sectors of the economies in question are and have been since very early in their colonial history linked closely to the world economy. Moreover, he has correctly emphasised that this connection has not automatically brought about capitalist economic development, such as optimistic models (derived from Adam Smith) would have predicted, by means of which the development of trade and the division of labour inevitably would bring about economic development. Nevertheless, Frank's error (shared by the whole tradition of which he is part, including Sweezy and Wallerstein among the better known) lies in his attempt to explain this phenomenon using the same economic determinist framework of the model he purports to transcend; in fact, he merely turns it upside-down: the development of the 'core' necessarily requires the underdevelopment of the 'periphery'. Thus he criticises both the alternative proposed by the traditional Latin American left (the possibility of a democratic bourgeois revolution, because in this context the only political solution is a revolution of an immediately socialist character), and the policies put forward by ECLA.

Nevertheless, his critique is not directed towards the real weaknesses in the analysis made by the Latin American left — the mechanical determination of internal by external structures; on the contrary, he strengthens that mechanical determination in his attempt to construct a model to explain the mechanisms through which the expropriation of the surplus takes place. Probably still unduly influenced by his training as an economist at the University of Chicago, he constructs a mechanico-formal model which is no more than a set of equations of general equilibrium (static and unhistorical), in which the extraction of the surplus takes place through a series of satellite–metropolis relationships, through which the surplus generated at each stage is syphoned off.

It is not surprising that his method leads Frank to displace class relations from the centre of his analysis of economic development and underdevelopment. Thus he develops a circular concept of capitalism; although it is evident that capitalism is a system where production for profit via exchange predominates, the opposite is not necessarily true: the existence of production for profits in the market is not necessarily a signal of capitalist production. For Frank, this is a *sufficient* condition for the existence of capitalist relations of production. Thus for Frank, the problem of the origins of capitalism (and therefore the origins of the development of the few and the underdevelopment of the majority) comes down to the origins of the expanding world market *and not to the emergence of a system of free wage labour.*

Although Frank did not go very far in his analysis of the capitalist system as a whole, its origins and development, Immanuel Wallerstein tackled this tremendous challenge in his remarkable book, *The Modern World System: Capitalist Agriculture and the Origins of the European World-Economy in the Sixteenth Century* (1974a).

Frank has reaffirmed his ideas in a series of articles published jointly in 1969; a year later he sought to enrich his analysis with the introduction of some elements of Latin American class structure (Frank, 1970).

Frank has been criticised from all sides, and on almost every point in his analysis.[29] Prominent among his critics is Laclau (1971), who provides an excellent synthesis of Frank's theoretical model, and shows that the only way in which Frank can 'demonstrate' that all the periphery is capitalist and has been since the colonial period is by using the concept of capitalism in a sense which is erroneous from a Marxist point of view, and useless for his central proposition, that of showing that a bourgeois revolution in the periphery is impossible. As regards this point then, Laclau concludes that Frank makes no contribution, leaving the analysis exactly where it started.[30]

Robert Brenner (1977) takes Laclau's analysis of Frank (as well as Dobb's critique of Sweezy), and demonstrates how the work of Sweezy, Frank and Wallerstein — brilliantly summarised and analysed by him — is doomed to negate the model put forward first by Adam Smith in *The Wealth of Nations*, Book 1, but

> because they have failed ... to discard the underlying individualistic-mechanist presuppositions of this model, they have ended up by erecting an alternative theory of capitalist development which is, in its central aspects, the mirror image of the 'progressist' thesis they wish to surpass. Thus, very much like those they criticize, they conceive of (changing) class relations as emerging more or less directly from the (changing) requirements for the generation of surplus and development of production, under the pressures and opportunities engendered by a growing world market. Only, whereas their opponents tend to see such market-determined processes (the development of trade and the division of labour), as setting off, automatically, a dynamic of economic development, they see them as enforcing the rise of economic backwardness. As result, they fail to take into account either the way in which class structures, once established, will in fact determine the course of economic development or underdevelopment over an entire epoch, or the way in which these class structures themselves emerge: as the outcome of class struggles whose results are incomprehensible in terms merely of market forces (Brenner, 1977, p.27).

Thus the way in which Frank uses the concepts 'development' and 'underdevelopment' seems incorrect from a Marxist point of view; furthermore, they do not seem useful for demonstrating what Frank attempts to demonstrate. But as this critique can also be applied to other authors who adopt the same approach I shall reserve discussion on this point to later. To summarise, Frank's direct contribution to our understanding of the process of Latin American development is largely limited to his critique of dualist models for Latin America.[31] Nevertheless, his indirect contribution is considerable. By this I mean that his work has inspired a significant quantity of research by others (whether to support or rebut his arguments), in their respective disciplines, particularly in the sociology of development.

The central line of Frank's thought regarding the 'development of underdevelopment' is continued, though from a critical point of view, by the Brazilian sociologist Theotonio dos Santos,[32] for whom

> the process under consideration (Latin American development) rather than being one of satellization as Frank believes, is a case of the formation of a certain type of internal structures conditioned by international relationships of dependence' (1969, p.80).

Dos Santos distinguishes different types of relations of dependency (essentially colonial, industrial–financial and industrial–technological, the latter having grown up since World War II), and consequently distinguishes different kinds of internal structures generated by them. Dos Santos emphasises the differences and discontinuities between the different types of dependency and between the internal structures which result from them, while Frank himself stresses the continuity and similarity of dependency relations in a capitalist context. In other words, while Frank wishes to emphasise the similarities between economic structures in the times of Cortez, Pizarro, Clive and Rhodes, and between those and the structures typified by the activity of multinational corporations, dos Santos is more concerned with the differences and discontinuities between them.

There is within dos Santos's analysis the beginnings of an interesting attempt to break with the concept of a mechanical determination of internal by external structures which dominated the traditional analysis of the left in Latin America, and which particularly characterised Frank's work. One finds initially in his analysis the perception not only that both structures are contradictory, but that movement is produced precisely through the dynamic of the contradictions between the two. Nevertheless, as he proceeds in the analysis he re-establishes, little by little, the priority of external over internal structures, separating almost metaphysically the two sides of the opposition — the internal and the external — and losing the notion of movement through the dynamic of the contradictions between these structures. The analysis which begins to emerge is again one typified by 'antecedent causation and inert consequences'. The culmination of this process is his well known *formal definition of dependency, which because of its formal nature is both static and unhistorical*; it is found in his 1970 article in the *American Economic Review*:

> Dependence is a conditioning situation in which the economies of one group of countries are conditioned by the development and expansion of others. A relationship of interdependence between two or more economies or between such economies and the world trading system becomes a dependent relationship when some countries can expand through self-impulsion while others, being in a dependent position, can only expand as a reflection of the dominant countries, which may have positive or negative effects on their immediate development (1970, pp.289-90).

A further analysis along the same lines of Frank's 'accumulation of backwardness' and the 'development of underdevelopment' is that of Rui Mauro Marini (1972b). His work, which is fundamentally an attempt to develop a far more sophisticated model than that of Frank or dos Santos, can be summarised as primarily an attempt to apply Luxemburg's schema (1913) to the Latin American situation.[33]

Finally, Caputo and Pizarro (1974) and Hinkelammert (1970a, b, c) have made contributions to this approach to the study of dependency from this same perspective of the 'development of underdevelopment'.

This type of approach has inspired an unending stream of works, mostly theoretical,[34] the most thorough going critiques of this type of 'theory of underdevelopment', in addition to that of Laclau and Brenner already discussed, have come from Cardoso (1974), Lall (1975) and Weisskopf (1976).

Lall (1975) offers an interesting critique of a number of dependency studies.[35] He argues that the characteristics to which underdevelopment in dependent countries is generally attributed are not exclusive to these economies, but are also found in so-called 'non-dependent' economies, and that therefore they are properly speaking characteristics of capitalist development in general and not necessarily only of dependent capitalism. He further argues that such analyses are not surprisingly unable to show causal relationships between these characteristics and underdevelopment.

Thomas Weisskopf (1976) takes Lall's analysis as a starting-point and provides empirical data to substantiate it.[36] The most systematic critique is that of Cardoso, who argues that these 'theories' are based on five interconnected erroneous theses concerning capitalist development in Latin America. These are: (i) that capitalist development in Latin America is impossible; (ii) that dependent capitalism is based on the extensive exploitation of labour and tied to the necessity of underpaying labour; (iii) that local bourgeoisies no longer exist as an active social force; (iv) that penetration by multinational firms leads local states to pursue an expansionist policy that is typically 'sub-imperialist'; and (v) that the political path of the sub-continent is at the crossroads, with the only conceivable options being socialism or fascism.

After rejecting one by one these erroneous theses upon which this line of analysis of dependency is based, and showing that they have been developed in order to support one another, Cardoso argues that in the case of Brazil the writers in question have in fact identified some of the *conditions* which give capitalist development its *specificity*. He shows, in his own words that some 'pieces of the puzzle are the same, but the way they go together . . . is different' (1973, p.21).

For my part (see Palma, forthcoming), I would argue, following Cardoso's analysis, that these theories of dependency are mistaken not only because they do not 'fit the facts', but also — and more importantly — because *their mechanico-formal nature renders them both static and unhistorical*.

The central nucleus around which the analysis of these dependency writers is organised is that capitalism, in a context of dependency, loses its historical progressive character, and can only generate underdevelopment.[37] In this respect, I would argue that though it is not difficult to see that the specific forms of development adopted by capitalism in dependent countries are different from those of advanced countries (this development is marked by a series of specific economic, political and social contradictions — many of which have been correctly identified by these writers and these contradictions appear to have become sharper with the passage of time), to leap from that assertion to the claim that for that reason capitalism has lost, or never even had, a historically progressive role in Latin America, is to take a leap into the dark. We need only recall Lenin's critique to the Narodniks: their contemporaries are equally 'wrong in their facts'; for example, in my own analysis of the Chilean case (which covers the period from 1910 to 1970) I have shown that Lenin's criteria for assessing the progressiveness of capitalism — increase in the productive forces of social labour and in the socialisation of that labour — were both met during the period under study.

Now, if the argument is that such processes have been manifested differently than in other capitalist countries, particularly those of the centre, or in diverse ways in the different branches of the Chilean economy, or that they have generated inequality at regional levels and in the distribution of income, have been accompanied by such phenomena as underemployment and unemployment, and have benefited the élite almost exclusively, or again that they have taken on a cyclical nature, then it does no more than affirm that the development of capitalism in Latin America, as everywhere else and at all times, has been characterised by its contradictory and exploitative nature. *The specificity of capitalist development in Latin America stems precisely from the particular ways in which these contradictions have been manifested, and the different ways in which many Latin American countries have faced and temporarily overcome them, the ways in which this process has created further contradictions, and so on.* It is through this process that the *specific dynamic* of capitalist development in different Latin American countries has been generated. In this connection we should recall that the whole of Lenin's analysis of the development of capitalism in Russia was a detailed study of the specific ways in which capitalism there temporarily overcame its contradictions, and that he *criticised the Narodniks for transforming those contradictions into a proof that capitalism was impossible in Russia, and for failing to understand that the same contradictions were the very ones which were basic to capitalist development, and which took specific forms in Russia.*

I would also argue here that the form in which the concepts 'capitalist development' and 'capitalist underdevelopment' are used by these dependency writers does not seem adequate.[38] (I now take up the point discussed earlier.)

Capitalist development is essentially a process of capital accumulation which produces as it evolves modifications in the composition of the productive forces, in resource allocation, in class relations, and in the character of the state; that is, which produces as it evolves modifications in the different structures of society. Whether the cyclical nature of capital accumulation or the modifications and contradictions which this accumulation produces are or are not 'desirable' or 'optimal' is another question entirely.

To deny, as the 'contemporary Narodniks' do, that capitalist development is taking place in some countries in Latin America and in some parts of the rest of the periphery is no less than absurd. To recognise it, on the other hand, as Lenin told the Narodniks, is quite compatible with the full recognition of the negative side of capitalism, and in no way an apology for it.

If one agrees with Cardoso (1976, p.1) that the standard that one has to use to assess the analytical adequacy, the interpretative and predictive capacity and the creative strength of new explanatory schema in the social sciences is *the sensitivity with which they detect new social processes and the precision with which they are able to explain mechanisms of social reproduction and modes of social transformation*, one should agree that the dependency analyses which have attempted to construct a formal theory of underdevelopment are of relatively low standard; they have been unable to meet these requirements in their study of the economic development and political domination of the peripheral nations.[39]

Dependency as a reformulation of the ECLA analysis of Latin American development. Towards the middle of the 1960s the ECLA analyses were overtaken by a gradual decline, in which many factors intervened. The statistics relating to Latin American development in the period after the Korean War presented a gloomy picture (see Booth, 1975, pp.62-4) which was interpreted in different ways as indicating the failure of the policies ECLA had been proposing since its foundation. Furthermore, the first attempts to introduce into the traditional ECLA analysis a number of 'social aspects' (Prebisch, 1963), far from strengthening the analysis, revealed its fragility (see Cardoso, 1977, p.32).

One of the results of the relative decline in the influence of ECLA's analyses was the emergence of an attempt to reformulate its thought. Before this can be discussed, a brief review of the ECLA analyses themselves will be necessary.[40]

ECLA itself attempted to reformulate the conventional theory of economic development, just as Keynesianism had set out to do with the central body of conventional economic theory.[41] Baran (1957, p.24) summarises Keynes's contribution as demonstrating that strong tendencies towards instability, economic stagnation and chronic underutilisation of resources, both human and material, are intrinsic to the market economy. For Keynes these are only 'tendencies', for he always stresses that they can be managed if the adequate counteracting measures are taken. That is, if individual and anonymous decisions tend to produce a series of disequilibria (with consequences as serious as the depression of the 1930s), they can be avoided by the collective decisions of individuals through the state (Keynes, 1932, p.318). In this way Keynes was opposed not only to the conception of the 'harmony of unregulated classical liberal capitalism', but also to the traditional Marxist view that the growing and cumulative contradictions of capitalism would necessarily become unmanageable in the end. The Keynesian tradition did not only emphasise the need for corrective state intervention in the economy, but also introduced into conventional economic analysis a series of variables previously considered 'exogenous' or 'irrational', such as income distribution, the interests of individuals, groups and nations, and market imperfections.[42]

That the ECLA analyses should have drawn their inspiration from Keynesianism in no way denies their originality; this lay in the way in which they applied the Keynesian analysis to the Latin American situation, and to the theory of economic development, to which the Keynesian tradition had hitherto paid little attention. The ECLA analysis produced the first major Latin American contribution to the social sciences, and furthermore went beyond the merely theoretical level to make concrete policy proposals on the basis of their theoretical work.

The nucleus of the ECLA analysis was the critique of the conventional theory of international trade (as expressed in the Hecksher–Ohlin–Samuelson model of Ricardo's theory of international trade); it aimed to show that the international division of labour which conventional theory claimed was 'naturally' produced by world trade was of much greater benefit to the centre (where manufacturing production is concentrated) than to the periphery (which was destined to produce primary products, be they agricultural or mineral). The analysis by ECLA has a unity and an internal coherence which is not always perceptible at first sight, as its component parts are scattered through numerous documents published over a period of years. Several contributions had their origins in the examination of specific problems, around which a series of theoretical arguments were articulated, in an attempt to isolate their causes and to justify the economic policy measures recommended to resolve them.

The key to the internal unity of ECLA thought lies in its early postulation of the original ideas and hypotheses around which its subsequent contributions would be organised. The starting point was the idea that the world economy was composed of two poles, the 'centre' and the 'periphery', and that *the structures of production* in each differed substantially. That of the centre was seen as *homogeneous and diversified*, that of the periphery, in contrast, as *heterogeneous and specialised*; heterogeneous because economic activities with significant differences as to productivity existed side by side, with the two extremes provided by an export sector with relatively high productivity of labour, and a subsistence agriculture in which it was particularly low; specialised because the export sector would tend to be concentrated upon a few primary products, with production characteristically confined to an 'enclave' within the peripheral economic structure, or, in other words, having very limited backward and forward linkage effects with the rest of the economy. It was this structural difference between the two types of economy which lay behind the different function of each pole in the international division of labour, and this in turn had the effect of reinforcing the structural difference between the two.

Thus the two poles were closely bound together, and mutually and reciprocally conditioning. Therefore, the structural difference between centre and periphery could not be defined or understood in static terms, as the transformation of either pole would be conditioned by the interaction between them. Centre and periphery formed a single system, dynamic by its very nature.

The principal elements of the long-term dynamic of the centre-periphery system, according to ECLA, could be summarised as follows: (i) the structure of production in the periphery remains backward, finding it difficult to generate technical progress or to integrate it into its productive activity. Thus the productivity of labour increases more slowly in the periphery than in the centre, and the primary export sector of the former advances more slowly in this respect than the manufacturing sector of the latter; (ii) the sectors in the periphery with low productivity (especially subsistence agriculture) generate a continuous excess labour supply, which exerts a strong downward pressure on wages in the modern sector. Low unionisation also contributes to this phenomenon, which not only would affect the level of internal effective demand, but also the level of prices in the peripheral export sector, becoming one of the factors behind the deterioration in the terms of trade between the two poles; (iii) both phenomena — differences in productivity and the deterioration in the terms of trade — explain why levels of average real income tend to diverge in the two poles of the system; and (iv) there is therefore a tendency towards unequal development in the two poles which constitute the system, in terms of levels of average real income, the degree of creation, penetration and diffusion of technical progress (homogeneity), and the degree of integration of the structures of production (diversification).

From this manner of defining the principal characteristics of the long-term dynamic of the centre-periphery system the *structuralist* nature of ECLA's thought emerges clearly: the determining factors in the relationship are given by the difference of structure of production in each pole. We have the definition of a system — centre-periphery — and the inequalities considered inherent in its dynamic; the structures of production of each pole are not only the basis of the relationship, but develop in the interaction between the two poles, while the differences between the two (and average real income) tend to persist.

Thus the ECLA analysis turns on three tendencies which are considered inherent to the development of the periphery: unemployment of the labour force, external disequilibrium, and the deterioration of the terms of trade.

(i) **Structural heterogeneity and unemployment.** The problem of employment in the periphery has two facets: the absorption of additions to the active population, and the re-absorption of the labour force in the most backward sectors into economic activities in which productivity is higher. As the ECLA analysis assumes that demand for labour is proportionate to the level of investment (its rate of growth is directly related to the rate of capital accumulation), and this takes place only in the modern sector, full employment of the labour force at adequate levels of productivity can only be achieved if the rate of capital accumulation in the export sector and in import substituting manufacturing activities is sufficient not only to absorb the growth in the whole of the active population, but also to re-absorb labour from the traditional sector. Thus the level of employment depends on the balance between the growth of the active population and the rhythm of the expulsion of labour from the traditional sector, and on the level of capital accumulation in the modern sector. It is from the heavy demand on the modern sector to provide full employment in the economy at adequate levels of productivity that the structural tendency toward unemployment in the peripheral economies is deduced.

(ii) Specialisation in production and external disequilibrium. The structure of production in the periphery is specialised in a double sense: only primary products are exported, and the economies are in general poorly integrated. From this it follows that the demand for manufactured products is oriented in the main towards imports, and given that their income elasticity is greater than unity, imports tend to grow faster than the level of real income or of exports. The opposite is the case in the centre, as imports consist essentially of primary products, for which income elasticity is less than unity; hence they grow less rapidly than real income and exports.

Thus for a given rate of growth of real incomes in the centre, the disparity between the income elasticities of imports at each pole will impose a limit upon the rate of growth of real income in the periphery.[43] This will not only tend to be less than that of the centre, but to be less in proportion to the degree of the disparity between the respective income elasticities of demand for imports. If the periphery attempts to surpass this limit, it will necessarily expose itself to successive deficits in its balance of trade; the only alternative will be an increased effort to satisfy demand for manufactured products with internal production. Only a process of import substitution, given these assumptions, can allow the periphery to enjoy a rate of growth of real incomes higher than that determined by the rate of growth in the centre and the disparity between income elasticities of demand for imports.

As this process of import substitution also generates a need for imports which can exceed the availability of foreign currency deriving from the slow expansion of primary exports, ECLA argues in its documents that there is a role for foreign capital in the first stages of the process, both to remedy the shortage of foreign currency, and to complement internal savings.

(iii) Specialisation, heterogeneity, and the deterioration in the terms of trade. The explanation for the phenomena of deteriorating terms of trade and the disparity in incomes which it brings with it are, in the thought of ECLA, a logical analytical deduction from the phenomena of specialisation and heterogeneity.

If it is assumed that exports in the periphery are not to diversify, the disparity in income elasticities of demand for imports generates deficits in the peripheral pole which in turn force successive devaluations; this stimulates increases in the volume of exports, and changes the structure of relative prices, shifting some of the internal demand for manufactured goods to the internal market, and thus promoting import substitution. As a result, exports will grow faster than will demand for them, and this will produce a fall in their relative prices. If we assume also, with ECLA, that the return on capital is constant, this fall in unit income is passed on to wages; this is possible because of the surplus of labour in the peripheral economy and the low level of unionisation among the employed. But as new manufacturing activities are created exclusively with the internal market in mind, its limited dimensions mean that productive capacity would grow more rapidly than demand, affecting the productivity of labour and average real industrial income.

The deterioration in the terms of trade in the primary export sector and the difference in the productivity of labour in import substituting manufacturing industry in the periphery and manufacturing industry in the centre mean that differences in income between the two poles not only persist, but may even increase. It is in this way that the analysis incorporates the basic ideas of the initial conceptualisation of the unequal character of development of the centre-periphery system.

According to ECLA, it is possible to escape from this vicious circle of underdevelopment only through a process of transformation of the economic structure of the periphery capable, ideally, of providing that economy with a rapid and sustained rate of growth, and avoiding unemployment, external disequilibrium, and the deterioration in the terms of trade. The central element in this structural transformation is the process of import substitution; thus Prebisch, in a recently published article, summarises ECLA's task as having been that of 'showing that industrialisation was an unavoidable prerequisite for development' (1980, p.viii). Furthermore, the article in question appears at times to use the concepts 'industrialisation' and 'development' as synonyms.

In other words, to achieve accelerated and sustained economic growth in Latin America a necessary condition (and, some ECLA writings seemed to suggest, a sufficient one) was the development of a process of industrialisation. But this process could not be expected to take place spontaneously, for it would be inhibited by the international division of labour which the centre would attempt to impose, and by a series of structural obstacles internal to Latin American economies. Consequently, a series of measures was proposed, intended to promote a process of deliberate or 'forced' industrialisation; these included state intervention in the economy both in the formulation of economic policies oriented towards these ends and as a direct productive agent. Among the economic policies suggested were those of 'healthy protectionism', exchange controls, the attraction of foreign investment into Latin American industry, the stimulation and orientation of national investment, and the adoption of wage policies aimed at boosting effective demand. The intervention of the state in directly productive activity was recommended in those areas where large amounts of slow-maturing investment were needed, and particularly where this need coincided with the production of essential goods or services.[44]

The dimensions of the thought of ECLA are based then not only upon its breadth and internal unity, but also upon its structuralist nature. The three most important characteristics of the development of the economy in the periphery – unemployment, external desequilibrium, and the deterioration of the terms of trade – are derived directly from the characteristics of the structure of production in the periphery; thus the possibility of tackling them is seen in terms of ideal patterns of transformation, which indicate the conditions of proportionality which must hold if those features are to be avoided.[45] This leads to the formulation, tacitly or explicitly, of the law of proportionality in the transformation which will avoid heterogeneity and thus allow full employment at adequate levels of productivity, the avoidance of specialisation and thus permit the escape from external desequilibria, and, through avoidance of the relative decline in the price of exports from the periphery, the escape from the deterioration in the terms of trade.

Nevertheless, it is also in this very same structuralist nature that the limitations of ECLA thought lie; at this level of analysis no consideration is given to the social relations of production which are at the base of the process of import-substituting industrialisation, and of the transformation in other structures of society that this brings in its wake.

ECLA proposes an ideal model of sectoral growth – and hence of global growth – designed in such a way that the tendencies peculiar to economic development of the periphery – unemployment, external desequilibrium, and the deterioration of the terms of trade – are not produced; from this are derived the necessary conditions of accumulation which will allow the proportionality required in the transformation of the different sectors of material production. Nevertheless, even when pushed to the limits of its potential internal coherence, the structural approach is inadequate for the analysis of the evolution in the long term of the economic system as a whole, as it clearly involves more than the transformation of the structure of production alone.

The theories of ECLA describe and examine certain aspects of the development of the forces of production (to the extent that they deal with the productivity of labour and the degree of diversification and homogeneity of the structures of production), but do not touch on relations of production, nor, as a result, on the manner in which the two interact.

Furthermore, the analysis of the inequalities of development cannot be carried out solely in terms of the pattern of accumulation necessary to avoid the creation of certain disproportions between the different sectors of material production, as inequalities of development are clearly linked to the possibility of saving and accumulation in each pole. That is to say, the requirements as far as accumulation is concerned are derived from these disproportions, but their feasibility depends more upon the general conditions in which accumulation occurs at world level than upon those disproportions. In other words, if the intention is to analyse the bipolarity of the centre-periphery system, it is not enough to postulate the inequality of development of the forces of production; it is necessary also to bear in mind that those forces of production develop in the framework of a process of generation, appropriation and utilisation of the economic surplus, and that process, and the relations of exploitation upon which it is based, are not produced purely within each pole, but also between the two poles of the world economy.

Perhaps the other distinctive aspect of this line of Latin American thought was that it made a basically *ethical* distinction between 'economic growth' and 'economic development'. According to this, development did not take place when growth was accompanied by: (i) increased inequality in the distribution of its benefits; (ii) a failure to increase social welfare, in so far as expenditure went to unproductive areas – or even worse to military spending – or the production of unnecessarily refined luxury consumer durables; (iii) the failure to create employment opportunities at the rate of the growth in population, let alone in urbanisation; and (iv) a growing loss of national control over economic, political, social and cultural life.

By making the distinction in these terms, their research developed along two separate lines, one concerned with the obstacles to *growth* (and in particular to industrial growth), the other concerned with the perverse character taken by *development*. The fragility of such a formulation consists in its confusing a socialist critique of capitalism with the analysis of the obstacles of capitalism in Latin America. (For a review of these issues see Faria (1976, pp.37-49).[46])

It is not particularly surprising that ECLA should have attracted its share of criticism, particularly as it went beyond theoretical pronouncements to offer packages of policy recommendations. It was criticised from sectors of the left for failing to denounce sufficiently the mechanisms of exploitation within the capitalist system, and for criticising the conventional theory of international trade only from 'within' (see, for example, Frank, 1967, and Caputo and Pizarro, 1974). On the other hand, from the liberal right the reaction was immediate and at times ferocious: ECLA's policy recommendations were totally heretical from the point of view of conventional theory, and threatened the political interests of significant sectors. A leading critic in academic circles was Haberler, who accused ECLA of failing to take due account of economic cycles, and argued that single factorial terms of trade would be a better indicator than the simple relationship between the prices of exports and imports.

On the political front, the liberal right accused ECLA of being the 'Trojan horse of Marxism', on the strength of the degree of coincidence between both analyses. Without doubt there was a significant degree of coincidence — both ideological and analytical — between the thought of ECLA and the post-1920 Marxist view of the obstacles facing capitalist development in the periphery, despite the fact that the language that they used and the premises from which they started were different. As I have shown, the central line of Marxist thought after 1920 argued that capitalist development in Latin America was necessary, but hindered by the 'feudal-imperialist' alliance; thus the anti-imperialist and 'anti-feudal' struggle had become at the same time a struggle for industrialisation, with the state and the 'national bourgeoisie' depicted as potential historical agents in this necessary capitalist development. In the case of ECLA, as with the Marxists, the principle obstacle to development (ECLA chose to speak of the 'principal obstacle' rather than the 'principal enemy') was located overseas, and ECLA shared with the Marxists the conviction that without a strenuous effort to remove the internal obstacles to development (the traditional sectors) the process of industrialisation would be greatly impeded.

Furthermore, the coincidence between crucial elements in the analysis of the two respective lines of thought is made more evident by the fact that the processes of reformulation in each occurred *simultaneously*. Thus when it became evident that capitalist development in Latin America was taking a path different from that expected, a number of ECLA members began a process of reformulation of the traditional thought of that institution, just at the time that an important sector of the Latin American left was breaking with the traditional Marxist view that capitalist development was both necessary and possible in Latin America, but hindered by the 'feudal-imperialist' alliance. Not only did the different processes of reformulation take place at the same time, but despite the apparently growing divergencies (particularly seen in the vocabulary adopted), they had one extremely important element in common: *pessimism* regarding the possibility of capitalist development.

As regards the attempt to reformulate the thought of ECLA, it was undoubtedly the sombre picture presented by their own statistics on Latin America (ECLA, 1963) which wrought the effect which the Cuban revolution had had on thinking within the other group. In the terminology of Kuhn (1962, 1972), they sought to change their paradigm. The process of import-substituting industrialisation which ECLA recommended seemed to aggravate balance-of-payments problems, instead of alleviating them; foreign investment was not only in part responsible for that (as after a certain period of time there was a net flow of capital away from the sub-continent), but it did not seem to be having other positive effects that ECLA had expected; real wages were not rising sufficiently quickly to produce the desired increase in effective demand — indeed, in several countries income distribution was worsening; the problems of unemployment were also growing more acute, in particular as a result of rural-urban migration; industrial production was becoming increasingly concentrated in products typically consumed by the élites, and was not having the 'ripple effect' upon other productive sectors of the economy, particularly the agricultural sector.

The bleak panorama of capitalist development in Latin America led to changes in the 'pre-theoretical entity' (to return to the language of Kuhn) in ECLA thinkers, but it strengthened the convictions of the dependency writers I reviewed earlier.[47] The former were faced with the problem of trying to discover why some of the expected consequences of industrialisation on the course of development were not being produced, the latter denied with greater vehemence the least possibility of dependent capitalist development.

The pessimism with regard to the possibilities of capitalist development in Latin America which was the keynote of the works written by both groups during this period was in each case accompanied by the same error: the failure to take duly into account the cyclical pattern characteristic of capitalist development.

The irony was that while both groups were busy writing and publishing different versions of stagnationist theories (the most sophisticated perhaps being Furtado, 1966), international trade was picking up, the terms of trade were changing in favour of Latin American exporters of agricultural and mineral products, and some countries were able to take advantage of the favourable situation and accelerate rapidly the rhythm of their economic development. Thus, as Cardoso (1977, p.33) remarks, 'history had prepared a trap for pessimists'. To put it in another way, the optimistic vision of the 1950s of the transformative power of industrialisation must yield to the realisation that in order to overcome the obstacles of a structural nature which hinder the functioning of the socio-economic system as a whole and impede its transformation, it is necessary to promote and carry through changes in the different structures of society.

Latifundist land-holding, consolidated during the period of outwardly oriented growth, the monopolistic character, the inefficiency and dependent nature (particularly as regard technology, finances and capital goods) of the industrial sector, shaped during the period of inwardly oriented growth, and the presence of foreign capital in the export sector are all at the base of a distribution of power, property and income which is both concentrated and exclusive. Furthermore, the new analysis indicates that political, economic and social structures hinder the functioning of accumulation and of management, causing the process of industrialisation to lose dynamism, and the structures in question to be gripped by relative inertia.

Thus agrarian reform is no longer presented as an option, but as a necessity. The structure of industrial ownership and the role of the state in the economy are moving to the centre of the debate; ownership of the export sector and the surplus it generates is openly discussed, in an atmosphere of growing nationalism. Perhaps the political and economic programme of the Popular Unity in Chile owed more to this new vision of peripheral development than to the current of Marxist thought already analysed. The work of Vuscovic is significant in this respect, particularly as regards his discussion of the concentrated and exclusive character of Latin American development (1970) and the alternative proposed to overcome them by the government of Allende (1973).[48]

These stagnationist theories, which characterised so much of Latin American thought at the end of the sixties and into the seventies, were first criticised in a substantial way by Tavares and Serra (1970). Pinto (1965, 1974) has made significant contributions to the analysis of structural heterogeneity, and of the continuous process of 'marginalisation' of the periphery (with Knakal, 1973). Sunkel provides a global and systematic presentation of this new conceptualisation of development (with Paz, 1970), and in a subsequent series of contributions analyses the process through which the greater degree of integration of the world economy leads to the greater disintegration of societies and economies in the periphery (1972, 1973 b, 1974). He has subsequently written, with Cariola, a revealing study of the relationship between the expansion of nitrates in Chile and the socio-economic transformation which came with it, a study which is openly critical of the 'underdevelopmentalist' theses which played such an important part in the post-ECLA analysis.

Subsequent contributions can generally be grouped into three categories: the first seeks to analyse the most recent transformations in the world capitalist system and their effects on the economies of the periphery, giving particular weight to the process of transnationalisation; the essays collected in Villamil (ed., 1979) are important contributions in this respect. The second concentrates upon the study of the theoretical and methodological implications of the application of the centre-periphery framework to Europe, and the potential fruitfulness of such an approach is well attested by the collection edited by Seers, Schaffer and Kiljunen (1979), and Seers and Vaitsos (1980). The third relates to the study of some of the most important issues in the contemporary international economy, such as transformations in international financial markets, and problems of energy and environment.

A methodology for the analysis of concrete situations of dependency. In my critique of the dependency studies reviewed so far I have already advanced the fundamental elements of what I understand to be the third of the three approaches within the dependency school. It is primarily related to the work of the Brazilian sociologist Fernando Henrique Cardoso, dating from the completion in 1967 of *Dependencia y Desarrollo en America Latina*, written with the Chilean historian Enzo Faletto.

Briefly, this third approach to the analysis of dependency can be expressed as follows:

(i) In common with the two approaches discussed already, this third approach sees the Latin American economies as an integral part of the world capitalist system, in a context of increasing internationalisation of the system as a whole; it also argues that the central dynamic of that system lies outside the peripheral economies and that therefore the options which lie open to them are limited by the development of the system at the centre; in this way the particular is in some way conditioned by the general. Therefore a basic element for the understanding of these societies is given by the 'general determinants' of the world capitalist system, which is itself changing through time; *the analysis therefore requires primarily an understanding of the contemporary characteristics of the world capitalist system*. However, the theory of imperialism, which was originally developed to provide an understanding of that system, had remained practically 'frozen' where it was at the time of the death of Lenin until the end of the 1950s. During this period, capitalism underwent significant and decisive stages of development and the theory failed to keep up with them. The depression of the 1930s, World War II, the emergence of the United States as the undisputed hegemonic power in the capitalist world, the challenge of the growing socialist bloc, and its attendant creation of new demands on the capitalist world if its system were to be maintained, the decolonisation of Africa and Asia, and the beginning of the process of the transnationalisation of capitalism had all contributed to create a world very different from that which had confronted Lenin. As the theory of imperialism once again began to place itself at the centre of Marxist analysis this failure to make any theoretical advance began to make itself felt; the transformations which had occurred and which continued to occur were slowly if at all incorporated into its analysis. Contributions as important as those of Gramsci[49] and Kalecki have remained almost unintegrated until very recently.[50]

One characteristic of the third approach to dependency, and one which has been widely recognised, has been to incorporate more successfully into its analysis of Latin American development the transformations which are occurring and have occurred in the world capitalist system, and in particular the changes which became significant towards the end of the 1950s in the rhythm and the form of capital movement, and in the international division of labour. The emergence of the so-called multinational corporations progressively transformed centre-periphery relationships, and relationships between the countries of the centre. As foreign capital has increasingly been directed towards manufacturing industry in the periphery,[51] the struggle for industrialisation, which was previously seen as an anti-imperialist struggle, has become increasingly the *goal* of foreign capital. Thus dependency and industrialisation cease to be contradictory and a path of 'dependent development' becomes possible.[52]

(ii) Furthermore, the third approach not only accepts as a starting-point and improves upon the analysis of the location of the economies of Latin America in the world capitalist system, but also accepts and enriches their demonstration that Latin American societies are structured through unequal and antagonistic patterns of social organisation, showing the social asymmetries and the exploitative character of social organisation which arise from its socio-economic base, giving considerable importance to the effect of the diversity of natural resources, geographic location, and so on of each economy, thus extending the analysis of the 'internal determinants' of the development of the Latin American economies.

(iii) But while these improvements are important, the most significant feature of this approach is that it goes beyond these points, and insists that from the premises so far outlined *one arrives at a partial, abstract and indeterminate characterisation of the Latin American historical process*, which can only be overcome by understanding how the general and specific determinants interact in particular and concrete situations. It is only by understanding the specificity of movement in these societies as a dialectical unity of both, and a synthesis of these 'internal' and 'external' factors, that one can explain the particularity of social, political and economic processes in the dependent societies. Only in this way can one explain why, for example, the single process of mercantile expansion should have produced in different Latin American societies slave labour, systems based on the exploitation of indigenous populations, and incipient forms of wage labour.

What is important is not simply to show that mercantile expansion was the basis of the transformation of the Latin American economies, and less to deduce mechanically that that process made them capitalist, but to avoid losing the specificity of history in a welter of vague abstract concepts by explaining how the mercantilist drive led to the creation of the phenomena mentioned, and to show how, throughout the history of Latin America, different sectors

> of local classes allied or clashed with foreign interests, organized different forms of state, sustained distinct ideologies or tried to implement various policies or defined alternative strategies to cope with imperialist challenges in diverse moments of history (Cardoso and Faletto, 1977, p.12).

The study of the dynamic of the dependent societies as the dialectical unity of internal and external factors implies that the conditioning effect of each in the movement of these societies can be separated only by making a static analysis. Equally, if the internal dynamic of the dependent society is a particular aspect of the general dynamic of the capitalist system, that does not imply that the latter *produces* concrete effects in the former, but finds *concrete expression in them*.

The system of 'external domination' reappears as an 'internal' phenomenon through the social practices of local groups and classes, who share its interests and values. Other internal groups and forces oppose this domination, and in the concrete development of these contradictions the specific dynamic of the society is generated. It is not a case of seeing one part of the world capitalist system as 'developing' and another as 'underdeveloping', or of seeing imperialism and dependency as two sides of the same coin, with the underdeveloped or dependent world reduced to a passive role determined by the other, but in the words of Cardoso and Faletto,

We conceive the relationship between external and internal forces as forming a complex whole whose structural links are not based on mere external forms of exploitation and coercion, but are rooted in coincidences of interests between local dominant classes and international ones, and, on the other side, are challenged by local dominated groups and classes. In some circumstances, the networks of coincident or reconciliated interests might expand to include segments of the middle class, if not even of alienated parts of working classes. In other circumstances, segments of dominant classes might seek internal alliance with middle classes, working classes, and even peasants, aiming to protect themselves from foreign penetration that contradicts its interests (1977, pp.10, 11).

There are of course elements within the capitalist system which affect all the Latin American economies, but it is precisely the *diversity within this unity* which characterises historical processes. *Thus the effort of analysis should be oriented towards the elaboration of concepts capable of explaining how the general trends in capitalist expansion are transformed into specific relationships between men, classes and states, how these specific relations in turn react upon the general trends of the capitalist system, how internal and external processes of political domination reflect one another, both in their compatibilities and their contradictions, how the economies and politics of Latin America are articulated with those of the centre, and how their specific dynamics are thus generated.*

Nevertheless, I do not mean to support a naive expectation that a 'correct' approach to the analysis of dependency would be capable of explaining everything; or that if it does not yet do so, it is *necessarily* due to the fact that the method was wrongly applied, or has not yet been developed enough. I do not have any illusions that our findings could explain every detail of our past history, or should be capable of predicting the exact course of future events, because I do not have any illusions that our findings can take out from history all its ambiguities, uncertainties, contradictions and surprises. As it has done so often in the past, history will undoubtedly continue to astonish us with unexpected revelations as unexpected as those that astonished Lenin in 1917.

In my view, some of the most successful analyses within the dependency school have been those which analyse specific situations in concrete terms. A case in point is Chudnovsky (1974), who after analysing the effect of multinational corporations in Colombia, goes on to relate it to the theory of imperialism. For other successful attempts at concrete analysis, one should consult the already mentioned works of Laclau (1969), Pinto (1965, 1974), Cariola and Sunkel (1976, 1977), and Singer (1971).

By way of conclusion

Throughout this survey I have shown first that there is no such thing as a single Marxist theory of underdevelopment; under this label we find approaches so different that it may probably be more appropriate to speak of 'Marxist inspired' theories of underdevelopment, if one wishes to contain them all under one heading.

I have also shown how the metamorphosis which the Marxist view of underdevelopment has undergone is due in some cases to changes in diagnosis and in others to the circumstances under which capitalism in the backward countries is developing. Among the former, the new way of looking at the relationships between capitalist and pre-capitalist structures in the peripheral areas of the world stands out. Since the Russian experience of capitalist development, this process has ceased to be analysed by most Marxist writers as one of pure destruction and replacement of pre-capitalist structures by capitalist ones; and has begun to be analysed as a far more complex process of interplay between both structures.

As concerns the 'changes in circumstances', the form in which Marxism analyses the relationships between advanced capitalism and the peripheral areas of the world (i.e. the way in which the backward countries serve the needs of advanced capitalist countries), passes through three different phases. In the first, the one on which Marx and Engels dwelt, the analysis is concerned with the way in which capitalist countries exported their manufactures to the peripheral countries while at the same time plundering wealth and slaves.

In the second, which stands out in Lenin's writings, the analysis had to do with the export of capital, the competition for supplies of raw materials and the process of monopolisation in advanced capitalist countries. In the third phase, the analysis deals with a much more complex post-colonial dependency of the peripheral countries, where foreign capital (in particular international corporations), profit repatriation, adverse changes in the terms of trade (i.e. unequal exchange) work together to hinder and distort economic development and industrialisation.

In so far as we are concerned with the dependency school which has arisen since the beginning of the sixties,[53] we can conclude that its principal contribution is the attempt to analyse peripheral societies through a 'comprehensive social science', which stresses the socio-political nature of the economic relations of production; in short, the approach is one of *political economy*, and thus an attempt to revive the nineteenth and early twentieth century tradition in this respect.

From this perspective, there is a critique of those who divide reality into dimensions analytically independent of each other and of the economic structures of a given society, as if these elements were in reality separable. Thus, the dependency school offers an important critique of such approaches as Rostow's stages of growth, 'modern-traditional' sociological typologies, dualism, functionalism, and in general all those which do not integrate into their analysis an account of the socio-political context in which development takes place (or fails to take place).

Nevertheless, as I have attempted to show, not all the approaches within the dependency school are successful in showing *how* these distinct spheres — social, economic and political — are related. While we find in the dependency analyses a methodology adequate for the analyses of concrete situations of underdevelopment, we also find writers who fail to understand the specificity of the historical process of the penetration of capitalism into the peripheral countries, and only condemn its negative aspects, complementing their analysis with a series of stagnationist theses in an attempt to build a formal theory of underdevelopment. These analyses are mistaken not only because they do not 'fit the facts', but because their mechanico-formal nature renders them both static and unhistorical. Such writers have thus developed schemas that are unable to explain the specificity of economic development and political domination in the backward countries; indeed, their models lack the sensitivity to detect the relevant social processes, and are unable to explain with precision the mechanisms of social reproduction and modes of social transformation of these societies. This leads them to use vague and imprecise concepts, as vague and imprecise as those used at the other end of the political spectrum, as for example the 'Brazilian miracle'.[54] To use their own language, by transforming their analyses into a mechanico-formal theory of peripheral underdevelopment — thus losing the richness that a dialectical analysis would provide — these writers have underdeveloped their contribution to the dependency school.

Notes

1. Earlier versions of this paper have appeared in *World Development* (Vol.6, No. 7/8, 1978; pp.881-924) and *Thames Papers in Political Economy* (Summer 1978). An extended version will be published by Academic Press in the series of titles in political economy of which Dr. John Eatwell is the series editor. We would like to thank the said publishers for permission to reproduce material used in the respective versions.

   I would like to thank Paul Cammack, Carlos Fortin, Stephany Griffith-Jones, Francoise Mandroux, Blanca Muniz, Luis Ortega, Dudley Seers, Elizabeth Spillius, Thamos Skouras and Bob Sutcliffe for their stimulating cooperation.

2. In this respect, see Lenin, 1899, pp.65-8; dos Santos, 1968; Barratt-Brown, 1972, pp.43-7; Sutcliffe, 1972a, pp.180-5; Caputo and Pizarro, 1974, pp.118-23.

3. This is due in part to the experience of the transitions of socialism, and to the existence today of developed socialist economies which can provide what otherwise would have been obtained from capitalist development.

4. For further discussions of the Asiatic mode of production, see Hobsbawm, 1964, dos Santos, 1968; Averini, 1968, 1976; D'Encausse and Schram, 1969; Batra, 1971; Foster-Carter, 1974.

5. The great importance of these statements towards the end of Marx's life is that they show that he saw history not as a mechanical continuum of discrete stages through which each society must pass, but as a process in which the particularity

of each historical situation had an important role to play. His position regarding the Russian case illustrates well the flexibility of his approach, which was informed by the dialectical unity of subjective and objective factors. Stalin (1934, p.104)̇ would later pervert this approach, stating that the Soviet form of dictatorship of the proletariat was 'suitable and obligatory for all countries without exception, including those where capitalism is developed', thus condemning all countries except the USSR to have no history of their own.

6. On Rosa Luxemburg, see Sweezy, 1942, pp.124-9; Robinson, 1963; Lichtheim, 1971, pp.117-25; Barratt-Brown, 1974, pp.50-2; Caputo and Pizarro, 1974, pp. 148-66; Furtado, 1974, pp.229-33; Nettl, 1975; Bradby, 1975, p.86.

7. For a further discussion, see Caputo and Pizarro, 1974, pp.135-45; O'Brien, 1975, p.21.

8. Similarly, Lukacs stresses, in his preface to the 1967 edition of *Geschichte und Klassenbewusstein* (1923), that his work should be read with an eye to the factional disputes of the time at which he wrote it.

9. Even less could it explain why it was precisely the social democratic groups of France, Italy, Germany and England who were the first to break the agreements taken in Congress after the Second International during the Second International to oppose the war on account of its imperialist nature. The only ones to stand by those agreements were the Russians, both Bolsheviks and Mensheviks, and some minority groups in other countries, such as Luxemburg's followers in Germany. The Russian left opposed the granting of war credits in the Duma. Later the Mensheviks followed the line of social democrats elsewhere, as did some Bolshevik groups. Those in Paris enrolled in the French Army, and Plekhanov the 'father of Russian Marxism' and collaborator with Lenin for many years, went so far in their support according to Lenin's widow, Krupskaya, (1930, p.247) as to 'make a farewell speech in their honour'.

10. This point is emphasised by Lukacs, 1924, p.75; it is important not to seek in the essay what Lenin did not set out to provide, an 'economic theory' of imperialism; in this respect Lenin is largely content to follow Hobson, 1902, and Hilferding, 1910. The substantive element of his contribution is in the analysis of the effect which economic changes have on the world capitalist system in general, and on the class struggle in individual countries in particular. Approaches to Lenin's work from different points of view have led to some misdirected criticism; for a summary of it, see Sutcliffe, 1972b, pp.370-5.

11. I am here following Rudenko, 1966.

12. For further discussions of Lenin's work and its relation to other work on imperialism, see Varga and Mendelson (eds.), 1939; Kruger, 1955; Kemp, 1967, 1972; L. Shapiro and P. Reddaway, 1967; Horowitz, 1969; Pailloix, 1970; Hinkelammert, 1971; Lichtheim, 1971; Barratt-Brown, 1972, 1974.

13. The Narodniks were a group of intellectuals and a series of terrorist groups who were the leading Russian revolutionaries during the last three decades of the nineteenth century, reaching their peak in the 1870s. From this group emerged later the 'Social Revolutionaries', a party which played an important role in the period from February to October 1917, and of which Kerensky was a member. The base of the party was fundamentally peasant, although it had some strength in the towns, dominating the first democratic municipalities, many soviets, and some sectors of the army. The Narodniks were a complex group of eighteenth century Enlightenment materialists and radicals in the tradition of the French Revolution; their theoretical roots were in Marxism, their political practice was inspired by anarchism. The first translation of *Capital*, by a Narodnik, appeared as early as 1872.

14. The peasant commune, a system of common land tenure with periodical redistribution of individual allotments, prevailed under serfdom and survived its abolition in 1861.

15. They went on to explain the ambiguity of the class position of the peasant as follows: 'If by a chance they are revolutionaries, they are so only in the view of their impending transfer to the proletariat; they thus defend not their present, but their future interest; they desert their own standpoint to place themselves at that of the proletariat'.
16. A year later, and only a year before he died, Marx (with Engels) returned to the theme in a new preface to the Russian edition of the *Communist Manifesto* using similar arguments. Ten years later, Engels would affirm that if there had ever been a possibility of avoiding capitalist development in Russia there was no longer. The Russian commune was by then part of the past, and Russia could therefore not escape passage through the stage of capitalism.
17. Thus, for example, a year before (in February 1898) in the founding Congress of the 'Russian Social Democratic Workers' Party' (the first concerted attempt to create a Russian Marxist party on Russian soil, and the forerunner of the Russian Communist Party (Bolshevik)), delegates stressed that the principal dilemma of the Russian revolution was the incapacity of the bourgeoisie to make its own revolution; from that they derived the consequent need to extend to the proletariat the leadership in the bourgeois democratic revolution. In this context they stated, 'The farther east one goes in Europe, the weaker, meaner and more cowardly in the political sense becomes the bourgeoisie, and the greater the cultural and political tasks which fall to the lot of the proletariat' (cited in Carr, 1966, Vol.1, p.15).
18. It was only some years later that Stalin developed his well-known thesis of 'Socialism in one country',
19. Lenin's widow herself has testified to the great surprise with which Lenin received the news of the February revolution. See Krupskaya, 1930, p.286.
20. For a general discussion of the problems of late industrialisation, see Gerschenkron, 1952; for a discussion of the impact of the expansion of capitalism into backward nations, see Rey, 1971.
21. In 1824 the British Chancellor, Lord Canning, made an oft-quoted statement: 'Spanish America is free, and if we do not badly mismanage our affairs, she is English'. History would prove that his optimism was justified.
22. It is surprising that other lines of Marxist analysis were practically absent in the debate; Trotsky's work, for example, was not influenced, or at least, not acknowledged as influential, despite his important contributions, and in particular that of 1930, in which he insisted that the specific historical circumstances of individual countries would preclude their repeating the path to capitalist development traced out by the advanced nations.
23. It should be noted that this did not preclude, for example, an alliance with small rural producers. For a full account of the whole controversy mentioned briefly here, see Suarez, 1967.
24. ECLA (United Nations' Economic Commission for Latin America).
25. A characterisation is abstract in the Marxist sense when it is based *on partial or indeterminate relationships*. See Luporini, 1965, and Sassoon, 1965.
26. Baran enriches the theoretical framework of this line of Marxist thought. See also Baran and Sweezy, 1966, and Mandel, 1968.
27. Hence, according to Frank, the continual failure of attempts, such as those in Latin America in the 1830s, to weaken the metropolis-satellite chain. See Frank, 1967, pp.57–66.
28. For the presentation of dualist analyses, see Lewis 1954, 1958; Jorgenson, 1961, 1967; Fei and Ranis, 1964. Other critiques of dualism have come from Griffin, 1969; Laclau, 1969; Novack, 1970; Singer, 1970; Rweyemamu, 1971; Cole and Saunders, 1972; and Seligson, 1972. The thesis that Latin America had been capitalist since colonial times had previously been advanced by Bagu, 1949, and Vitale, 1966.

29. Frank himself has kept his audience up to date with the growing bibliography relating to his own work (Frank, 1972, 1974, 1977). Here we would only mention a critique commonly made of Frank, of other dependency writers, and of Marxists in general, regarding the role of ideology in their analysis (see, for example, Nove, 1974). Marxist analysis, as a general rule, springs simultaneously from political and intellectual praxis, and therefore only on a logical level is it possible to make a clear distinction between 'concept' and 'history' and between 'theory' and 'practice'. From this point of view it is only of formally scholastic interest to claim that a concept is generated 'impure', and 'stained' with ideology. This is how any theory emerges in the social sciences. As Cardoso (1974, p. 328) states, 'Ideology reflects the real inversely and at times perversely'. To criticise Frank and other authors because their concepts are 'impregnated' with ideology is only to state the obvious; to criticise them because their ideology reflects reality perversely may be an important element of a critique of their work. For further ideas relating to this subject, see Larrain, 1977.

30. Laclau (1971) points out that by restricting his analysis to the circulation of capital Frank fails to realise that integration into the world economy sometimes even strengthens pre-capitalist relations of production; it does not follow however that if such relations were not capitalist they were feudal (Cardoso, 1974b). In my judgement, the frequent use of the term 'feudal' to characterise pre-capitalist relations of production in Latin America illustrates the folly of purely theoretical analysis. It is precisely the lack of concrete analysis which leaves a vacuum, and there is a tendency to fill it with concepts developed for other situations. It is time to attempt to analyse the Latin American experience in terms of categories derived from its own history, rather than continue to squeeze her history into West European categories. For interesting studies of pre-capitalist relations in Latin America, see Cardoso, 1960, 1962; Glaucer, 1971; Barboza-Ramirez, 1971.

31. Frank of course also criticised models of economic development such as that of Rostow,which claimed that all nations could and should follow the same path. For a discussion of Frank and Rostow, see Foster-Carter, 1976.

32. For an analysis of the work of dos Santos, see Fausto, 1971.

33. For a critique of Marini, see Laclau, 1971, pp. 83-8; Cardoso, 1973, pp. 7-11. See also Marini's earlier works (Marini, 1969, 1972a).

34. See (among others) Lebedinsky, 1968; Galeno, 1969; Petras, 1969. 1970; Cecena Cervantes, 1970; Fernandez, 1970; De la Pena, 1971; Bagchi, 1972; Cockroft, Frank and Johnson (eds.), 1972; Malave-Mata, 1972; Meeropol, 1972; Alschuler, 1973; Muller, 1973.

35. Although Lall (and later Weisskopf) appears to direct his critique at the whole dependency school, it is applicable in fact only to those whom I classify as attempting to build a mechanico-formal theory of dependent development.

36. We should note here the figures for industrial growth of many less developed countries should be regarded with caution. They may be inflated due to monopoly pricing; the industrial sector may be so small as to make its rate of growth appear misleadingly high; the repatriation of profits carried by foreign capital may be high, and in that case the growth rate of industrial production may overstate, in some cases significantly, the growth in national income derived from industry.

37. This error is the reverse of that committed by others, who (as we shall see later) focus upon the high point of the cycle and project it as a permanent state of affairs. Both forget that the basic permanent features which capitalism has shown are the cyclical character of capital accumulation and the spontaneous tendency towards the concentration of income and wealth, particularly when the state does not take measures to avoid this.

38. See, for example, the works of Regis Debray, 1970.
39. A series of empirical works related to this approach to dependency has been produced. For a critique of these, refer to Palma (1978, pp. 905-6).
40. Among the better analyses of the thought of ECLA are those of Hirschman (1961, 1967); ECLA (1969), and Cardoso (1977). The most recent and most complete is Rodriguez (1980), on which much of the following analysis is based.
41. It is not coincidental that Prebisch published a study of Keynes before he made his first contributions to ECLA. For a short and systematic exposition of Prebisch's main ideas, see Bacha (1974); for a full bibliography, see Di Marco (ed.), (1972).
42. That is, instead of initiating analysis from a perspective such as that of Hicks (1969, p. 160: 'If there were no nations . . . the absorption of the whole human race into the ranks of the developed world would be relatively simple', Keynesian theory takes the existence of nations as the starting-point for economic analysis, not as an obstacle to it (Robinson, 1970; Knapp, 1973, etc.). For an interesting analysis of the different perspectives of neo-classical, Keynesian and Marxist economics, see Barratt-Brown, 1974.
43. If the rate of growth of income in the centre is Y_c and E_p and E_c the income elasticity of demand for imports in the periphery and the centre respectively, the expression $Y_c \times E_c = Y_p \div E_p$ indicates the rate of growth of income in the periphery which will permit the external equilibrium of both economies to be maintained in the long term, assuming that no variation in the prices or movement of capital occurs. See Rodriguez (1980, p. 254). The expression shows that the greater the disparity in elasticities, the lower the rate of growth of income in the periphery must be.
44. This is the case, for example, with steel, where heavy investment is called for with no prospect of an early return, where the productive process involved and particularly the crucial importance of internal economies of scale, practically ensure that the market will be dominated if not monopolised by a single producer, and where the strategic role of the product as an essential input for a wide range of industrial production makes it particularly important that a producer should not exploit his monopoly or oligopoly position; it was therefore considered an ideal case for state investment.
45. For an analysis of these laws of proportionality, see Rodriguez (1980).
46. For discussion of stagnationist theses and that regarding 'distorted' development, see above.
47. In other words, if the Cuban revolution provided the basis for the adoption by other sectors of the left of the analysis which called for an immediate transition to socialism, it was the 'bleak panorama of capitalist development' in the early 1960s which finally brought them into that camp.
48. For a collection and discussion of articles concerning the different aspects of the government of the Unidad Popular, see Palma (ed.), 1973.
49. For a good collection of Gramsci's work (the most original contribution to Marxist thought since Lenin), see Gramsci, 1971.
50. For attempts to up-date the theory of imperialism, see Rhodes (ed.), 1970; Owen and Sutcliffe (eds.), 1972; Barratt-Brown, 1974; and Radice (ed.), 1975.
51. For empirical evidence on this point, see O'Connor, 1970; Bodenheimer, 1970; Quijano, 1971; Fajnzylber, 1971; Cardoso, 1972; Barratt-Brown, 1974; and Warren, 1973.
52. This does not mean, as Warren (1973) seems to argue, that it became possible *throughout* the periphery.
53. For other surveys of dependency lieratture, see Chilcote, 1974 and O'Brien, 1975. For a survey of the literature relating to the Caribbean, see Girvan, 1973.
    I have not attempted in this essay to integrate the growing literature related

to Africa. For a recent survey article on this subject, see Shaw and Grieve, 1977; see also Harris, 1975. I would like to mention that from the point of view of the subject covered, this literature has placed particular emphasis on analysis of the way in which political independence has been followed by a process of strong economic and social 'dependence' (Amin, 1972; Fanon, 1967; Jorgenson, 1975; Okumu, 1971); and how these relationships of dependence have developed in an increasingly complex framework (Bretton, 1973; Rothchild and Curry, 1975; Selwyn 1975 b and c); and considerable attention has been given to the particular role that the new ruling classes have played in it (Cronje, Ling and Cronje, 1976; Green, 1970; Markovitz, 1977; Shaw, 1975; Shaw and Newbury, 1977; Wallerstein, 1973 and 1975; and Zartman, 1976).

The possibilities of a capitalist development for the African countries are analysed from all points of view (Amin, 1973; Davidson, 1974; Fanon, 1970 a and b; Nyerere, 1973; Wallerstein, 1973 and 1974b); and special emphasis has been placed on the problem involved in the elaboration of alternative development strategies (Falk, 1972; Green, 1975; Ghai, 1972 and 1973; Huntington and Nelson, 1976; Rood, 1975; Schumacher, 1975; Seidman, 1972; Selwyn, 1975a; Thomas, 1974, 1975 and 1976; Vernon, 1976; Wallerstein 1971 and 1974b). Finally, for analysis of specific African countries, see Vallaway, 1975; Cliffe and Saul (eds.), 1972; Godfrey and Langdon, 1976; Green, 1976; Grundy, 1976; Johns, 1971 and 1975; McHenry, 1976; Pratt, 1975; Rweyemanu, 1973; Sandbrook, 1975; Saul, 1973; Seidman, 1974; and Shaw, 1976.

54. It is not surprising therefore that the most penetrating analyses of Brazilian economic development are found in dependency analyses already cited, or in those which place the post-1967 boom in its historical context. For example, Bacha (1977) shows how the aggregate Brazilian economic growth from 1968 to 1974 is not a 'miracle', but conforms rather closely to the cyclical growth pattern of the Brazilian economy in the post-war period.

Bibliography

Editions cited are those quoted in the text of the paper itself; however, given the importance of the date of writing or first publication this is placed in brackets immediately after the author's name, both in this bibliography and in the text.

Some of the works cited are unpublished; I would like to thank those who made them available to me and allowed me to discuss and quote them freely.

Alschuler, L.R. (1973), 'A sociological theory of Latin America underdevelopment', *Comparative Studies*, Vol. VI (April 1972), pp. 41-60.

Amin, S. (1972), 'Underdevelopment and dependence in Black Africa: origins and and contemporary forms', *Journal of Modern African Studies*, Vol. 10, No. 4, pp. 503-25.

Amin, S. (1973), *Neocolonialism in West Africa*, Harmondsworth, Penguin.

Avineri, S. (1968), *Karl Marx on Colonialism and Modernization: His Despatches and Other Writings on China, India, Mexico, the Middle East and North Africa*, New York, Doubleday.

Avineri, S. (1976), 'Karl Marx and colonialism and modernization', in M.C. Howard and J.E. King, *Marx*, Harmondsworth, Penguin.

Bacha, E.L. (1977), 'Issues and evidence on recent Brazilian economic growth', *World Development*, Vol. 5, Nos. 1 and 2, pp. 47-68.

Bagchi, A.K. (1972), 'Some international foundations of capitalist growth and underdevelopment', *Economic and Political Weekly*, Special Number, pp. 155-70.

Bagu, S. (1949), *Economias de la Sociedad Colonial*, Buenos Aires, Atenco.

Baran, P. (1975), *La Economia Politica del Crecimiento*, Mexico, F.C.E., 1969.

Baran, P., and Sweezy, P. (1966), *Monopoly Capital: An Essay on the American*

Economic and Social Order, New York, Monthly Review Press.

Barbosa-Ramirez, A.R. (1971), *La Estructura Economica de la Nueva Espana*, Mexico, Siglo XXI Editores.

Barratt-Brown, M. (1974), *Economics of Imperialism*, Harmondsworth, Penguin.

Bath, C.R., and James, D.D. (1976), 'Dependency analysis of Latin America: some criticisms, some suggestions', *Latin American Research Review*, Vol. XI, No. 3, pp. 3-54.

Batra, R. (1971), *El Mondo de Produccion Asiatico*, Mexico, ERA.

Beckford, G. (1972), *Persistent Poverty: Underdevelopment in Plantation Economics of the Third World*, New York, Oxford University Press.

Bettelheim, C. (1970), *Chine et URSS: Deux Modèles d'Industrialisation*, Paris, Temps Modernes.

Bodenheimer, S. (1970), 'Dependency and imperialism', *Politics and Society*, pp. 327-58.

Booth, D. (1975), 'Andre Gunder Frank: an introduction and appreciation', in I. Oxaal, T. Barnett and D. Booth, *Beyond the Sociology of Development*, London, Routledge and Kegan Paul.

Bradby, R. (1975), 'The destruction of natural economy', *Economy and Society*, Vol. 4, No. 2, pp. 127-61.

Brenner, R. (1977), 'The origins of capitalist development: a critique of neo-Smithian Marxism', *New Left Review*, No. 104, pp. 25-93.

Bretton, H. (1973), *Power and Politics in Africa*, Chicago, Aldine.

Bukharin, N.I. (1915), *Imperialism and World Economy*, London, Martin Lawrence, 1929.

Bukharin, N. (1926), *Der Imperialismus und die Akkumulation des Kapitals*, Berlin/Vienna.

Bukharin, N., and Preobrazhensky, F. (1917), *The ABC of Communism*, Harmondsworth, Penguin, 1969.

Callaway, B. (1975), 'The political economy of Nigeria', in R. Harris (ed.) (1975).

Cammack, P. (1977), 'Dependency, class structure and the state in the writings of F.H. Cardoso' (Ms. 1977).

Caputo, O. y Pizarro (1974), *Dependencia y Relaciones Internationales*, Costa Rica, EDUCA.

Cardoso, F.H. (1960), *Core e Mobilidade Social en Florianopolis*, Sao Paulo, Editora Nacional.

Cardoso, F.H. (1962), *Capitalismo e Escravidao no Brasil Meridional*, Sao Paulo, Difusao Europeia do Livro.

Cardoso, F.H. (1970), 'Teoria de la dependencia o analysis concretos de situaciones de dependencia?' F.H. Cardoso (1972b).

Cardoso, F.H. (1972a), 'Dependency and development in Latin America', *New Left Review*, No. 74, pp. 83-95.

Cardoso, F.H. (1972b), *Estado y Sociedad en America Latina*, Buenos Aires, Ediciones Nueva Vision.

Cardoso, F.H. (1973), 'The contradiction of associated development' (Ms, 1973); reprinted in 'Current theses on Latin American development and dependency: a critique' (1976a).

Cardoso, F.H. (1974a), 'Notas sobre el estado actual de los estudios sobre la dependencia', in J. Serra (ed.), *Desarrollo Latinoamericano: Ensayos Criticos*, Mexico, F.C.E.

Cardoso, F.H. (1974b), 'The paper enemy', *Latin American Perspectives*, Vol. 1, No. 1, pp. 66-74.

Cardoso, F.H. (1976a), 'Current theses on Latin American development and dependency: a critique' (paper presented to the III Scandinavian Research Conference on Latin America, Bergen, 17-19 June 1976).

Cardoso, F.H. (1976b), 'The consumption of dependency in the US' (paper presented to the III Scandinavian Research Conference on Latin America, Bergen, 17-19 June 1976); reprinted in *Latin American Research Review*, Vol. XII, No. 3 (1977), pp. 7-24.

Cardoso, F.H. (1977), 'The originality of the copy: ECLA and the idea of development' (Ms. 1977).

Cardoso, F.H. and Faletto, E. (1976), *Dependencia y Desarrollo en America Latina*, Mexico, Siglo XXI Editores, 1969.

Cardoso, F.H. and Faletto, E. (1977), *Dependency and Development in Latin America*, American ed. with new preface, forthcoming.

Cariola, C., and Sunkel, O. (1976), 'Expansion salitrera y transformaciones socio-economicas en Chile 1860-1930' (Ms. 1976).

Cariola, C., and Sunkel, O. (1977), 'Some preliminary notes on nitrate expansion and class formation in Chile in the period 1860-1930' (Ms. 1977).

Carr, E.H. (1966), *The Bolshevik Revolution*, Harmondsworth, Penguin.

Cecna-Cervantes, J.L. (1970), *Superexploitacion, Dependencia y Desarrollo*, Mexico, Editorial Nuestro Tempo.

Chilcote, R.H. (1974), 'Dependency: a critical synthesis of the literature', *Latin American Perspective*, Vol. 1, No. 1, pp. 4-29.

Chudnovsky, D. (1974), *Empresas Multinacionales y Ganancias Monopolicas en una Economia Latinoamericana*, Buenos Aires, Siglo XXI Editores.

Cliffe, L., and Saul, J.S. (eds.) (1972), *Socialism in Tanzania*, Vols. 1 and 2, Nairobi, East African Publishing House, 1972 and 1973.

Cockcroft, J.D., Frank, A.G., and Johnson, D.K. (1972), *America's Political Economy*, New York, Doubleday and Co.

Cole, W., and Sanders, R. (1972), 'A modified dualism model for Latin American economies', *Journal of Development Areas*, Vol. II, pp. 185-9.

Conquest, R. (1972), *Lenin*, London, Fontana.

Cronje. S., Ling, M., and Cronje, G. (1976), *Lonrho: Portrait of a Multinational*, Harmondsworth, Pelican.

Davidson, B. (1974), *Can Africa Survive? Arguments against Growth without Development*, Boston, Little Brown.

Debray, R. (1970), *Strategy for Revolution: Essays on Latin America*, written between 1965 and 1969 and edited in 1970 by R. Blackburn, London, Jonathan Cape.

Degras, J. (ed.), (1960), *The Communist International, 1919-1943: Documents, Vol. 2, 1928-1938*, London, Oxford University Press.

De Kadt, E., and Williams, G. (1974), *Sociology and Development*, London, Tavistock Publications, with an introduction by E. de Kadt, pp. 1-19.

De la Pena, S. (1971), *El Antidesarrollo de America Latina*, Mexico, Siglo XXI Editores.

D'Encause, H.C., and Schram, S.R. (1969), *Marxism in Asia*, London, Allan Lane.

dos Santos, T. (1968), 'Colonialismo, imperialismo y monopolios en "El Capital" ', in CESO, *Imperialismo y Dependencia Externa*, Santiago, CESO.

dos Santos, T. (1969), 'The crisis of development theory and the problems of dependence in Latin America', in H. Bernstein (ed.), *Underdevelopment and Development*, Harmondsworth, Penguin, 1973.

dos Santos, T. (1970), 'The structure of dependence', *American Economic Review*, Vol. 60, No. 2, pp. 231-6.

ECLA (1965), *El Proceso de Industrialization de America Latina*, Santiago, ECLA.

ECLA (1969), *El Pensamiento de la CEPAL*, Santiago, Editorial Universitaria.

Fajnzylber, F. (1971), *Sistema Industrial e Exportacao de Manufacturados: Analise da Experience Brasiliera*, Rio de Janeiro, IPEA/INPES.

Falk, R.A. (1972), 'Zone II as a world order construct', in J.N. Rosenau, V. Davis, and M.A. East (eds.), *The Analysis of International Politics*, New York, Free Press.

Fanon, F. (1967), *The Wretched of the Earth*, Harmondsworth, Penguin.

Fanon, F. (1970a), *Black Skins: White Masks*, London, Paladin.
Fanon, F. (1970b), *Towards the African Revolution*, Harmondsworth, Pelican.
Faria, U. (1976), 'Occupational marginality, employment and poverty in urban Brazil' (unpublished Ph.D. dissertation, Harvard University).
Fausto, A. (1971), 'La nueva situacion de la dependencia y el analisis sociopolitico de Theotonia dos Santos', *Revista Latinoamericana de Ciencias Sociales*, Nos. 1/2, pp. 198-211.
Fei, J.C.H., and Ranis, G. (1964), *Development of the Labour Surplus Economy: Theory and Policy*, New Haven, Yale University Press.
Fernandez, F. (1970), 'Patrones de dominacion externa en America Latina', *Revista Mexicana de Sociologia*, Vol. XXXII, pp. 1439-59.
Fernandez, R., and Ocampo, J. (1974), 'The Latin American revolution: a theory of imperialism not dependency', *Latin American Perspective*, Vol. I, No. 1, pp. 30-61.
Flanders, J. (1973), 'Prebisch on protectionism: an evaluation', *Economic Journal*, Vol. 74, No. 6, pp. 305-26.
Ford, H. (1922), *My Life and Work*, London, William Heinemann.
Foster-Carter, A. (1974), 'Neo-Marxist approaches to development and underdevelopment', in E. de Kadt and G. Williams (1974).
Foster-Carter, A. (1976), 'From Rostow to Gunder Frank: conflicting paradigms in the analysis of underdevelopment', *World Development*, Vol. 4, No. 3, pp. 167-80.
Frank, A.G. (1966), 'The development of underdevelopment', *Monthly Review*, Vol. 18, No. 4, pp. 17-31.
Frank, A.G. (1967), *Capitalism and Underdevelopment in Latin America: Historical Studies of Chile and Brasil*, New York, Monthly Review Press.
Frank, A.G. (1969), *Latin America: Underdevelopment or Revolution*, New York, Monthly Review Press.
Frank, A.G. (1970), *Lumpenbourgeoisie: Lumpen Development, Dependence, Class and Politics in Latin America*, reprinted, New York, Monthly Review Press, 1972.
Frank, A.G. (1972, 1974 and 1977), 'Dependence is dead, long live dependence and the class struggle: an answer to critics' (Ms. University of Dar es Salaam, 1972); *Latin American Perspectives*, Vol. I, No. 1 (1974), pp. 87-106; and *World Development*, Vol. 5, No. 4 (April 1977), pp. 355-70).
Furtado, C. (1966), *Subdesarrollo y Estancamiento en America Latina*, Buenos Aires, C.E.A.L.
Galeno, E. (1969), 'The de-nationalization of Brazilian industry', *Monthly Review*, Vol. XXI, No. 7, pp. 11-30.
Gerschenkron, A. (1952), 'Economic backwardness in historical perspective', in B. Hoselitz (ed.), *The Progress of Underdeveloped Areas*, Chicago, Chicago University Press, reprinted in A. Gerschenkron (1962), *Economic Backwardness in Historical Perspective*, Cambridge, Mass., The Bleknap Press.
Ghai, D.P. (1972), 'Perspectives on future economic prospects and problems in Africa', in J.N. Bhagwati (ed.), *Economics and World Order*, New York, Macmillan.
Ghai, D.P. (1973), 'Concepts and strategies of economic independence', *Journal of Modern African Studies*, Vol. 11, No. 1, pp. 21-42.
Girvan, N. (1973), 'The development of dependency economics in the Caribbean and Latin America: review and comparison', *Social and Economic Studies*, Vol. 22 (March 1977), pp. 1-33.
Glaucer, K. (1971), 'Origenes del regimen de produccion vigente en Chile', in *Cuadernos de la Realidad Nacional*, No. 6, Santiago, pp. 78-152.
Godfrey, M., and Langdon, S. (1976), 'Partners in underdevelopment?: the transnationalisation thesis in a Kenyan context', *Journal of Commonwealth and Comparative Politics*, Vol. 14, No. 1, pp. 42-63.
Gramsci, A. (1971), *Selection from his Prison Notebooks*, London, Lawrence and Wishart.
Green, R.H. (1970), 'Political independence and the national economy: an essay on

the political economy of decolonisation', in C. Allen and R.W. Johnston (eds.), *African Perspectives: Papers in the History, Politics and Economics of Africa, presented to Thomas Hodgkin*, Cambridge, Cambridge University Press.

Green, R.H. (1975), 'The peripheral African economy and the MNC', in C. Widstrand (ed.), *Multinational Firms in Africa*, Uppsala, Scandinavian Institute of African Studies.

Green, R.H. (1976), 'Tanzanian goals, strategies, results: notes toward an interim assessment' (Ms., Seminar on Socialist Development in Tanzania since 1967, Toronto, April 1976).

Griffin, K. (1969), *Underdevelopment in Spanish America*, London, Allen and Unwin.

Grundy, K.W. (1976), 'Intermediary power and global dependency: the case of South Africa', *International Studies Quarterly*, No. 20, pp. 553-80.

Harris, R. (ed.) (1975), *The Political Economy of Africa*, Cambridge, Mass., Schenkman.

Hilferding, R. (1910), *Finanz Kapital: eine Studie uber die junte Entwicklung des Kapitalismus*, Vienna.

Hinkelammert, F. (1970a), *El Subdesarrollo Latino-americano: Un Caso de Desarrollo Capitalista*, Santiago, Ediciones Nueva Universidad, Universidad Catolica de Chile.

Hinkelammert, F. (1970b), 'La teoria clasica del imperialismo, el subdesarrollo y la acumulacion socialista', reprinted in M.A. Garreton (ed.), *Economia Politica en la Unidad Popular*, Barcelona, Libros de Confrontacion, 1975.

Hinkelammert, F. (1970c), 'Teoria de la dialectica del desarrollo desigual', *Cuadernos de la Realidad Nacional*, No. 6, pp. 15-220.

Hinkelammert, F. (1971), *Dialectica del Desarrollo Desigual*, Valparaiso, Ediciones Universitarias de Valparaiso, 1970.

Hirshman, A. (1958), *The Strategy of Economic Development*, New Haven, Yale University Press.

Hirshman, A. (1861), 'Ideologies of economic development', reprinted in *A Bias for Hope*, New Haven, Yale University Press, 1971.

Hobsbawm, E. (1964), *Introduction to Karl Marx: Pre-capitalist Economic Foundations*, London, Lawrence and Wishart.

Hobson, J.A. (1902), *Imperialism — A Study*, London, Allen and Unwin, 1938.

Hobson, J.A. (1911), *The Economic Interpretation of Investment*, London, The Financial Review of Reviews.

Hodgson, J.L. (1966), 'An evaluation of the Prebisch thesis' (unpublished Ph.D. dissertation, University of Wisconsin, Madison).

Horowitz, D. (ed.) (1968), *Marx and Modern Economics*, New York, Monthly Review Press.

Horowitz, D. (1969), *Imperialism and Revolution*, Harmondsworth, Penguin.

Huntington, S.P., and Nelson, J.M. (1976), *No Easy Choice: Political Participation in Developing Countries*, Cambridge, Mass., Harvard University Press.

Johns, S. (1971), 'Parastatal bodies in Zambia: problems and prospects', in H. and U.E. Simonis (eds.), *Socio-Economic Development in Dual Economies: The Example of Zambia*, Munich, Welform Verlag, for African Studies Institute.

Johns, S. (1975), *State Capitalism in Zambia: The Evolution of the Parastatal Sector*, San Francisco, African Studies Association.

Jorgenson, D.W. (1961), 'The development of a dual economy', *Economic Journal* (June), pp. 309-34.

Jorgenson, D.W. (1967), 'Surplus agricultural labour and the development of a dual economy', *Oxford Economic Papers*, pp. 288-312.

Jorgenson, J.J. (1975), 'Multinational corporations in the indigenization of the Kenyan economy', in C. Widstrand (ed.), *Multinational Firms in Africa*, Uppsala, Scandinavian Institute of African Studies.

Kahl, J.A. (1976), *Modernization, Exploitation and Dependency in Latin America*,

New Jersey, Transaction Books.

Kalecki, M. (1933, 1934 and 1935), *Selected Essays on the Dynamics of the Capitalist Economy 1930-1970*, Cambridge, Cambridge University Press, 1971.

Kautsky, K. (1914), 'Ultra imperialism', *New Left Review* (January-February 1970).

Kay, G. (1975), *Development and Underdevelopment: A Marxist Analysis*, London, Macmillan.

Kemp, T. (1967), *Theories of Imperialism*, London, Dobson Books.

Kemp, T. (1972), 'The Marxist theory of imperialism', in R. Owen and B. Sutcliffe.

Keynes, J.M. (1938), *The General Theory of Employment, Interest and Money*, London, Macmillan, 1960.

Kierman, V.G. (1967), 'Marx on India', *Socialist Register 1967*, London, Merlin Press.

Kruger, D.H. (1955), 'Hobson, Lenin and Schumpeter on Imperialism', *Journal of the History of Ideas*, pp. 250-60.

Krupskaya, N. (1930), *Memories of Lenin*, London, Lawrence and Wishart, 1970.

Laclau, E. (1969), 'Modos de produccion, sistemas economicos y poblacion excedente: aproximacion historica a los casos Argentinos y Chilenos', *Revista Latinoamericana de Sociologia*, Vol. 2, No. 2, pp. 776-816.

Laclau, E. (1971), 'Feudalism and capitalism in Latin America', *New Left Review* (May-June), pp. 19-38.

Lall, S. (1975), 'Is dependence a useful concept in analysing underdevelopment?', *World Development*, Vol. 3, No. 11, pp. 799-810.

Larrain, J. (1977), 'The concept of ideology: some theoretical and methodological questions' (unpublished Ph.D. dissertation, Sussex University).

Lebedinsky, M. (1968), *Del Subdesarrollo al Desarrollo*, Buenos Aires, Editorial Quipo.

Lenin (1899), *The Development of Capitalism in Russia*, Moscow, Progress Publishers, 1967.

Lenin (1915), *Philosophical Notebook*, Moscow, Progress Publishers, 1967.

Lenin (1916), *Imperialism, the Highest Stage of Capitalism*, Peking, Foreign Languages Press, 1970.

Lenin (1917), *1905 — Jornadas Revolucionarias*, Santiago, B.E.P., 1970.

Lenin (1920), '1920 theses', in *La Guerra y la Humanidad*, Mexico, Ediciones Frente Cultural, 1939.

Lewis, A. (1954), 'Economic development with unlimited supplies of labour', *Manchester School of Economic and Social Studies*, Vol. 22, No. 2, pp. 139-92.

Lewis, A. (1958), 'Unlimited labour: further notes', *Manchester School*.

Lukacs, G. (1923), *History and Class Consciousness: Studies in Marxist Didactics*, London, Merlin Press, 1971.

Lukacs, G. (1924), *Lenin: A Study on the Unity of his Thought*, London, New Left Books, 1970.

Luporini, C. (1975), 'Reality and historicity: economy and dialectics in Marxism', *Economy and Society*, Vol. 4, No. 2, pp. 206-321, and Vol. 4, No. 3, pp. 283-308.

Luxemburg, R. (1913), *The Accumulation of Capital*, London, Routledge and Kegan Paul Ltd., 1963.

Mandel, E. (1968), *Marxist Economic Theory*, London, Merlin Press.

Mandel, E. (1970), *La Formacion del Pensamiento Economico de Marx*, Mexico, Siglo XXI Editores.

Malave-Mata, H. (1972), 'Dialectica del subdesarrollo y dependencia', *Problemas de Desarrollo*, No. III, pp. 23-52.

Marini, R.M. (1969), *Subdesarrollo y Revolucion*, Mexico, Siglo XXI Editores.

Marini, R.M. (1972a), 'Brazilian sub-imperialism', *Monthly Review*, No. 9, pp. 14-24.

Marini, R.M. (1972b), 'Dialectica de la dependencia: la economia exportadora', *Sociedad y Desarrollo*, No. 1, pp. 5-31.

Markovitz, L.L. (1977), *Power and Class in Africa: An Introduction to Change and Conflict in African Politics*, Englewood Cliffs, Prentice Hall.

Marx, K. (1848), 'The Communist Manifesto', in L. Feuer (ed.), *Marx and Engels: Basic Writings on Politics and Philosophy*, London, Fontana Library, 1969.

Marx, K. (1853), 'Future results of British rule in India', *New York Daily Tribune* (25 June 1853), reprinted in L. Feuer (ed.), *Marx and Engels: Basic Writings on Politics and Philosophy*, London, Fontana Library, 1969.

Marx, K. (1859), *Grundrisse Foundations of the Critique of Political Economy*, Harmondsworth, Penguin, 1973.

Marx, K. (1867), *El Capital*, Vol. 1, Mexico, F.C.E. 1946.

Marx, K. (1877), 'Russia's pattern of development', Letter to the Editorial Board of the Otechestvennige Zapiski, reprinted in L. Feuer (ed.), *Marx and Engels: Basic Writings on Politics and Philosophy*, London, Fontana Library, 1969.

Marx, K. (1885), *El Capital*, Vol. II, Mexico, F.C.E. 1946.

Marx, K. (1894), *El Capital*, Vol. III, Mexico, F.C.E. 1946.

McGowan, P. (1976), 'Economic dependence and economic performance in Black Africa', *The Journal of Modern African Studies*, Vol. 14, No. 1, pp. 25-40.

McHenry, D.E. (1976), 'The underdevelopment theory: a case-study from Tanzania', *The Journal of Modern African Studies*, Vol. 14, No. 1, pp. 621-36.

Meeropol, M. (1972), 'Towards a political economy analysis of underdevelopment', *Review of Radical Political Economy*, Vol. IV, pp. 77-108.

Muller, R. (1973), 'The multinational corporation and the underdevelopment of the third world', in C.K. Wilbee (ed.), *The Political Economy of Development and Underdevelopment*, New York, Random House.

Nettl, P. (1975), *Rosa Luxemburgo*, Mexico, ERA.

Novack, G. (1970), 'The permanent revolution in Latin America', *International Press*, Vol. III, pp. 978-83.

Nove, A. (1974), 'On reading Andre Gunder Frank', *Journal of Development Studies*, Vol. 10, Nos. 3 and 4, pp. 445-55.

Nyerere, J.K. (1973), *Freedom and Development*, Dar es Salaam, Oxford University Press.

O'Brien, P. (1975), 'A critique of Latin American theories of dependency', in I. Oxaal, T. Barnett and D. Booth (eds.), *Beyond the Sociology of Development*, London, Routledge and Kegan Paul.

O'Connor, J. (1970), 'The meaning of imperialism', in R.I. Rhodes (1970).

Okumu, J. (1971), 'The place of African states in international relations', in A. Schou and A. Brundtland (eds.), *Small States in International Relations*, Stockholm, Almqvist and Wiksell, Nobel Symposium 17.

Owen, R., and Sutcliffe, B. (eds.) (1972), *Studies in the Theory of Imperialism*, London, Longman.

Palloix, C. (1970), 'La question de l'impérialisme chez V.I. Lenin et Rosa Luxemburg', *L'Homme et Société* (January-March 1970).

Palma, G. (ed.) (1973), *La Vie Chilena al Socialismo*, Mexico, Siglo XXI Editores.

Palma, G. (1978), 'Dependency: a formal theory of underdevelopment, or a methodology for the analysis of concrete situations of underdevelopment?', *World Development*, Vol. 6, No. 7/8, pp. 881-924.

Palma, G. (forthcoming), 'Essays on the development of the Chilean manufacturing industry: a case of capitalist associated development',

Petras, J. (1969), *Politics and Social Forces in Chilean Development*, Berkeley, University of California Press.

Petras, J. (1970), *Politics and Social Structure in Latin America*, New York, Monthly Review Press.

Pinto, A. (1965), 'La concentracion del progreso tecnico y de sus frutos en el desarrollo' *Trimestre Economico*, No. 25, pp. 3-69; reprinted in A. Pinto (1973).

Pinto, A. (1973), *Inflacion: Raices Estructurales*, Mexico, F.C.E.

Pinto, A. (1974), 'Heterogencidad estructural y el metodo de desarrollo reciente' in J. Serra (ed.), *Desarrollo Latinoamericano, Ensayos Criticos*, Mexico, F.C.E.

Pinto, A., and Knakel, J. (1973), 'The centre-periphery system 20 years later', *Social and Economic Studies*, pp. 34-89.

Pratt, R.C. (1975), 'Foreign policy issues and the emergence of socialism in Tanzania, 1961-68', *International Journal*, Vol. 30, No. 3, pp. 445-70.

Poulantzas, N. (1972), *Poder Politico y Clases Sociales en el Estado Capitalista*, Mexico, Siglo XXI Editores.

Prebisch, R. (1963), *Hacia una Dinamica del Desarrollo Economico*, Mexico, F.C.E.

Prebisch, R. (1980), 'Prologo', in O. Rodriguez (1980).

Quijano, A. (1971), 'Nationalism and capitalism in Peru: a study of neo-imperialism', *Monthly Review* (July-August).

Radice, H. (ed.) (1975), *International Firm and Modern Imperialism*, Harmondsworth, Penguin.

Ray, D. (1973), 'The dependency model of Latin American underdevelopment: three basic fallacies', *Journal of Interamerican Studies and World Affairs*, Vol. XV, pp. 4-20.

Rey, P.P. (1971), *Les Alliances des Classes*, Paris, Maspero.

Rhodes, R.I. (ed.) (1970), *Imperialism and Underdevelopment: A Reader*, New York, Monthly Review Press.

Robinson, J. (1963), *Introduction in Rosa Luxemburg, Accumulation of Capital*, London, Routledge and Kegan Paul.

Rodriguez, O. (1980), *La Teoria del Subdesarrollo de la CEPAL*, Mexico, Siglo XXI Editores.

Rood, L.L. (1975), 'Foreign investment in African manufacturing', *Journal of Modern African Studies*, Vol. 13, No. 1, pp. 19-34.

Rothchild, D., and Curry, R.L. (1975), *Beyond the Nation-State: The Political Economy of Regionalism*, San Francisco, American Political Science Association.

Rudenko, G. (1966), *La Metodologia Leninista en la Investigacion del Imperialismo*, Havana, Publicaciones Economicas.

Rweyemamu, J.F. (1971), 'The causes of poverty in the periphery', *Journal of Modern African Studies*, Vol. IX, pp. 453-5.

Rweyemamu, J. (1973), *Underdevelopment and Industrialization in Tanzania*, Nairobi, Oxford University Press.

Salera, V. (1971), 'Prebisch's change and development', *Interamerican Economic Affairs*, Vol. 24, No. 4, pp. 67-79.

Sandbrook, R. (1975), *Proletarians and African Capitalism: The Kenyan Case 1960-1972*, London, Cambridge University Press.

Sassoon, D. (1975), 'An introduction to Luporini', *Economy and Society*, Vol. 4, No. 2, pp. 194-205.

Saul, J.S. (1973), 'Socialism in one country: Tanzania', in G. Arrighi and J.S. Saul, *Essays on the Political Economy of Africa*, New York, Monthly Review Press.

Schumacher, E.F. (1975), *Small is Beautiful: Economics as if People Mattered*, New York, Harper and Row.

Seers, D., Schaffer, B., and Kiljunen, K.-L. (eds.) (1979), *Underdeveloped Europe: Studies in Core-Periphery Relations*, Hassocks, Sussex, Harvester Press.

Seidman, A. (1972), *Comparative Development Strategies in West Africa*, Nairobi, East African Publishing House.

Seidman, A. (1974), 'The distorted growth of import-substitution industry: the Zambian case', *Journal of Modern African Studies*, Vol. 12, No. 4, pp. 601-31.

Seligson, M. (1972), 'The "dual society" thesis in Latin America: a re-examination of the Costa Rica case', *Social Forces*, Vol. LI, pp. 91-8.

Selwyn, P. (ed.) (1975a), *Development Policy in Small Countries*, London, Croom Helm.

Selwyn, P. (1975b), *Industries of the Southern African Periphery*, London, Croom Helm.

Serra, J. (ed.) (1974), *Desarrollo Latinoamericano, Ensayos Criticos*, Mexico, F.C.E.

Shapiro, L., and Reddaway, P. (1967), *Lenin: The Man, The Theorist, The Leader*, London.

Shaw, T.M. (1975), 'The political economy of African international relations', *Issue*, Vol. 5. No. 4, pp. 29-38.

Shaw, T.M. (1976), *Dependence and Underdevelopment: The Development and Foreign Policies of Zambia*, Papers in International Studies, Africa Series No. 28, Athens, Ohio University.

Shaw, T.M., and Newbury, M.C. (1977), 'Dependence or interdependence; Africa in the global political economy', in M.W. Delancey (ed.), *African International Relations*, New York, Africana.

Shaw, T.M., and Grieve, M. (1977), 'Dependence or development: international and internal inequalities in Africa', *Development and Change*, No. 8, pp. 377-408.

Singer, H.W. (1970), 'Dualism revisited: a new approach to the problems of the dual society in developing countries', *Journal of Development Studies*, Vol. VII, pp. 60-75.

Singer, P. (1971), *Forca de Trabalho e Emprego, no Brazil 1920-1969*, Saõ Paulo, CEBRAP, Cuaderno, Numero 3.

Stalin, J. (1934), *Problems of Leninism*, Moscow, Cooperative Publishing Society of Foreign Workers in the USSR.

Stenberg, M. (1974), 'Dependency, imperialism and the relations of production', *Latin American Perspective*, Vol. 1, No. 1, pp. 75-86.

Sunkel, O. (1972), 'Big business and dependency', *Foreign Affairs*, Vol. 24, No. 1, pp. 517-31.

Sunkel, O. (1973a), 'The pattern of Latin American development', in V.I. Urquidi and E.R.Thorp (eds.), *Latin America in the International Economy*, London, Macmillan.

Sunkel, O. (1973b), 'Transnational capitalism and national disintegration in Latin America', *Social and Economic Studies*, Vol. 22, No. 1, pp. 132-76.

Sunkel, O. (1974), 'A critical commentary on the United Nations Report on multinational corporations in world development', IDS, Sussex.

Sunkel, O., and Paz, P. (1970), *El Subdesarrollo Latinoamericano y la Teoria del Desarrollo*, Mexico, Siglo XXI Editores.

Sutcliffe, B. (1972a), 'Imperialism and industrialization in the third world', in R. Owen and B. Sutcliffe (1972).

Sutcliffe, B. (1972b), 'Conclusions', in R. Owen and B. Sutcliffe (1972).

Suarez, A. (1967), *Cuba: Castroism and Communism: 1959-1966*, Cambridge, Mass., MIT Press.

Sweezy, P. (1942), *La Teoria del Desarrollo Capitalista*, Mexico, F.C.E. 1969.

Tavares, M.C., and Serra, J. (1970), 'Mas alla del estancamiento', in J. Serra (1974).

Thomas, C.V. (1974), *Dependence and Transformation: The Economics of the Transition to Socialism*, New York, Monthly Review Press.

Thomas, C.V. (1975), 'Industrialization and the transformation of Africa: an alternative to MNC expansion', in C. Widstrad (ed.), *Multinational Firms in Africa*, Uppsala, Scandinavian Institute of African Studies.

Thomas, C.V. (1976), 'Class struggle, social development and the theory of the non-capitalist path', Scandinavian Seminar on Non-capitalist Development in Africa, Helsinki, August 1976.

Trotsky, L. (1930), *Historia de la Revolucion Rusa*, Santiago, Quimantu, 1972.

Varga, E., and Mendelson, L. (eds.) (1939), *New Data for V.I. Lenin's Imperialism, the Highest Stage of Capitalism*, London, Lawrence and Wishart.

Vernon, R. (1976), 'The distribution of power', in R. Vernon (ed.), *The Oil Crisis*, New York, W.W. Norton.

Villamil, J. (ed.) (1979), *Transnational Capitalism and National Development: New Perspectives on Dependence*, Hassocks, Sussex, Harvester Press.

Viner, J. (1951), 'Seis conferencias', *Revista Brasileira de Economia*, Vol. 2, Rio de

Janeiro.

Vitale, L. (1966), 'America Latina: feudal o capitalista', *Estrategia*, No. 3.

Vuscovic, P. (197), 'Distribucion del ingreso y opciones de desarrollo' reprinted in M.A. Garrteon, *Economica Politica de la Unidad Popular*, Barcelona, Libros de Confrontacion, 1975.

Vuscovic, P. (1973), 'La politica economica del gobierno de la Unidad Popular', in G. Palma (1973).

Walicki, A. (1969), *The Controversy over Capitalism*, London, Oxford University Press.

Wallerstein, I. (1971), 'The range of choice: constraints on the policies of governments of contemporary African independent states', in M.F. Lofchie (ed.), *The State of the Nations*, Berkeley, University of California Press.

Wallerstein, I. (1973), 'Africa in a capitalist world', *Issue*, Vol. 3, No. 3, pp. 1-12.

Wallerstein, I. (1974a), *The Modern World System: Capitalist Agriculture and the Origins of the European World-Economy in the Sixteenth Century*, New York, Academic Press.

Wallerstein, I. (1974b), 'Dependence in an interdependent world: the limited possibilities of a transformation within the capitalist world economy', *African Studies Review*, Vol. 17, No. 1, pp. 1-26.

Wallerstein, I. (1975), 'Class and class conflict in contemporary Africa', *Monthly Review*, No. 26, pp. 34-42 (originally published in the *Canadian Journal of African Studies*, Vol. 7, No. 3, pp. 375-80).

Warren, B. 91973), 'Imperialism and capitalist industrialization', *New Left Review*, pp. 3-44.

Weisskopf, T.E. (1976), 'Dependence as an explanation of underdevelopment: a critique' (Ms., University of Michigan, 1976).

Zartman, I.W. (1976), 'Europe and Africa: decolonization or dependency?', *Foreign Affairs*, Vol. 54, No. 2, pp. 325-43.

2 DEPENDENCY AND THE NEWLY INDUSTRIALISING COUNTRIES (NICs): TOWARDS A REAPPRAISAL

Manfred Bienefeld

Dependency is a label which encompasses such a diversity of arguments that any discussion of it must take care to distinguish between different usages if it is not to add further confusion to an already obscure debate.

Some exponents and most critics appear to define the approach in terms of certain of its conclusions, which have all too often taken the rather ahistorical and paradoxically static form of statements asserting or implying a permanent division of the global economy into a core and a periphery and treating capitalist development in the periphery as an impossibility. In this context, 'analysis' has often been reduced to a one-sided and tautological account of how economic, social, political and cultural factors interact to reproduce this pattern. Given the inevitable fact that in such an interdisciplinary analysis there are many unquantifiable factors, it has rarely proved difficult to reach this effectively predetermined conclusion in any particular instance.

Such conclusions were never analytically defensible, and the events of the 1970s have served to expose their fallacy more clearly than ever. While this is as it should be, it does not deny the importance or the value of the dependency perspective as such, because that perspective cannot be defined primarily in terms of a particular set of conclusions, although these were admittedly frequently drawn by exponents of this approach. In fact, given the historical, dynamic and interdisciplinary emphasis of that perspective, such static and ahistorical conclusions represent an anomaly which can be understood, though not therefore defended, only in ideological terms. For this it is necessary to consider the context within which dependency emerged.

In essence dependency should be understood as one part of the reaction against the free trade-modernisation orthodoxy which represented in many senses the mirror image of the crude dependency theory earlier discussed. Here the *a priori* conclusion was often the positive impact of economic and social integration into the 'modern' world. Here too there were enough qualitative variables to allow any reality to be squared with this conclusion. Tautology also did service in that failures to derive the expected benefits of integration became *prima facie* proof of internal ('traditional') impediments to change. In this case it was the static and ahistorical nature of the analysis which has to be understood in terms of the role it played in legitimising policies serving particular interests.

The generally ambiguous and often extremely polarising consequences

79

of integrationist policies when pursued in technologically relatively backward economies provided the material and political base from which alternative perspectives emerged.

The cruel fact was that for many developing economies the attempt to integrate themselves fully into the international economy as it actually existed revealed a situation in which devaluation had to be stopped long before it could produce anything like internal full employment. The reason devaluation could not be pursued to its logical conclusion ('the equilibrium exchange rate') lay in the fact that the associated real wage reductions first meet political limits, when social and political polarisation become acute, and then economic limits, when further wage reductions begin to increase unit labour costs (the reduced efficiency wage) and when capital flows are impaired by the above political developments. The resulting social polarisation and generally high levels of domestic unemployment, often of both capital and labour (Schydlowski 1976, Mezzera 1977) fuelled the search for an alternative perspective.

This could take the form of a direct advocacy of peasant based socialism, as derived (with some difficulty) from 'traditional' Marxist analysis in Maoist China. Alternatively it may take the form of a simple insistence that nationalist policies are necessary to counter various problems associated with integrationist policies when pursued by economically weak countries. The modern, post-mercantilist versions of this position generally consider such policies not as ends in themselves, but as means to the achievement of a relative economic advance which will then allow a fuller and more effective integration. This version of the argument, which can be traced back at least to the German nineteenth century economist List, received its greatest post-war impetus from the Latin American structuralist school associated with Prebisch and ECLA.

Dependency, as an extension of the structuralist position, stresses the need to incorporate into the analysis questions concerning the adequacy of the political base from which policies aimed at national structural change must be implemented. The position broadly accepts the importance of the structuralist problematic but argues that in addition to establishing the need for such nationally defined policies, it is also necessary to analyse these factors which may stand in the way of their formulation and implementation. This means, among other things, that all policy choices must also explicitly concern themselves with the impact which they themselves will have on the balance of political forces which will determine the future formulation of policy. These issues are analysed within an international context of asymmetrical interdependence in which relative technological backwardness and relative economic and political weakness are considered to constitute major (though not insurmountable) problems for 'national' policy formulation, because they increase both the intensity of, and the potential difficulties associated with, international (foreign) influence as mediated through economic, political and cultural channels.

Dependency, understood as an interdisciplinary attempt to analyse these issues for the purpose of identifying desirable long-term national strategies and policies, is not only defensible, but of great and increasing importance in a world which is integrating and polarising at one and the same time. While that discussion is not a substitute for specific disciplinary analysis, either of a theoretical or an empirical kind, it represents a perspective from which such analyses can be related to each other, and within which they should be required to confront certain aspects of the concrete reality of underdevelopment which they sometimes ignore. Unfortunately the actual debate which has developed from this perspective has suffered from two fundamental weaknesses, which in turn have led to many of the unwarranted conclusions mentioned at the outset.

Problems derived from a false point of departure

The weaknesses of the dependency debate are closely related to its strengths, namely its interdisciplinary approach and its orientation towards long-term strategic policy issues. The ambitious interdisciplinary orientation invites oversimplification while the concern with strategic policy creates intense pressures to draw broad conclusions quickly, and to become committed to the conclusions once drawn. These shortcomings neither excuse the weaknesses, nor invalidate the approach. As problems they should be recognised so as to be minimised. As inevitable concomitants of an interdisciplinary, long-term policy orientation they merely remind us that it is spurious to resolve those problems through achieving greater 'rigour' by pushing more of reality under the 'ceteris paribus' carpet, or by claiming objectivity in an area of social science with ideological, material and political consequences simply too direct and too visible to afford participants the luxury of this pretense.

The first problem with the debate as it has developed concerns the basic structuralist premise that nationally-oriented and formulated policy is desirable, in order to meet certain specified objectives more effectively. Much of the dependency debate accepts this premise as 'given', and all too frequently treats it as implicitly absolute. The consequence is a use of the concept of 'self-reliance', as if that conformed to the principle of 'the more the better', and a use of the notion of 'delinking' which implies that this is an end in itself, rather than a means to an end. A further consequence of these fallacies is to induce a concern with internal structures and price relativities, without significant regard for changing external circumstances. This is, of course, the antithesis of the dependency perspective.

The route by which the debate often reaches such contradictory and untenable conclusions leads through the above misconceptions, and follows on from those to the facile, but attractive, conclusion that therefore a 'socialist' alternative is shown to be necessary, because it is said to represent the only circumstance under which delinking can be sufficiently extensive to allow the necessary national 'self-reliant' policies to be formulated and implemented. While this conclusion may be correct in many cases, it cannot be reached by this route and there have been major differences between those who have reached it in this way, and those who have reached it via a more orthodox Marxist route. The discussion will return to that dispute.

The argument, which is built on the crude and indefensible premise of an unqualified need for 'national' policy, and which goes on to conclude that this is achievable only through virtually total disengagement, will be readily induced to assert the 'impossibility' of peripheral capitalist development on the grounds that sufficiently independent nationalist states, based on a capitalist economy, are not conceivable in the modern age.

Insofar as much of the dependency debate has explicitly and implicitly operated from such premises and drawn such conclusions, it has spread confusion and misunderstanding. Indeed, in many respects this part of the debate represented a backward step from the structuralist discussion, and in some areas it has obscured important distinctions being made in the development economics debate.

Inevitably this version of the argument has been unable to take on board the major changes in the international context, which have characterised the 1970s, although these events have undermined its foundations and exposed its fallacies. Those same events have, however, also emphasised the importance of further analysis from the dependency perspective properly understood, so that one must assume that those former exponents of the approach who have been induced by the events of the seventies to confess the sins of their past, and to renounce dependency, were operating with the crude arguments described above.

This crude dependency argument was always indefensible. In fact the case for extensive nationally-oriented policy intervention always had to be established in relation to specific sets of circumstances: a country's particular physical (resources, population, location)[1] and social (cultural cohesion, skills) characteristics; with due regard to the international context, in terms of resource availability and demand, financial flows, and general competitive conditions; and, finally, in relation to the possibilities of consistent and effective political intervention. In addition, it always had to be established with reference to a particular set of objectives, reflecting some pattern of socially and politically defensible priorities and including some specified notion of social time preference.

This does not mean each case is unique. Generalisations are possible at various levels of abstraction and in relation to various common characteristics of the economics being analysed. Furthermore, because the debate is concerned with the impact of certain types of external linkage, it must evidently consider such issues separately for various economic systems in which economics are linked through different mechanisms. For this reason the fact that this paper, and the dependency debate in general, is primarily concerned with dependency in the capitalist context is not to be understood as suggesting that problems associated with asymmetric interdependence linked to technological backwardness and economic and political weakness do not exist under socialism. It simply means that such problems need to be identified and analysed in relation to that specific set of circumstances. Indeed, as we shall see later in this paper, it is of great importance that even the analysis of these issues within the capitalist context should make due allowance for significant changes in the operations of that system.

This means that the answer to the question of whether there can be a general discussion of dependency, or only an analysis of particular unique cases, is both 'yes' and 'no'.

The answer is 'no' insofar as the detailed conclusions to be reached in any particular policy debate must be derived from the specific circumstances of that case (though this should include its international context). The answer is emphatically 'yes', insofar as it is both possible and important to establish more generally applicable propositions identifying the broad characteristics of relationships within a particular systemic context. These general characteristics in turn become the background against which particular cases must be analysed. At this level there are a variety of propositions which have been raised to prominence in the analysis of capitalist dependency and which constitute points of departure for any analysis. These propositions do not apply uniformly to all cases, but they constitute general areas of difficulty for developing countries, the applicability of which must be assumed unless it can be shown that specific circumstances exist which deny their relevance in a particular case.

These propositions include the desirability of extensive state intervention to ensure that international competitive pressures do not become destructive, instead of being conducive to greater efficiency; state policy to concern itself directly with the generation of external economies through macro-economic measures; an explicit concern with the encouragement and achievement of an effective transfer of technology and the building up of technological capabilities; a concern with the ambiguous and potentially problematic consequences of international capital flows over the short and the long term; a clear awareness of the vital importance of the absorptive capacity of the industrial country markets, and the short-term limitations of that; a concern to define and pursue nationally-oriented policies in such a manner that international political and economic retaliation is both anticipated and counteracted; an awareness of the importance of sustaining the political coalitions on which such national policies necessarily depend; a recognition of the serious difficulty of attempt to reconcile more rapid development with democracy or a degree of social justice. This list could be extended, but these few examples illustrate the point. That point is *not* that these problems are raised only in a dependency frame. This is clearly not true. It is rather that it is in that debate that these, and other points, are brought to bear on the issues simultaneously, and free from the *a priori* assumption that there exists a free market which will resolve them as best as could be expected. Naturally, these points must not be raised on the opposite *a priori* assumption, namely that the real market transforms each of them into absolute blockages implying that no technology is transferred, or that international capital flows produce only problems.

Hence dependency does not deny the possibility of capitalist development in the periphery. It simply derives from both historical and theoretical sources an appreciation of the enormous difficulties which are placed in the way of that possibility, when some or all of the following conditions apply: a large technological gap; extensive market instability; a high degree of market concentration and compartmentalisation (most extreme in the case of markets internal to vertically integrated firms); large international wage differentials, with developing country wages so low as to limit the scope for further reduction without increasing unit labour costs; significant impediments to international capital flows determined by the interests of capital exporting economies; a high level of foreign capital involvement in the primary export sectors of developing countries; and the existence of important external economies associated with industrial development.

When many of these conditions apply, as they do to most developing countries in the post-war world, and to some of the weaker industrial countries as well, the case for extensive state intervention becomes powerful. The experience of the 1970s reinforces this conclusion, even though the current suggestion that policy is primarily a matter of 'getting the prices right' (in relation to international prices) seems to suggest otherwise. Before turning to that issue let us consider the second major weakness of the dependency debate.

A second weakness: the unspecified destination

Having suggested that much of the dependency debate has been deeply problematic because it has based itself on a false premise, it is necessary to suggest further that that debate has frequently aimed at a destination which it has also treated in a rather cavalier manner. All too often the socialism which it posited as the 'solution', was given the tautological meaning of being that form of society or state which, through its control of the means of production, could and would produce the desired more rapid, more integrated development together with socialist democracy. So long as capitalist development was defined as impossible, the relative desirability of this alternative was easy to assert, even when serious problems were recognised. However, once capitalist development in the periphery is considered possible, even though extremely difficult, then the problems of the proposed alternative loom rather larger, and require more explicit treatment than they have generally received.

It is not surprising that the conclusion that socialism is necessary in peripheral economies because of their need to disengage (in some absolute sense) from the international economy, has generated considerable and legitimate criticism from those who derive an espousal of socialism from a more traditional Marxist analysis. The latter group has been deeply concerned by the equation of socialism with disengagement from the international economy and by the idea that there are areas of the globe to which capitalism will not extend. They have also been unhappy about the implication: that phenomena like marginalisation are particular to peripheral capitalism or that the need for socialism is confined to the peripheral economies. They have finally been most disturbed by the fact that much of the dependency debate assumes the possibility of a humane, democratic and progressive socialism in the periphery.

These concerns are clearly justified and they do establish the irreconcilability of Marxist analysis with those versions of dependency which stress the need for total disengagement, speak of permanent cores and peripheries, and assert socialism as the correct objective of political struggle without considering seriously the necessary material and political conditions which would allow such a socialism to produce the desired results.

However the dependency perspective does not necessarily involve these untenable assumptions, and when it does not, it stands in no fundamental contradiction with Marxist analysis. Indeed, the clear Marxist emphasis on the uneven nature of capitalist development is a foundation on which that analysis invites the development of a dependency perspective. In that case there is no conflict whatsoever between the simultaneous acceptance of a globally expanding and growing capitalism, and the identification of a 'special' set of problems and consequences associated with economically and technically less advanced regions. Equally, marginalisation does not contradict the basic notion of capitalism's periodic regeneration of the reserve army of labour, but appears as a particular form of that process in which its consequences are distributed unevenly throughout the global system. From such an analysis the conclusion readily follows that the contradictions of capitalism are deeper within such peripheral areas, that the possibility of releasing tensions through material concessions are more constrained, and that hence radical political pressures are more likely to build up. However, the conclusion that is likely to produce socialism cannot be reconciled so readily with a Marxist analysis and remains a major point of contention.

While it is clear that a Marxist analysis is not compatible with the assumption that socialism is a universally available alternative to capitalism, a vigorous debate contests the question whether the possibility of socialism is totally precluded by that analysis in all situations where the forces of production are not relatively advanced. Some interpretations do assert this impossibility and are led thereby to an emphasis on the concept of 'premature socialism' (Warren 1973), or to the conclusion that socialism is conceivable only as international socialism. The escape from this form of determinism is effected either through the Maoist concept of 'peasant socialism', or through the notion of the 'relative autonomy' of the state in the less advanced countries (Alavi 1972, Saul 1974). The latter position is based effectively on the idea that in that context the relative weakness of socialist forces is often paralleled by an equivalent weakness of opposing class forces. While this is an important argument, it essentially relates to the conditions which might bring a radical progressive regime to power, and much less to the question of whether such a regime is likely to be able to bring to fruition its good intentions.

This latter point has frequently diverted the debate into an essentially sterile and ultimately semantic argument about whether or not the reality in any particular country meets some author's minimum requirements to qualify for the category, socialist. This debate was naturally linked to the crude version of dependency which treated socialism as an adequate description of the solution to the dilemma of underdevelopment. On the other hand, the defensible version of dependency is based on the more plausible and less restrictive assumption that socialism could be regarded as a potentially desirable object of immediate political struggle in the context of many developing countries, not because it held out the promise of an immediate transformation to an ideal type of socialism, but because it raised the possibility that in spite of political weaknesses and obstacles a substantial increase in the social control exercised over the economic process could prove to be progressive, in the sense defined above. In an international context this control would, of course, initially be exercised through the agency of the state, and its orientation would necessarily be based on some definition of a national interest. While that was often a spurious cover for sectional or international interests, this was not necessarily always the case to the same degree. In effect, this approach induces dependency to take a more detailed and active interest in the differences between the entire range of state interventions. It does after all make a difference to a country's working people where it stands in the international capitalist hierarchy. Indeed this is the basic premise of dependency.

To escape that dilemma a debate about 'the transition to socialism' has emerged, and insofar as this debate does not collapse into an excessively literal search for evidence of annual unilinear movement towards the ultimate objective (suitably defined), it allows the issue to be posed in a more useful manner. This means that it should ask the question whether or not a greater degree of social control can be imposed on the development process through the mechanism of the state, and whether this control can be (or is being) exercised in the interests (short- or long-term) of the great majority of the members of that society.

Such a phrase need only be written to convince even the most optimistic of the enormous difficulty of attempting to answer it. However, it has to be posed and addressed in this way. It cannot be avoided by an *a priori*, and potentially tautological, definition of the socialist state as the sole means of producing such a result. Nevertheless, the dependency debate's unacceptable tendency to reject all cases of state intervention within a non-socialist framework as necessarily incapable of generating any significant short- or long-term benefits for the working people involved, had a political rationale, and an analytic foundation, and the unwarranted crudeness of such a conclusion should not be allowed to obscure its substantial grain of truth.

This conclusion appears somewhat less crude once it is accepted that in general the dependency argument must be understood to address the possibility of a development which generates benefits diffused throughout society and compatible with a relative reduction in levels of political, social and economic repression. Given this objective, its tendency to reject state capitalist alternatives is more understandable and also less challenged by the events of the 1970s. However, while dependency's scepticism with respect to the possibility of peripheral capitalist development, even when there is substantial state involvement, is made much more defensible by this formulation, it still cannot and should not be seen in terms of an impossibility. At the same time, to look at the possibility of capitalist development in this way is not a confusion of morality and analysis (Palma 1978), but rather the politically and analytically most important way of posing the question of capitalist development in the periphery (Bienefeld 1980b).

The challenge of the 1970s to this formulation of dependency is not in fact very far-reaching, though sufficient to undermine the notion of impossibility. The challenge arises because in a very few cases capitalist development has proceeded to the point of beginning to diffuse benefits and pushing up unskilled real wages, but the important issue is to analyse that process in detail and to clarify the stringent national and international conditions which have helped to produce these results. This is a prime task for analysis from a dependency perspective, and in order to undertake it, a much broader range of state intervention will have to be considered than that allowed by a simple dichotomous distinction of socialist and non-socialist states.

What is a separate though closely related question is whether policies which achieve a relative advance within the capitalist context are sustainable or desirable in the long run, or whether they necessarily lead to intra-capitalist conflict in the context of periodic crises. This is a question which the dependency perspective cannot address directly because its basic concern is too narrow to encompass that issue. The next section will show, however, that dependency must accept the challenge of incorporating into its analysis the consequences of changes in the phases of development of the international economy, and ultimately the possibility of major contradictions developing within international capitalism.

The NICs from a dependency perspective

The 1970s produced a variety of highly contradictory trends. For many developing countries it was a period of extreme difficulty, mounting indebtedness and social and political polarisation. For some oil producers it was a period of phenomenal growth in incomes, but very slow movement in their attempts to translate this wealth into a broadly based process of economic and social change. For the industrial countries it was a period of growing uncertainty, rising unemployment and economic instability. Finally, for a few newly industrialising countries (NICs)[2] it was a period of sustained and phenomenally rapid growth, based on an equally remarkable expansion of manufactured exports.

These developments, especially the explosive growth of the NICs, have been interpreted in many different ways. The most prevalent explanation of the NIC phenomenon has placed very heavy emphasis on the internal policies pursued by the respective countries, with special stress on their efforts to get their prices right in relation to international opportunity costs and thereby to promote exports by nullifying previous biases against exports (Bhagwati 1978, Little 1979). From this it has been widely concluded that such policies have a crucial importance and a wide applicability in other developing countries intent upon reproducing the NIC experience (Keesing 1979).

For the dependency perspective these conclusions represent a considerable challenge in that they assert in a generalised way the prime importance of internal policy, the adequacy of market price signals as guides to resource allocation, and the effective insignificance of the potential problems which might be associated with the role of foreign capital, the transfer of technology, or the generation of external economies in the course of industrialisation.

More challenging still are the arguments which suggest that the cases of South Korea and Taiwan[3] show that if such policies are pursued for a long enough time they will diffuse benefits throughout the society as labour shortage begins to push up unskilled wages (Rao 1978, Westphal 1977). Linked to this observation concerning material benefits is the idea that social and political liberalisation can and will follow in the wake of such a relaxation of material constraints.

It has been argued repeatedly that these developments clearly contradict the crude versions of dependency. The question to be posed now is to what extent they require a major adjustment in the basic premises from which the dependency perspective views the development process. While the following discussion should be regarded primarily as indicative of the issues around which such an assessment must turn, it will tentatively suggest that these premises are likely to be strengthened rather than weakened by such an exercise.

With respect to the issue of the need for extensive state intervention to construct a nationally defined set of priorities and prices, the experience of the majority of NICs allows the initial observation that there can be no doubt about the extent to which power was generally centralised within monolithic states, nor about the extent to which that power was exercised directly in the economic sphere. Such intervention has included widespread intimidation and repression practised in the labour market; direct state involvement in production to establish and support major projects considered to be of particular national significance; heavy state involvement in international financial markets spreading many risks to the national economic level; an extensive and continuing use of tariff protection and export subsidy, carefully adjusted over time in accordance with perceived changes in the competitive strength of various sectors of production (Kim 1980).

This latter point leads to two further observations. Firstly, the carefully controlled, and product-specific adjustment of this set of tariff/subsidies suggests the possibility that the coincidence which has been established between the broad exchange rate policies of the NICs and their phenomenal growth (Bhagwati 1978) should be understood to some extent at least as reflecting a growing competitive strength which allowed such policies to be pursued over a long period without their being choked off by their domestic economic and political consequences. This possibility naturally poses questions regarding the source of this competitive strength, and these lead to the second observation. The gradual and highly differentiated adjustment of levels of protection and subsidy emphasise the fact that it is generally agreed, even by strong supporters of the export promotion policy (Stecher 1980, Yanagihara 1979), that the import substitution phase was a necessary precursor of the later policy, and in the case of Brazil an authoritative source even speaks of the entire recent policy in terms of varying phases of import substitution (Campos 1980). This implies, of course, that the import substitution versus export promotion debate is not a debate about alternatives, but about the transition from the former to the latter which should determine the optimal form of import substitution and the appropriate timing of the transition. In short, import substitution appears as one necessary condition for attaining the manufacturing capability from which a NIC strategy could be launched.

The fact that import substitution as such is not a sufficient condition for achieving greater relative efficiency and hence competitiveness need hardly be stated. In this connection it is the diversity rather than the similarity of the NIC experience which poses two questions for further consideration. The first is that this diversity, when combined with the almost simultaneous emergence of these processes in the larger NICs (Hong Kong and Singapore having begun rather earlier, along with Puerto Rico which has since lost its status as an economists' miracle), draws attention to a possible general, and hence international, change and to this we shall turn in a moment. The second question raised by the diversity of the earlier import substitution processes in the NICs relates to the dependency perspective's broad concern with the potential ambiguities associated with foreign investment, which accept that there are benefits associated with foreign investment, but urges the need to consider the possibility of associated difficulties. It is hence of some interest to note analysts explaining the particular strength of the South Korean experience by reference to the fact that in that case 'there was no involvement of foreign enterprises during the import substitution phase' (Yanagihara 1979). To this one must add that even subsequently South Korea has effectively minimised the role played by direct foreign investment in many areas of basic and heavy industry, thereby recalling the Japanese practice to the present time.

At the same time, Senor Campos, one of the early architects of the 'Brazilian miracle', shows in a recent paper that Brazil's import substitution had occurred with a very extensive, if not dominant, participation of foreign capital and follows this with a plea for an 'urgent need to re-assess the role of the foreign sector at the present stage of the Brazilian ISI' (Import Substituting Industrialisation) (Campos 1980).

It would be of some interest to pursue the hypothesis that this difference has been critical in enabling Korea to formulate and implement a strategy of which it has been said that 'it is difficult not to be struck by the bold vision and imaginative approach of Korea's long-term strategy' (Hasan 1976). It is of the essence of bold, long-term strategies that they require a political and economic base which is sufficiently strong and independent to assume the attendant risks and short-term costs. Here again the Japanese example provides an important analogy (Singh 1978). Finally, it goes without saying that such strategies require the extensive state involvement earlier discussed.

These issues also relate directly to the question of technology and its acquisition. Here again it is clear that the strategic dimension of Korean policy has, like the Japanese policy, at its core a technological rationale. Both are based on an argument which holds that when industrialisation produces full employment competitiveness will be sustained only by a relative improvement in productivity and this will then require extensive technical capabilities. This need not imply, as Luc Soete's paper suggests,[4] a capacity to invent new technologies across the industrial spectrum, but merely the need to develop the capacity to innovate, or to apply the most recent technologies on an expanding scale. The long-term strategies formulated by Korea and Japan[5] are based on a belief in the vital importance of this capability and on a rejection of the assumption that these capabilities will develop of their own accord. The developments of the past fifteen years would appear to suggest the Japanese perception of this issue may well be the correct one. In the context of the NICs the issue reappears in the Brazilian case where the stage of import substituting capital goods has now been blocked for some time by the fact that such a capability was not built up more strongly much earlier, and that attempts to do so at this late stage are defeated by the short-term cost increases which they transmit to the entire industrial structure.

On balance it is at least plausible to suggest that the NIC phenomenon strengthens the basic premises of dependency which stress the relative importance for developing countries of extensive state intervention in the economy; of protection against external competition provided it is adjusted gradually and selectively in accordance with changing relative levels of efficiency; of the need to be concerned about the long-term consequences of direct foreign investment; and of the need to consider explicitly and actively policies which will accelerate the domestic acquisition of techno-logical capabilities and the national generation of external economies.

The next issue to consider is that of the relative importance of inter-national conditions as opposed to national circumstances and policies. As indicated earlier, the simultaneity of the NIC explosion suggests a possible common cause. This supposition is strengthened when it is recalled that this development occurred at a time when the international economy underwent major changes. What connections can one establish between these two sets of developments?

The developments of the 1970s are fundamentally related to a long-term decline in the competitiveness of the United States (and of a lesser significance the British) economy, which is most graphically reflected in the long-term productivity trends for the major industrial countries. Within the formal structure of the Bretton Woods arrangements (relatively fixed exchange rates and convertibility of dollars into gold) this under-lying trend was reflected in a growing outflow of dollars combined with increasing doubts about the 'real' value of those dollars. The Vietnam war accelerated this process dramatically, making the point that this economic decline (Meier 1977) undermined the entire basis of the international political balance, dependent as that was on the dominant geo-political role of the United States. The response of the United States was to use its power in the spheres of finance, defence, energy and food to counter these trends, thus illustrating the fact that what is sometimes considered to be economics can only be understood as political economy (Bienefeld 1980a). Associated with these trends was a sustained period of growth and econo-mic expansion which generated two further phenomena of great importance: the first was a rapid increase in the demand for various raw material inputs, and the second was a secular decline in rates of profit in the OECD econo-mies (OECD 1979b) which reflected both a gradual tendency towards the over-building of industrial capacity to produce production goods (Forrester 1977) and the coming on stream in the latter half of the 1960s of the enormous quantities of industrial capacity which the Japanese had installed in the context of the long-term strategy earlier discussed, and which raised its share of global manufacturing capacity from 4.8 to 7.8 per cent in the space of five years.

In any event, whatever the preferred causal sequence the fact was that the differential productivity trends in the major industrial economies, the declining rates of profit, the emergence of persistent and widespread levels of unemployment and of excess installed industrial capacity, and the related increasing importance of the struggle over monopoly rents based on the control of resources or of technology, defined the sense in which the period from the late 1960s is to be described as one of intensifying competitive pressure in the international economy.

These pressures were in turn responsible for generating the conditions which must be considered as the necessary background to the NIC pheno-menon, in the sense that they are necessary to understand its scale, if not its nature. After all, the share of global manufacturing production accounted for by the developing world had remained largely unchanged for more than fifteen years prior to 1973 (UNIDO 1979).

The features of these global developments which led to the NIC pheno-menon included the increasing need to reduce costs of production, the intensified need to find markets for installed producer goods capacities, and the accumulation of financial resources encountering increasing diffi-culty in finding investment opportunities in production which would yield an acceptable real rate of return. The result was a new world in which both producers and retailers sought new sources of supply from a few, politically reliable and economically relatively advanced cheap labour economies. The consequent access to industrial country markets represented the context in which the relevant state dominated economies could embark on a new highly expansionist and outward looking strategy. Their scope in this respect was further increased by the existence of enormous quantities of finance which the states in question could borrow for a very long time at no charge, that is with interest rates below international rates of inflation (OECD 1979a). It was this dimension of the process which permitted the South Korean definition and pursuit of its 'bold and imaginative long-term strategy'.

To summarise this part of the discussion, it is not being suggested that the NICs were passive recipients of an internationally determined stimulus, but that major changes in the international economy created conditions and opportunities which a few countries which had certain geo-political, and internal economic and political characteristics, were able to utilise to produce very rapid growth and industrialisation. In short, the dependency perspective's insistence on a strong emphasis on the international context would appear to be vindicated. Furthermore, the very fact that these new conditions proved so dramatically effective in liberating productive capa-bilities in a range of developing economies suggests that the previous international context may indeed have constituted an impediment to this process. This suggestion is, of course, also strengthened by the many previous instances when disturbances in the global economy — through war or depression — have led to a discontinuous and rapid increase in industrial and economic growth in a wide range of developing countries.

From this perspective it seems as foolish to extrapolate this ten-year experience into the future, as it was to assume that the more restrictive conditions prevailing until the mid-sixties would continue forever. There are many indications at present that those international conditions which have been described as the critical background for the NIC expansion, are under severe pressure. A prolonged deflation of the United States market or a further relative restriction in the availability of international finance would introduce an extremely discontinuous break into this process. Already numerous governments of more recent export promoting economies, acting upon the simplistic versions of the export promotion advice prevalent today, are finding that the world is not so simple as that analysis would suggest.

Finally, there is the question of the social and welfare consequences of the capitalist growth of the NICs. Here there are two clearly discernible facts. The first is that extremely high levels of political repression and violence have accompanied NIC strategies from their inception, and to the present (that is, after fifteen or more years) there has been very little relaxation of these pressures. At the same time, in South Korea and Taiwan significant material benefits have been diffused to unskilled workers over the past decade. In Brazil however income distribution has not improved, and even the absolute levels of wages of unskilled workers have changed little over the whole of the period of the miracle.

From a dependency perspective it seems relevant to ask whether it is not strange that the implicit trade-off between 'freedom' and 'material benefits' seems to undergo some remarkable transformations within the policy debate. It has been common to argue that if the 'socialist' alternative could produce the material benefits, it remained unacceptable because of its costs in terms of 'freedom'. Many who were fond of that argument are now found among those who extol the NICs on the grounds that they have produced the material benefits. At times double-think is so highly developed that the same person can extol the virtues of the South Korean model, while violently denouncing the repression of the Tanzanian state, which in fact pales into insignificance in comparison to that of Korea.

The second problem raised by this issue is the question of how the national interest is defined. Since in the NIC model there can be no question of democratic control, because the implicit social time preference is unlikely to be acceptable on any democratic basis, the authoritarian, militaristic and politically unresponsive states on which these strategies depend provide no assurance whatsoever that they will define that national interest in a way which objectively represents the long-term interests of the population as a whole. While the South Korean case suggests that it is nevertheless possible that such a state could define its own interests in terms of a long-term policy aimed at moving the national economy upwards in the international economic hierarchy, there can be no guarantee that such a choice would be made, or that it would be sustained if it required sacrifices by those in control of that state at some stage.

It is also necessary to emphasise that the diffusion of material benefits is in any case at a very early stage, and has occurred only in South Korea and Taiwan in a very clear manner. Furthermore, it is agreed by most analysts that the main reasons those two have followed a relatively egalitarian pattern have to do with the egalitarian pattern of landholding, the post-war destruction of the major concentrations of private capital, and the consequent pattern and degree of state involvement in the economy. Even so the South Korean state has had to take special measures to keep the urban-rural gap from widening during the past decade (Hong 1980, Yanagihara 1979, Westphal 1977, Rao 1978).

In summary of this last section, there would seem to be no reason to suppose that the NIC experience represents an adequate and acceptable pattern of development which meets the objective of seeking more rapid growth together with a degree of social control ensuring a diffusion of benefits, and some responsiveness to popular demands and priorities. There is no basis therefore for suggesting that this experience obviates the importance of the search for a more responsive, more humane form of state which is also capable of generating the material advance which is one major objective for development.

On balance, the 1970s and the NICs provide solid grounds for a further development and refinement of analysis from the dependency perspective.

Notes

1. See Chapter 6 this volume.
2. Used here in the sense of the OECD (1979), to include Brazil, South Korea, Hong Kong, Singapore, Mexico and Taiwan, but excluding the South European communities which raise similar problems but in a significantly different context.
3. Hong Kong and Singapore are not addressed in this discussion, since their minute size, and the absence of any rural economy, make them very special cases indeed. They do illustrate, however, that in such a confined context and in the presence of certain social, locational, political and economic conditions, international capital (both in the form of industrial and merchant capital), when concentrated on such locations, can relatively readily produce full employment and some diffusion of benefits. The struggle to withstand the economic consequences of that development by moving up the technological ladder dominates the policies of these city states at present.
4. See Chapter 10 this volume.
5. This is most clearly stated in the now famous statement of Mr. Ojimi, Vice-Minister of Japan's Ministry of International Trade and Industry:

    The MITI decided to establish in Japan, industries which require intensive employment of capital and technology, industries that in consideration of comparative cost of production should be the most inappropriate for Japan, industries such as steel, oil-refining, petrochemicals, automobiles, aircraft, industrial machinery of all sorts, and electronics, including electronic computers. From a short-run static viewpoint, encouragement of such industries would seem to conflict with economic rationalism. But, from a long-range viewpoint, these are precisely the industries where income elasticity of demand is high, technological progress rapid, and labour productivity rises fast. It was clear that without these industries it would be difficult to employ a population of 100 million and raise their standard of living to that of Europe and America with light industries alone; whether right or wrong,

Japan had to have these heavy and chemical industries. (OECD 1978, cited in Singh 1978).

Bibliography

Alavi, H. (1972), 'The State in Post-Colonial Societies', *New Left Review, No. 74*, July/August.

Bhagwati, J. (1978), *Foreign Trade Regimes and Economic Development: Anatomy and Consequences of Exchange Control Regimes*, Cambridge, Mass., Ballinger for National Bureau for Economic Research.

Bienefeld, M.A. (1980a), 'Impact on Industry' in D. Seers and C. Vaitsos (eds.), *The Second Enlargement of the EEC: Integration of Unequal Partners*, London, Macmillan, forthcoming 1981.

Bienefeld, M.A. (1980b), 'Dependency in the Eighties', *IDS Bulletin*, Vol. 12, No. 1, forthcoming.

Campos, Ambassador Roberto de Oliveira (1980), 'Prospectives of the New Industrial Countries — Brazil', Paper presented to the International Conference on Old and New Industrial Countries in the 1980s, Sussex European Research Centre, The University of Sussex, 6-8 January.

Forrester, J.J., Low, G.W. and Mass, N.J. (1977), 'Capital Formation and the Long Wave in Economic Activity', Report on a Meeting of Corporate Sponsors of the System Dynamics National Project, Massachusetts Institute of Technology, Boston, 11 March.

Hasan, Parvex (1976), *Korea: Problems and Issues in a Rapidly Growing Economy*, Baltimore and London: Johns Hopkins University Press for the World Bank.

Hong, W. (1980), 'Trade, Industrial Growth and Income Distribution in Korea', Seoul University, mimeo.

Keesing, D.B. (1979), 'Trade Policy for Developing Countries', *World Bank Staff Working Paper No. 353*, Washington.

Kom, K.W. (1980), 'Economic Prospects for Korea in the 1980s', Paper presented to the International Conference on Old and New Industrial Countries in the 1980s, Sussex European Research Centre, University of Sussex, 6-8 January.

Little, I.M.D. (1979), 'The Experience and Causes of Rapid Labour-Intensive Development in Korea, Hong Kong and Singapore: And the Possibilities of Evaluation', ILO-ARTEP, WP 11-1, Working Paper, Geneva.

Meier, H.D. (1977), *Der Konkurrenzkampf auf dem Weltmarkt*, Frankfurt and New York, Campus.

Mezzera, J. (1977), 'Trade Policy and Industrial Job Creation', OIT (ILO), PREALC, Monograph 7.

OECD (1979a), *The Impact of the Newly Industrialising Countries on Production and Trade in Manufacturers*, Paris.

OECD (1979b), *The Measurement of Profit* by Peter Hill, OECD, Paris.

Palma, G. (1978), 'Dependency: A Formal Theory of Underdevelopment or a Methodology for the Analysis of Concrete Situations of Underdevelopment?', *World Development*, Vol. 6, No. 7/8. Chapter 1 above is a revised version.

Rao, D.C. (1978), 'Economic Growth and Equity in the Republic of Korea', *World Development*, Vol. 6, No. 3.

Saul, J.S. (1974), 'The State in Post-Colonial Societies — Tanzania', *Socialist Register for 1974*, London.

Schydlowsky, D.N. (1976), 'Capital Utilisation, Growth, Employment and Balance of Payments and Price Stabilisation', *Centre for Latin American Development Studies, DP 22*, Boston.

Singh, Ajit (1978), 'The Reconstruction of UK Industry' in F. Blackaby (ed.), *De-Industrialisation*, London, Heinemann and the National Institute for Economic and Social Research.

Stecher, B. (1980), 'The Nature of New Industrial Countries', Paper presented to the International Conference on Old and New Industrial Countries in the 1980s', Sussex European Research Centre, University of Sussex, 6-8 January.

UNIDO (1979), *World Industry since 1960: Progress and Prospects*, New York.

Warren, W. (1973), 'Imperialism and Capitalist Industrialisation', *New Left Review*, No. 81.

Westphal, L.E. (1977), 'Industrial Policy and Development in Korea', *World Bank Staff Working Paper No. 263*, Washington.

Yanigahara, Toru (1979), 'The "Korea Model" and its Applicability to Southeast Asian Countries: A Preliminary Consideration', Paper presented to the International Symposium on 'New Directions of Asia's Development Strategies', Institute of Developing Economics, Tokyo, 13-16 March.

3   RAPID CAPITALIST DEVELOPMENT MODELS: A NEW POLITICS OF DEPENDENCE?

Geoff Lamb *

A central feature of one dominant stream of dependency theory, as of the theory of imperialism, has been the notion of blocked development: that is, that dependence prevents development and industrialisation save of a special, distorted kind. The tendency associated with the name of André Gunder Frank has given to this notion an impossibilist or stagnationist gloss, moreover, which presents socialist transformation as the only — and largely untheorised — means of escape. A solution may be, as Gabriel Palma's work suggests, to emphasise Marxist elements in dependency theory: in that case, however, it would seem that dependency is reduced merely to a sub-set of Marxist theory about unequal capitalist development, rather than a distinctive intellectual contribution.

The problem is rather sharply demonstrated if we consider the phenomenon of the 'fast developers', or so-called newly industrialising countries (NICs).[1] To the extent that they can be regarded as a group (and there are evident problems) their emergence in the world economy as industrial producers and exporters from the ranks of 'underdevelopment' requires explanation. Internally, too, it is difficult to find in dependency categories the dynamic for the economic and political transformation which these countries have so quickly undergone. Particularly when the NIC experience is generalised as a 'model' for other countries to envy or emulate, it does not seem that the most familiar tendencies in dependency theory have much to offer analytically.

It is possible to show that the 'fast developers' of Latin America, Southern Europe and South East Asia are still indeed 'dependent' on the metropolitan countries, in different ways and sometimes more markedly than a decade or two ago. But the development of a machine tool industry in Korea, for example, or of a large financial sector in Singapore, demands an analytical apparatus capable of tracing through the full domestic and international implications of rapid sectoral development in these underdeveloped economies. And whatever their intellectual and political attractions, dependency theories have tended to be long on rather general theorising and description, and short on analysis and concrete prescription which can grapple with these problems.

*This paper contains the views of the author only and not necessarily those of the World Bank.

Dependency theories and politics

The tendency towards general description has been most apparent in dealing with political phenomena: it is indeed tempting and convenient to see politics as a residual category to be read off in a straightforward manner as the effect of other (mainly economic) structures. This can have two paradoxical outcomes. Political life may be seen as the expression of dependency and metropolitan domination at the level of the State: politics is therefore part of the 'system of dependency' and must be overturned or displaced. On the other hand, many dependency theories would hold that the populations in the modern, transnationalised enclaves have an objective interest in the maintenance of dependent structures — an effect of employment, consumption standards and tastes, ideology and so on. Since they are also the socially conscious and organisationally mobilised groups, the political impetus for change is unlikely to be sustained in such an 'infected' environment.

So an ambivalence about the possibility of change develops — a combination often of radical pessimism and revolutionary voluntarism — with political outcomes which have included extreme guerrilla experiments. Gramsci's slogan, 'pessimism of the intellect, optimism of the will', here comes to express not steely political determination like his, but something which has more in common with the dark heart of European political romanticism; and it is not accidental that in this political tradition the line between revolutionary armed action and fascist terrorism becomes extremely tenuous. As with political ideology, so with political analysis. The conflation of national and psycho-social generalisations in many dependency theories means that they are impatient or uneasy with the elements of political analysis, which tend to be intermediate with respect to the poles of nation and individual: social class, political organisation and articulation, complex, differentiated and mobilised political interests, and so on. One consequence is a considerable difficulty in dealing with the State, and hence with what is conveniently but problematically termed the 'room for manoeuvre' on the part of dependent regimes.

On the whole, dependency theories have tended to minimise the room for manoeuvre, or indeed to question whether the issue can be conceived in that way (the second point has more substance than the first). Since the society as a whole is dependent on an external metropolis or on the international system as a whole, and since it is in particular the dependent State which reproduces and perpetuates that external domination, there is, on this view, no point in presuming any impetus to tamper with the structures of domination themselves. Consequently, as in the work of Frank, there is an explicit denial of an autonomous political role for a national bourgeoisie, or for a State dominated by or representing such a class.

Imperialism and class alliances

In Marxist theories of imperialism, by contrast, which have at their centre a notion of exploitation rather than one of dependency, the national bourgeoisie is accorded a crucial political place. The possibility of development and economic transformation in imperialist-dominated countries has as its *political* condition an alliance of anti-imperialist forces — the usually small but politically strategic working class, the national capitalists, 'patriotic intelligentsia' and the broad masses of poorer peasants. The viability of this (necessarily uneasy) alliance is in fact predicated on a national bourgeoisie which has interests crucially in conflict with imperialism. The argument is that economic domination by imperialist firms seriously inhibits the possibility of accumulation by national capitalists, whose interests would therefore be served by more 'patriotic' policies of nationalisation, control of foreign trade, and the political and economic inhibition of traditionally pro-imperialist groups such as traditional rulers, landlords and merchants dependent on the imperial connection.

The problem with this idea is that a great deal depends on the strength and viability of the national bourgeoisie, a class which in dependent or imperialist dominated countries is *by definition* weak, inhibited and of somewhat uncertain political orientation. The great strength of the Marxist notion of political development, on the other hand, is its robustly political view of the State and its possibilities. There is no suggestion here of the benign State or of the State as the embodiment of the national interest. On the contrary, the character of the State and its actions is seen as the direct outcome of the balance of social forces within the 'progressive alliance' itself — which in turn depends on the political organisation and consciousness of the contending classes, and indeed on the degree of political activity which the State apparatus itself permits.

Here it is worth pointing to a secondary weakness in Marxist theory which is now beginning to be remedied. The tendency to view the State as mere instrument (the 'executive committee of the bourgeoisie', in the words of the Communist Manifesto) underestimates the political significance of the bureaucratic apparatus itself, including its military wing. The connections of that apparatus with imperialism are of critical importance, whether they stem from military technology transfers, counter-insurgency programmes, salary comparability and career transfers between the public service and multinational corporations, or merely from the diffuse consciousness produced by foreign education and participation in the international conspiracy of expertise.

An intervening model?

The rapidly developing capitalist countries of the underdeveloped world can be put forward as a sort of intervening model challenging these two

views of dependence or imperialist domination and demanding their reformulation in important respects. Firstly, they have indeed experienced rapid
development, a rise in the level of productive forces, and diversification of
economic activities.[2] Secondly, however, this has certainly not happened
as a consequence of a broad, progressive national coalition. On the contrary,
in most of the 'new industrialisers' an apparent condition of successful
accumulation and diversification has been the effective exclusion of the
broad masses of the population from political processes. Now clearly the
explanation for this 'intervening model' lies primarily in the international
economy and the changing international division of labour and, secondly,
in particular characteristics of the main national examples. Neither aspect
is central to this paper.

It may be worthwhile, instead, to explore the possible political implications of the more or less explicit adoption of such models by other
developing countries with ambitions to follow the 'rapid development'
path. Examples will be drawn primarily from two such countries, Trinidad
and Sri Lanka. These are not, of course, classified as NICs, nor should they
be. But their commitment to rapid accumulation and 'openness' — long-
standing in the case of Trinidad, dramatically recent in Sri Lanka — may
provide valuable insights into the 'politics of NIC emulation', and a commentary on some of the theoretical problems in dependency and Marxist
thought alluded to above.

The two countries chosen are quite good examples of the emulation of
more or less explicit 'models' of rapid development. Trinidad has since
Independence in 1956 explicitly followed the example of Puerto Rico
(itself almost archetypally a 'dependency' model) with subsequent modification to take account of the dramatic economic failure in Puerto Rico
and of Trinidad's energy advantages. In Sri Lanka since the change of
government in 1977 the government's intention has been to repeat some
of the experiences of the South East Asian industrialising countries, with
the 'Singapore model' often mentioned, particularly in labour matters. A
crucial point in assessing the practical viability and theoretical importance
of such models, of course, is that they are imitated or applied across
countries with different endowments and cultures; and in this respect it
will be apparent that Trinidad and Sri Lanka have more in common with
many other Third World countries than with the models they seek to
emulate, particularly in the relative absence of indigenous capital and a
native capitalist class.

Development strategies

The central features of Trinidad's economic strategy are, firstly, the construction of major industrial facilities based either on high energy use or
on petrochemical down-stream manufacturing, using an increasing proportion of the oil and natural gas currently exported, and, secondly, expanding

Trinidad's role as an exporting and manufacturing centre for the Caribbean region as a whole. The centre-piece of this policy is the Point Lisas industrial development area, which will combine petrochemical facilities (a liquid ammonia plant, a fertilizer factory, and facilities for gas liquefaction and methanol manufacturing) and energy-intensive heavy industry, including an iron and steel mill and an aluminium smelter. Rapid development of energy-based industrialisation is seen as involving the closest possible partnership between government and multinationals. The nitrogen plant is a joint venture between government and the United States multinational W.R. Grace; the fertilizer plant a joint venture with Amoco; the LNG project between government, Tenneco and People's Gas Corporation of Illinois; the Iron and Steel Company of Trinidad is a wholly-owned government corporation, but with extensive construction and technology contracts with United States and Japanese firms. The Point Lisas Industrial Development Corporation is clearly the cutting edge of government strategy. Trinidad already occupies a pre-eminent place in the regional trade of the English-speaking Caribbean and is using its financial muscle from oil revenues to expand; the problems of rapidly inflating production costs and foreign exchange outflows for small-scale protected manufacturing, however, have somewhat tempered enthusiasm in this direction. In both types of industrialisation, energy/petrochemical and regional manufacturing, the commitment to foreign investment, indeed actual foreign domination, is complete.

In Sri Lanka government strategy since 1977 has had three major components. Firstly, there has been a drastic speeding up of the timetable of the giant Mahaweli River irrigation project, in which 900,000 acres of presently dry land would be brought under irrigated agriculture, mainly for rice. The target period for the project's completion has been shortened from thirty to six years. Secondly, the government has embarked on a huge construction programme centred on Colombo, primarily of urban housing (500,000 were planned over five years from 1978, with 100,000 in the public sector) but also envisaging the construction of new infrastructure and a new legislative and administrative capital. Thirdly, the leading component of government strategy has been the encouragement of industrialisation in a free trade or export manufacturing zone primarily located in the Greater Colombo area, and administered by a Greater Colombo Economic Commission with considerable though vague administrative powers and an enormous amount of political influence.

Main political features

We cannot here review in full the consequences of these strategies, which concentrate on hoped-for comparative advantage in one case from exhaustible resources, and in the other from land and cheap labour. But some conclusions may be drawn about the political implications of adoption or transfer of these models: not so much because the politics of these countries is a simple consequence of their eager 'openness', but because open dependence encourages or intensifies many political tendencies already present in most Third World countries. Some of the leading features may be summarised as follows:

1. A sustained attempt to demobilise the organised power of labour, and so in the longer term to lower real wages and reduce political opposition to government policies favouring capital and the 'leading sectors'. One might note that such policies can quite easily be given a superficially 'progressive' gloss: for example, described as reducing the power of a labour aristocracy, or as favouring the unemployed as against those with jobs, or (as has been advanced in the case of South Korea) a commitment to equality and the maintenance of low urban-rural income differentials.

In both Sri Lanka and Trinidad there have been attempts — in the latter over a much longer period than in the former — at legal and administrative restraint on the trade unions. Trinidad has had a series of 'anti-subversive' commissions of enquiry into labour unrest, and two major pieces of industrial relations legislation which make it legally very difficult to organise workers, to form large multibranch unions, and to strike. The new Sri Lanka government has attempted to introduce trade union legislation along broadly similar lines, but has in the event held off from implementing its full intentions as a result of strong reaction — even from its own supporters — in the trade union movement.

What is important in both these cases, as in other capitalist developing countries trying to industrialise rapidly, is not merely specific anti-working-class action, but the general identification of labour as the major policy constraint or obstacle. There is consequently a tendency to curb and delimit working class organisation and influence — to make life awkward for unions, to make it more difficult for them to recruit in the new factories of the industrialisation programme, quietly to encourage police harrassment, to consider modifying health, safety and minimum wage laws in new enterprises, and so forth.

2. The development of a strong and by its nature growing political constituency committed to sustaining 'openness' and dependent capitalist development.

In the Caribbean this has of course particular historical connections, for example through migration. But new forces arise from or are immeasurably strengthened by the rapid development commitment. One important element is the educational and professional interest of the middle classes and intelligentsia. In both Trinidad and Sri Lanka efforts at educational reform have either been reduced to a bogus veneer of authenticity (unique Caribbean culture, etc.) or are straightforwardly dismantled, for example, the fate of the substantial 'national' curriculum reforms of the Bandaranaike government in Sri Lanka.

Instead schooling becomes more and more explicitly oriented not merely to the leading foreign-dominated economic sectors (this would after all have some economic justification), but to international transferability and the possibility of educational escape. Educational achievement in Trinidad, for example, is measured less by the standards of the University of the West Indies, than by going 'out of the island' to foreign universities and colleges, mainly in North America. In Sri Lanka the former linkage between education and foreign travel and Englishness is being aggressively re-established: newspaper editorials can without irony welcome the prospective reintroduction of A-level examinations because 'secondary schooling is intended to prepare pupils for higher education overseas'.

The same tendencies hold true for professional qualifications: a determined political defence of the international transferability of skills. In the 1960s Trinidad lost something like two-thirds of its total professional cadre through emigration. This rate has abated somewhat in the 1970s with the rise in opportunities for professionals within the country, but most people with higher education would still expect to spend a substantial part of their working career outside Trinidad.

Sri Lanka has lost the majority of its qualified and experienced engineers to the Middle East, while medical emigration to that area and to Nigeria is likely to be accelerated by the Jayawardene government's easing of public service requirements as part of its general policy of freedom for the propertied classes. (It might be noted in passing that a concomitant of medical 'freedom' and the open liberal economy has been the reintroduction of freedom to import branded drugs and pharmaceuticals — a reversal of the highly regarded Sri Lankan practice of state controlled import and manufacture of a much smaller and cheaper range of generic medicines.)

3. The external economic interests of paramount importance to the regime's strategy rapidly assume overwhelming political influence, often informal in character. In Trinidad that role is filled by Texaco, Amoco and W.R. Grace; in Sri Lanka the new entrepreneurs are not yet well established, so it is the providers of aid for infrastructure and other development who occupy the favoured position: the aid missions, with the IMF representative perhaps as *primus inter pares*.

4. State employment becomes even more crucial a political resource than in most developing countries. For the socially advantaged, state or public sector employment is one of the few ways of creaming off some benefits from a process of development which is predominantly in the hands of foreign firms. In both Trinidad and Sri Lanka there have been large expansions in the public sector and rises in pay considerably greater than in the economy as a whole. In Sri Lanka, additionally, income tax has been abolished for state employees. For the lower classes there is a political rationale for government to provide considerable state employment even of a makework kind, or alternatively to offer (or appear to offer) welfare and other benefits for the sake of political quiescence.

5. The politics of primary exploitation. Sri Lankan strategy is dependent on the fortunes of tea, and to a lesser extent rubber, in the international economy: until recently the relatively buoyant market placed the regime in a good position to finance imports and to launch, under appropriate political auspices, the major drive for international capital which — certainly in terms of public finance — has been conspicuously successful in the short term. Trade figures for 1979, however, showed a record deficit of US $420m., after two years of surpluses.[3] Government measures resulting from these and other economic difficulties affected even the relatively privileged public sector employees, and provoked an attempted general strike in mid-1980. In Trinidad, of course, state and corporate oil revenues provide the surplus for energy-based and petrochemical industrialisation.

But there is another, political, aspect of this provision of surplus: in both cases policy depends to a considerable degree on the government being able to make the population bear the costs of this transfer from primary to industrial development. In Sri Lanka, quite apart from the history of exploitation represented in the accumulated capital of the estates (whatever present wage improvements), the concentration on the 'big three' projects in fact involves direct costs for the rest of the population — wildly inflated urban land prices, declining or more expensive services, particularly in health and utilities, and relative neglect of non-Mahaweli agriculture. It also makes increasingly vulnerable welfare gains such as the food subsidy and ration system which, despite often criticised economic inefficiency, has probably been the most important single factor in Sri Lanka's very favourable longevity and nutrition record.[4] The subsidies and ration entitlements that still remain are to be abolished during 1980. In Trinidad the State accumulated large surpluses in the seventies partly by allowing the Trinidad dollar to drift downwards for long periods against the United States dollar, thus dramatically driving up consumer prices (given the United States origin of· most of Trinidad's imports), while the State received its oil revenues in United States dollars.

6. A tendency to hive off high-growth activities and provide political protection for these enclaves. Special regional-cum-functional development authorities, for example, have been set up in both Trinidad and Sri Lanka for the leading development projects (Point Lisas in Trinidad, Mahaweli and Greater Colombo in Sri Lanka). These powerful institutions provide little or no access for political representatives (save for the most obvious pork-barrel reasons), no voice for workers or ordinary recipients (who are 'targets', not subjects), but direct access for state functionaries, for powerful economic interests, and for technocrats who are often little more than the transmission agents for foreign capital.

The obverse of this hiving-off and exclusion is, in some cases, the confinement of democratic and constitutional politics to relatively peripheral and residual resources and decisions, in which personal intercession and influence-peddling are the stuff of politics. Government and administration then often tend to become mere bureau-shuffling. There may well be neither political intention nor capacity to provide substantial resources outside of favoured activities. Government must, however, be seen to be performing and providing, and there is certainly a need to justify the endless expansion of state bureaucracy, jobs and perquisites. This is perhaps much more marked in Trinidad, where the proliferation of special funds and agencies emulates the bureaucratic profusion of another fast developer, Brazil. In this process the *appearance* of activity and development can be created by establishing new funds, consolidating and amalgamating existing agencies, setting up working parties and commissions to examine implementation, and so on. This tendency is less developed in Sri Lanka, although the fate of the much vaunted district development ministries is suggestive of much bureaucratic activity, a great deal of political propaganda, certain concrete benefits flowing to local politicians, and apparently little benefit so far for the population at large.

Political outcomes

It is difficult to draw anything other than tentative conclusions from such a cursory and partial discussion. It will be fairly clear, however, that the two countries we have been discussing are not so much different in kind from developing countries in general, as experiencing the accentuation of common features of post-colonial and developing states. In the process, there is a strikingly rapid accretion of economic commitments and political tendencies with very long-term implications. In Trinidad and Sri Lanka, as in comparable countries, major projects with substantial economic ramifications and a long life have been quite rapidly set in train. The industries set up under the Greater Colombo Economic Commission or by the Point Lisas Industrial Development Corporation will be *there* (the former probably more transiently than the latter). Their agreements will have to be honoured, their royalty payments made, their capital repatriation permitted, their taxes written off, their infrastructure debts serviced, their local political representatives paid off, their labour kept under control – or else substantial, perhaps crushing, political costs will have to be faced. The economic consequences of these lines of development in the long term are perhaps open to question: there seems very little doubt, however, that the *political* effect of this rapid capitalist development is to raise very substantially the costs of anything but incremental political change which accepts as given the existing set of international, political and economic relationships and which accedes to the domestic political constituency fostered by those relationships.

If we turn the question the other way around, however, we may ask: what are the political requirements for sustaining the line of rapid capitalist development represented by Sri Lanka and Trinidad? One tempting but oversimple answer is that it requires in the longer term repressive, probably military rule — Brazil, South Korea, Singapore may be cited as convenient examples. It seems premature to reach so apocalyptically authoritarian a conclusion, although there can be little doubt about the *tendency* toward repression, as the earlier discussion should have made clear. Rapid development strategies in Sri Lanka and Trinidad have produced attempts to clamp down on labour, and to restrict the area of operation of representative constitutional politics. These policies have not been entirely successful, however: we have cited labour resistance to proposed trade union laws in Sri Lanka, and in Trinidad there have been considerable concessions in practice in recognition of the effectiveness of working-class organisation. In both countries also political representation, particularly of ethnic minorities (Tamils in Sri Lanka, East Indians in Trinidad) has produced amelioration for vulnerable groups: some relaxation of rationing and welfare administration in Sri Lanka, and state assistance for workers during phases of sugar industry contraction in Trinidad are recent examples. So political struggle, however delimited, has a perceptible effect.

Objectively, however, as the costs of rapid development mount sharply, so does the impetus towards control and repression. In both countries one might, with only a hint of paranoia, discern an atmosphere of dress rehearsal in the activities of the security forces: in Sri Lanka in action against secessionists and small guerrilla groupings, or in Trinidad where troops have been used against strikers. In the latter case, additionally, the domestic use of the repressive apparatus is complemented by the 'regional role' accorded to favoured reliable status — compare South Korean involvement in the United States' Asian adventures with current American concern over 'radicalism' in the Caribbean and the consequent grooming of Trinidad to shoulder some of the responsibility for maintaining regional political order.

The likely outcome therefore is not entirely clear, even though the balance seems tilted toward political conflict and repression. The political resolution of such struggles, however, depends obviously on organisation and the outcome of conflict at earlier stages — and here we might make two tentative generalisations about strategic variables.

The first is that it is the strength of the working class and the labour movement — both organised and inchoate, traditional and explosive — which is the fundamental political constraint on the forms of rapid development which capitalist regimes may impose. How 'progressive' the outcome of labour's resistance might be in any particular case is dependent on other factors: for example, on whether the working class is numerically and politically the most important popular social force, as in Trinidad in an intermediate position, as in Sri Lanka, or a very small and relatively privileged minority, as in many African countries. The political role of labour in opposing fast-track policies is likely to be similarly important in each case: the political-economic origin and consequences of such opposition is likely to differ substantially between types.

The second major variable, to return to the discussion of theories about imperialism and underdevelopment, is the allegiance, orientation and 'tendency of polarisation' of the middle strata of the population. In theoretical terms these determine the outcome of the debate over the national-democratic, anti-imperialist revolution. More importantly, in terms of concrete politics, the viability of dependent rapid development requires the collaboration of actual and potential indigenous capitalists, of the professions, and of the educated servants of the modern State. There is little sign, it must be said, of major incapacity in either Trinidad or Sri Lanka to service these groups by the application of the regimes' policies so far, nor of substantial dissent amongst them. At the same time, the extent to which foreign dependence ultimately constrains the national bourgeoisie in material and ideological terms is worth considering: the experience of, say, Brazil and South Korea in recent years suggests that 'anti-imperialist contradictions' have tended to re-emerge after even long periods of repression, involving tenuous but real political links between labour and other classes.

The fast developers — both the prototypes and the emulators — are unlikely to 'disprove' any particular theory of development. They do perhaps compel a more painful confrontation with reality than dependency theorists and academic Marxists have been willing to undertake. The same applies to many neo-classical commentators: see, for example, the grotesque attempts to hold up Korea, Taiwan, Brazil, etc. as triumphs for the free play of market forces, when in fact they are among the more corporate, planned and *dirigiste* economies in the world; and they certainly make more awkward the recitation of clichés about blocked development, stagnant peripheries and the rest.

Perhaps the sharpest cut made by the NICs at dependency theory is at a political level — the economic record, particularly with current colossally mounting debt burdens, contains important ambiguities, after all. The political vacuousness of most dependency theory has become sharply apparent: its either-or simplifications of political questions cannot provide much analytical purchase on the political trajectory of development in the rapidly growing economies. The 'intervening model' — between the national-democratic State of Marxist theory and the dominated periphery of dependency — brings us back to the centrality of accumulation for development, and to the fact that accumulation is everywhere and at all times a *political* as well as economic process, over which the fiercest social struggles rage. Politics in developing countries is about who controls the process of accumulation and transformation of productive resources, and in whose interests: the best-known fast developers resolved the question unambiguously for a time, and now some of them find themselves under strong pressure from labour to reverse that trend. In the cases of emulators discussed in this paper, that pressure has emerged very early, and may yet be suppressed. In all these cases, it is clear that the style and pace of development depends primarily on the outcome of those proximate and urgent political struggles and mobilisations, rather than on a highly general set of world-structural conditions. That is not a plea for empiricism, but for 'radical' political analysis to develop the capacity to deal sensibly with the politics of accumulation — or to concede the field.

Notes

1.   They represent no problem of course for those 'theories' which are really the expression of a metaphysical cultural pathos about change and modernity: dependency as an emotional stance can regard all change as homologous.
2.   A convenient summary of their recent economic performance is to be found in the OECD study, *Trade with the Newly Industrializing Countries*, Paris, June 1979.
3.   See Paul Isenman, 'The Relationship of Basic Needs to Growth, Income Distribution and Employment: The Case of Sri Lanka'.
4.   *Financial Times*, 28 February 1980.

4 CAPITALISM IN NIGERIA AND PROBLEMS OF DEPENDENCE: SOME HISTORICAL COMMENTS

Jan J. Milewski

The purpose of this paper is to reconsider one aspect of dependent development: changes in the attitudes of people involved in the development of a dependent economy toward the very issue of dependence. This aspect seems to be neglected by the majority of those writing on the subject. They usually concentrate on quantitative aspects of the dependence of the economy of the countries studied. Such an approach is of course justified, but it does not exhaust the problem. Moreover, it often leads to over-simplification and even to false conclusions.

This oversimplification may be observed in work on so-called cultural dependence. Cardoso, for example, holds that if an economy is dependent, its people are also dependent in terms of their attitudes, mentality, consumption patterns, ideology, etc. The extent to which such a proposition can be regarded as generally applicable is discussed in this paper, using the example of early Nigerian capitalist groups.

The main characteristics of pre-colonial economic development

Pre-colonial structures have had a great influence on the development of the Nigerian capitalist-oriented economy from the late nineteenth century, because the period of colonial rule was very short. Up to 1860 Nigeria was entirely independent, in political terms, from Europe. The small colony of Lagos, created by Britain in that year, was for two further decades the only piece of Nigerian land ruled by Europeans. The conquest of the whole of today's Nigeria by Britain took place during the period from the 1880s to 1908. Since independence was won in 1960, most of the country was not ruled formally by a foreign power for more than six or seven decades. In these circumstances the whole range of pre-colonial structures, organisations, institutions, customs, etc. inevitably played a crucial role in changes in the colonial period.

The economic history of Nigeria from the late nineteenth century onwards is especially interesting. The myth that before colonial rule Nigerian societies were living in an entirely subsistence economy was destroyed long ago. Certainly, in most of them the subsistence factor was very important, even dominant. But even so, many societies were producing a substantial surplus, and were involved in active local exchange and often long distance trade. People living in the north had participated for centuries in trade with Western Sudan and also trans-Saharan commerce. Southerners, especially those on the coast, had been trading with Europeans from the early sixteenth century. This second direction of trade is of special interest because it was with an expanding capitalist Europe. In fact, it promoted dependence long before the colonial period.

The main export of the Nigerian coast from the sixteenth to the middle of the nineteenth centuries was slaves. The moral and demographic aspects of that trade are too well-known to be repeated. But it is worth recalling that economically the slave trade created a very peculiar type of dependency among some coastal societies. The famous trading states of the Niger Delta are good examples. Their whole socio-political and economic systems were adjusted to their role in the intercontinental slave trade: collecting slaves in the interior, transporting them to the ports, and keeping them until they were bought by European traders. The slave trade was the main source of the revenues of those societies. Highly sophisticated armaments, supplied by the slave traders, gave them military superiority over their neighbours.

The slave trade made these coastal societies dependent in two respects: income and security. Moreover, many goods which otherwise could be produced locally were replaced by imports, and local crafts declined. So, analysed simply in terms of dependence, the four centuries of slave trade also brought damaging results. Most of the productive abilities of the coastal societies were destroyed, and in spite of the relatively high income of their rulers, there was virtually no capital accumulation. Once the slave trade collapsed, most trading communities involved in it had either to adjust to other trades or disappear.

From the middle of the nineteenth century, European demand began to switch from slaves to the produce of Nigerian forests and fields: palm oil and kernels, cotton, from the end of the century cocoa, and from the beginning of the twentieth century groundnuts, rubber, timber, etc. The growing demand for these products created quite new conditions for the development of a market economy in Nigeria, and for dependent development as well.

Since the slave trade dominated the image of the Nigerian economy in the pre-colonial period, it may be worth reminding ourselves briefly of its other features which were significant for subsequent development. First, agriculture (cattle breeding in the north) was the main sector. Second, subsistence was the dominating factor in total output, but productive abilities allowed the production of a surplus, sometimes quite substantial. Third, in most of the rural economies large labour surpluses existed, which could be used to increase output with given technology. In some societies there were also surpluses of arable land. Fourth, systems of land tenure and social organisation, with their great differentiation, in most cases allowed members of the communities to take individual decisions when producing on communal land, and to dispose of their own output as they thought best. Fifth, long before the colonial period, as was already mentioned, many Nigerian societies had developed systems of local exchange, and medium and long distance trade. Trading customs and institutions were accepted and strictly respected. The social role of trade among many societies was much higher than one could expect from the fraction of output that was exchangeable. Sixth, in many societies specialised groups of traders and merchants had emerged. They had skills in trade, knowledge of market possibilities, and a great desire to expand their sales. At the end of the nineteenth century their organisational capacities were greatly in excess of their actual trade.

To summarise, the pre-colonial economies of Nigerian societies at the end of the nineteenth century had created a particularly good basis for the expansion of market agriculture, based on indigenous farmers and trading systems.

The evolution of agriculture and the question of dependence

It is usually taken for granted that if market-oriented agriculture expands as a result of foreign demand, its dependence on foreign markets will grow continuously. The Nigerian case shows that the process is more complex.

The chief interest of British firms expanding into Nigeria from the 1880s was trade, in particular purchasing Nigerian agricultural and forest products needed by European industries, and selling in exchange European products. Throughout the colonial period commerce was the main area of investment of foreign capital in Nigeria. Mining, the second area of activities of British firms, always played a secondary role in terms of both investment and policy.

From the beginning of colonial rule the main goods exported were of rural origin, thus two routes were open for colonial policy. First, foreign firms could have taken agricultural production into their own hands, depriving Nigerians of land and using them as a labour force. This was the solution imposed in many African colonies at the turn of the nineteenth and twentieth centuries. Alternatively, land and agricultural production could have remained in the hands of indigenous farmers. That solution was very rare in the colonial period, but it was applied in Nigeria. It came as a result of the colonial government accepting two assumptions: that Nigerian farmers would be able to meet the rising demand of British firms, and that any grabbing of the land of the indigenous population would cause violent opposition, which eventually might undermine colonial rule. Both assumptions proved to be right.[1]

Nigerian farmers responded very actively to growing market opportunities from the end of the nineteenth century. The dramatic growth of agricultural exports reflected rising demand combined with increases in total output and the purchase of surplus production from a growing number of farmers. It is not surprising that A. McPhee called this process in the early 1920s 'an economic revolution'.[2]

What factors prevented Nigerian agriculture oriented to foreign markets becoming *entirely* dependent? It is not possible to provide a satisfactory answer, but some historical factors should be remembered. First was the attitude of the indigenous societies towards the changes. As mentioned above, these systems allowed a considerable degree of freedom of participation in the new market economy. But this freedom had its limits, especially where land was individually owned. Second, foreign demand, in spite of its magnitude, may not have been strong enough to bring about a total transformation in a few decades. And third, the very fact that much of the proceeds of a farmer's output was taken by foreign firms in the system of exploitation possibly left him an income too small to stimulate faster changes. All in all, the rate of growth of agricultural exports from Nigeria from the beginning of the twentieth century was much higher than the rate of social transformation in agriculture.

For the reasons mentioned above, and several others, Nigerian farmers did not create, with a few exceptions, large agricultural units to produce for export. The growing output came from small-scale farmers, often operating only with family labour. This pattern of development oriented to foreign markets had several advantages for the farmers, but it did not encourage the fast development of capitalist-type units. The only exceptions were some cocoa farmers, a small proportion of the total rural population.

In the process of development of the dependent economy, the rise of small-scale, foreign market-oriented farms created a complex situation in Nigeria. The original acceleration of their market production was definitely channeled into a colonial type of foreign trade, subject to colonial exploitation. But at the same time only cocoa farmers were producing a cash crop which had no use domestically. All other export crops (palm oil, palm kernels, cotton, groundnuts, etc.) were consumed by the farmers themselves. They could be sold on the home market as well; with the growth of the export trade, urban centres were expanding after 1900, and the demand for foodstuffs was increasing there. Therefore Nigerian export farmers were protected in two ways, to some extent, against fluctuations in export prices. Moreover, the growth of foreign trade from the second decade of the twentieth century clearly encouraged the development of domestic agricultural production competitive with imports, e.g. kola nuts.[3] With the size of Nigeria's population, and diversification of the economy in terms of supply and demand for various types of foods, the increase in agricultural exports inevitably encouraged a growth of interregional trade and domestic markets. The beginnings of this process can be traced already in the 1920s.

When the expansion of interregional trade in locally produced and consumed goods accelerated after World War II, the domestic market was becoming a more effective factor limiting the dependence of the economy as a whole. Compared with most other African countries of the time, Nigeria was in a relatively much better position.

New commercial and entrepreneurial groups

The type of colonial economic expansion which took place in Nigeria from the end of the nineteenth century created a great demand for the services of local traders, middlemen and later entrepreneurs. As mentioned above, the first generation of big traders was crushed or limited in their activities by the expansion of European firms in Africa at the turn of the century, but the peculiar type of commercial expansion in Nigeria could not eliminate them entirely. Nigerian traders, transporters, clerks, etc., were needed, and the demand for them was growing with the growth of foreign trade. The only question was the scope of their activities, restricted by the colonial situation.

After 1900 a new division of labour between Nigerian and foreign traders emerged. Nigerian farmers, of course, had a place in this as well (see Table 4.1).

TABLE 4.1. The division of labour in Nigeria, post-1900

Type of economic activity	Nigerians	Foreign firms	Area of competition
Agricultural production	x		
Internal trade (local)	x		
Internal trade (local regional national)	x	x	x
Transport internal	x	x	x
Transport sea		x	
Operations on foreign markets		x	
Supplies of imported goods		x	
Distribution of imported goods	x	x	x
Banking	x *	x	x
Manufacturing	x	x	x

* From the 1930s (see text).

Banking and manufacturing were 'competitive' in that early Nigerian attempts were made to break the foreign monopoly in these fields long before independence. The struggle to set up Nigerian banks in the late 1920s and early 1930s eventually produced success in the establishment of the first African bank south of the Sahara, the National Bank of Nigeria, in 1933. It was not able to compete effectively with British banks at the time, but it survived. Industries of very small scale, such as bakery and printing, were run successfully by Nigerians from the beginning of the twentieth century.

Generally speaking, this division of labour between Nigerians and foreign firms existed from the early twentieth century till Independence, but some short-term changes should be mentioned. From the 1880s to the 1920s, when the pattern was actually established, former Nigerian monopolists in the coastal trade had to disappear. Many big merchants, firms and trading 'houses' went bankrupt; others were pushed out of the best markets and reduced to a smaller scale. Nevertheless, many traders not only survived the continental expansion, but considerably improved their professional skill and expanded their business during these years. They also moved, as was mentioned above, to new small industries in Lagos.

From the 1920s to 1945 there were great fluctuations in Nigerian terms of trade, and export and import volumes, due to the Great Depression and World War II. There was growing concentration of foreign capital operating in Nigeria with the creation of the United Africa Company (UAC) in 1929. The consequences of all these processes for the participation of Nigerian commercial groups in the market economy were very serious. However, in spite of increasing difficulties, Nigerian traders and entrepreneurs were able to increase their relative share of internal trade. They also managed to enter a new branch of business: motor transport. Their expansion was soon spectacular in the south-western part of the country. Nigerian lorry-owners there became dangerous competitors of the railways by the early 1930s. Their role in the transport of cocoa became in a short time so important for the economy of the area that the colonial government, in spite of railways management complaints, decided to leave them untouched.

The period of post-war recovery from 1945 to Independence in 1960 brought a fast expansion of the market economy, especially visible after 1950. New branches of business flourished, including early stages of indigenous industrialisation. The growth of the internal market was faster than ever. For various reasons, including changes in colonial policy, the share of Nigerian commercial groups in various types of enterprises quickly increased. In many branches, including construction, internal transport, real estate, and banking, they operated on a scale unknown before.

Generally, up to the late 1960s the expansion of Nigerian enterprise was based on two areas of economic activity, agriculture, producing both for export and home markets, and growing domestic trade. Although many Nigerian enterprises were clearly involved only in the export-import sector, many others were linked with it indirectly, through the mechanism of the domestic market. The drive of some entrepreneurs to invest in manufacturing, evident especially from the 1950s, was obviously aimed at the domestic market. Its enormous potential size, unknown in any other African country, was already well understood long before Independence.

The opening of the oil era in the economic history of Nigeria in the mid-1960s, undermined previous trends in the development of Nigerian enterprise. Although that period is outside the scope of this paper, a few short remarks may be useful. Oil money, as is well-known, opened so many new opportunities for entrepreneurs that some branches previously regarded as profitable became much less attractive. New import opportunities discouraged some entrepreneurs from moving into the industrial sector, as they had tried to do before. Agriculture was also found to be much less profitable. For these reasons the attitudes of many Nigerian entrepreneurs in the oil era and the pattern of their activities cannot be regarded as a mere continuation of their earlier involvement.

But a more important problem here is a certain contradiction between the attitudes of many people involved in commercial activities within dependent parts of the economy and their actual work. Entrepreneurs linked with cocoa trade and cocoa farmers illustrate the problem best. If we go back to the history of Lagos and its hinterland from the 1890s, three observations can be made. First, for obvious reasons the first groups of Nigerian (and other African) entrepreneurs of the capitalist type were rising in that field. Second, a lot of people belonging to this group were at the same time closely linked with nationalist, anti-colonial, movements. Third, nearly all the early national leaders of the 'modern' type from the end of the nineteenth century were directly or indirectly linked with some capitalist type of enterprise.

It is not surprising that the national leaders were very often simultaneously involved in the growth of the dependent sector as far as their professional work was concerned; yet they were building ideology and political movements to achieve independence. Moreover, the question of economic independence was very much alive in their writings and activities right from the 1890s. They usually knew what economic dependence means not (or not only) from theoretical works but from their own practical experience as businessmen, lawyers, merchants, publishers, etc.

Because of the economic system they lived in, most of these leaders-entrepreneurs were struggling not for economic freedom in the abstract but for the freedom to develop Nigerian, national capitalism. There is no room here to prove this statement, but it may easily be confirmed from the writings on economic issues by Nigerian national leaders from the end of the nineteenth century (those published in the press, or kept in Nigerian and other archives in the form of pamphlets, programmes, memoranda, personal letters, etc.[4]). Many dependence theories would benefit from this first-hand material, coming directly from practical experience, very often of wide horizons and with an unbeatable knowledge of the mechanisms of dependence in West Africa. Some plans for economic independence prepared by Ghanaian and Nigerian leaders in the 1920s and 1930s were decades ahead of practical possibilities but are nevertheless most interesting examples of independent economic thinking.[5]

Concepts of Nigerian capitalism

For a long time authors writing on the economic history of Nigeria were not concerned with the sort of economic system that had been developing from the beginning of the twentieth century. Many otherwise valuable studies discussed only the development of the 'open', 'mixed' and other economic systems.[6] It was not until the late 1960s that Polly Hill wrote about capitalism in West Africa, mainly in Ghana and Nigeria, for the first time. She was interested in processes in agriculture, and her stimulating approach and conclusions were related only to small parts of the rural economies of both countries. Nevertheless, the first step had been taken.

More general interpretations of trends of economic development in Nigeria in terms of the political economy were first undertaken by R.O. Ekundare, T. Turner, G. Williams, and jointly by P. Collins, T. Turner and G. Williams.[7]

The work of Ekundare is of particular interest. He wrote the first economic history of Nigeria, covering the crucial period of the expansion of the market economy (1860-1960), the period when the origins of Nigerian capitalism can be traced.

'Every economic history', writes Ekundare, 'is premised on a philosophy, explicitly stated or implied; a philosophy which reveals the conception of the economic world in which a people have lived. In substance, the philosophy behind the economic history of Nigeria is based on "Competitive Capitalism".'[8] Ekundare explains how, according to him, the system developed in Nigeria. 'The British administration in Nigeria between 1860 and 1960 was made relatively easy by the fact that it met with a philosophy of economic growth on which the modern system was built. The adoption of the indirect-rule policy by the British was made possible by the indigenous economic system which was not completely alien to the British, and which encouraged Britain to adopt the colonial economy as an arm of the British economic system.' 'The economics of the slave trade', continues Ekundare, 'and that of the legitimate trade which followed — and which had its foundation in "rural" agricultural capitalism — had strengthened the claim of a long-established competitive capitalism in Nigeria, (and) it was a slow but inevitable process of change in what was fast becoming a highly materialistic society'.[9] Leaving aside the question whether early capitalism ever, and especially under colonial conditions, is uncompetitive, the picture outlined by Ekundare, which includes a combination of private capitalist enterprise (corporate and individual), as well as government enterprise, seems to explain some of the characteristics of Nigerian development discussed above.

The views of Collins, Turner and Williams also deserve attention, since they made the first attempt at a comprehensive and systematic analysis of the mechanisms of the socio-economic system prevailing in Nigeria in the 1970s. They, especially Terisa Turner, applied the concept of commercial capitalism to Nigeria of the time. 'In a commercial capitalist political economy', she writes, 'the dominant business class is not composed of capitalists who organise labour, capital, raw materials and energy to produce a product for the market. Among the reasons for the near absence of productive entrepreneurship (*sic*!) are capital shortage, pre-emptive concentration of foreign firms, and more profitable alternatives. The absence of industrialisation is commonly explained by reference to a "Lack of appropriate technical skills and managerial know-how . . .". This explanation fails to take into account the fact that many nationals with these technical and managerial qualities become middlemen, not capitalists. Many middlemen have professional qualifications as accountants, business administrators, lawyers, etc., and have been diverted from the practice of their professions by more promising opportunities in commerce.'[10]

This view, right in principle, does not fit exactly the complex situation in Nigeria. The author seemed to be over impressed by the oil boom and its effects on enterprise in the mid-1970s, which could easily overshadow other branches of entrepreneurial activity.

The concept of 'nurture-capitalism' in Nigeria, developed by P.S. Schatz, is more concerned with the mechanisms of stimulation of the system.[11] Starting his analysis from the 1950s, Schatz emphasises the 'nurture' character of capitalism, especially clear in the mid-1970s. To some extent this view seemed to confirm our observation of the leaders-entrepreneurs relationship in earlier periods. And after all, one should ask why capitalism was 'nurtured' in Nigeria after independence. For the author it seemed, as stressed above, a logical continuation of the pattern of the economic basis of the political leadership.

The same problem was discussed by Soviet authors in a recent study on contemporary Nigeria.[12] When analysing the economy, they divided it into three sectors, using as a criterion the ownership of the means of production: governmental, capitalist (Nigerian and foreign) and traditional. (The last is of course disputable, but this is not important here.) They then analyse the processes of change in both parts of the capitalist sector. With such an approach it seems to be much easier to follow the dynamics of both Nigerian and foreign capitalism, and to understand differences in their development. It may also help to reveal mutual links of indigenous capitalism, foreign capitalism and the governmental sector, and to assess the possible role of the government in efforts to implement ideas of increasing economic independence.

Conclusions

In this paper it has been argued that capitalism as a system of organisation of economic life was regarded as a way of development in Nigeria long before Independence. It was caused by several factors, including the way Nigeria entered the world economy. The idea of national capitalism was therefore in a sense inherited by the post-Independence Nigerian leadership from the times of anti-colonial struggle. It was accepted as part of the nation's concept of development in the short-term programmes of all subsequent governments, both civilian and military after 1960, by all major political parties and ruling groups. The decision to achieve economic independence within the capitalist system was present in all subsequent economic development plans. In all these, however, the goal of full economic independence was also presented as one of the basic tasks.

The questions whether industrialisation, as a part of full independence, is possible in the post-colonial economy within the capitalist system, and whether the full economic independence of the post-colonial country within that system is possible, are outside the scope of this paper. But these questions are, one must stress, not new in Nigeria; they have been studied by a few generations of Nigerian intellectuals and political thinkers.

Notes

1. See Jan J. Milewski, 'The Great Depression of the Early 1930s in a Colonial Country: A Case Study of Nigeria', *Africana Bulletin*, No. 23, 1975, pp.7–46.
2. A. McPhee, *The Economic Revolution in British West Africa*, 1926.
3. Milewski, *op. cit.*, p.33.
4. This subject is developed in a book just completed, *Indigenous Capitalism in Nigeria, 1900-1939*.
5. Milewski, *op. cit.*
6. For example, G.K. Helleiner, *Peasant Agriculture, Government and Economic Growth in Nigeria*, 1966; P. Kilby, *Industrialisation in an Open Economy: Nigeria 1945-1966*, 1969; also A.G. Hopkins, *An Economic History of West Africa*, 1970.
7. G. Williams, 'Nigeria, A Political Economy', and P. Collins, T. Turner and G. Williams, 'Nigeria, Capitalism and the Coup', in G. Williams (ed.), *Nigeria: Economy and Society*, 1976; T. Turner, 'Commercial Capitalism and the 1975 Coup', in K. Panther-Brick, *Soldiers and Oil: The Political Transformation in Nigeria*, 1978.
8. R.O. Ekundare, *An Economic History of Nigeria 1860-1960*, 1973, p.383.
9. *Ibid.*, p.384.
10. T. Turner, 'Commercial Capitalism . . .', *op. cit.*, p.169.
11. P.S. Schatz, *Nigerian Capitalism*, 1978.
12. Nigeria, Sowremiennyj Etap Razwitja (*Nigeria, Contemporary Stage of Development*), Moscow, 1978.

5 TRADE, PRODUCTION AND SELF-RELIANCE

H. David Evans *

Within the dependency tradition, there is a strong current of thought which seeks to identify the relationship between the integration of peripheral areas into the world capitalist system and the limits thereby imposed on policies and prospects for national development. Within this context, the idea of the desirability of more 'self-reliant' national development has taken many forms.[1]

The early tradition of Prebisch and Singer sought to identify market and institutional structures which, in conjunction with a trading relationship dominated by an exchange of agricultural products for industrial products, led to an unequal distribution of the gains from trade. The 'self-reliant' development strategy was, of course, industrialisation via protected import-competing industrialisation required to realise externalities in the development process and to eliminate the structural causes of unequal benefits from trade.[2] The Emmanuel theory of unequal exchange has had rather similar concerns. The self-reliant development strategy prescribed is the collective imposition of export taxes by Third World countries to offset unequal exchange and to generate revenue for productive investment.

The political economy critique of the early import-substitution tradition has led to a greater emphasis on class relations. Writers such as Sunkel and Furtado have focussed on the relationship of national versus international capital, rather than unequal trading relations alone.[3] The 'dominators' are the transnational organisations and actors in alliance with various nationally based classes. The analysis of possible independent state action to redress imbalances in equalities in market and non-market relationships with the world economy becomes potentially far more complex, though the quest for simplification remains strong. Thus, for example, Seers (1979) attempts a taxonomy of nation states in the world economy by degrees of dependency, with a crucial determinant of the degree of dependency being the potential capacity of the nation state to move towards autarky, without great short-run economic cost (and possible long-run economic gain) in the pursuit of independent sovereign interests. In a stronger vein, the unequal exchange branch of the dependency tradition (to be distinguished from Emmanuel), characterised by such writers as Frank, Wallerstein, Amin and Saigal (henceforth Frank *et al.*), attempts to derive from the notion of

---

* In developing this paper I have benefited greatly from discussions with Diane Elson, Martin Godfrey, Robin Murray, Ennio Rodriguez, Dudley Seers, Keith Smith and Ian Steedman. I thank them all but implicate none.

exploitation of peripheral areas by the core areas of the world capitalist system and the 'development of underdevelopment', the conclusion that the inherent potential for semi-autarkic or more 'self-reliant' development is very great.[4]

In all this literature there is an underlying concern with the limits of national power and national sovereignty to formulate and implement more self-reliant development strategies. The specification of the alternative strategies is often ill-defined. Some authors, such as Sunkel and Seers, have what might be called a 'common sensical' approach to the formulation of alternatives. The Frank *et al.* 'unequal exchange' group has a conception of withdrawal into semi-autarkic socialism. Whether implicit or explicit, there is a strong vein in the dependency tradition which sees either retreat into relative autarky for the purposes of desired national development, or a temporary retreat for delinking, only to emerge as more equal trading units later, as a crucial aspect of all self-reliant development.[5]

Dependency theory and the theory of comparative advantage

The great contribution of dependency theory to the understanding of the questions of trade and development has been the strong reaction against both the formalism and narrow utilitarian economism of the standard neo-classical account of international trade and its relation to development. There has been a strong questioning of the realism of the assumptions which underlie the formal models of trade, such as the abstraction from power relationships, the degree to which internal market forces have developed to allow a division to be made between fully national and international trade, and the extent to which market processes will lead to full employment, and the distribution of the gains from trade.[6] Furthermore, the nation state as a unit of analysis has been seen as a rather more problematic entity than in the standard account of the theory of comparative advantage, requiring more careful study. Yet the reaction within the dependency tradition against more formal attempts to theorise trading relationships has surely gone too far. Whilst there have been some attempts to redress this balance by some of the unequal exchange writers referred to, there are at least three areas — the nation state and the conception of autarky, transitions between trading regimes, and distribution of the gains from trade — where I believe more abstract thought and formal specification of a theory of comparative advantage can be of considerable interest.

The nation state and the conception of autarky

The Ricardian theory of comparative advantage centres on the nation state as the unit of analysis. The pattern and potential gains from trade are then established by examining the process of price formation in a 'pre-trade' or 'autarkic' state and comparing this with a trading situation in which international prices have been formed. This procedure remains at the foundation of all theoretical accounts of international trade to date, though there are important differences about the defining characteristics of the national unit. In the Ricardian tradition differing endowments of nature and other aids to production govern the productivity of labour. It is the dichotomy between the internal and external mobility of capital and labour which, in conjunction with the delimiting of the areas of sway of national currencies, gives content to the national unit. The neo-classical tradition is dominated by Ohlin (1952), who builds both geography and space into the single market Walrasian general equilibrium system of mutual interdependence in an attempt to develop a more general theory of pricing in which there are a number of more or less closely related markets. The national unit then becomes a special form of regional unit, defined in relation to factor endowments, the effects of national borders on factor mobility, currency systems, community interests and social institutions. Here Ohlin (1952, p.244, fn.2) explicitly rejects views of the national economy as organic units in which the character of the whole is different from the sum of the parts, choosing to separate the analytical/quantitative problem of international trade from qualitative/social aspects. However, some neo-classical writers have attempted to give more content to the conception of the nation state.[7] The more recently developed neo-Ricardian and unequal exchange trade literature (see Steedman, 1979a, 1979b; Evans, 1980a, 1980b) is squarely within the Ricardian tradition, with national differences in the determination of income distribution and produced means of production brought onto centre stage. The neo-Ricardian theoretical framework has a more serious connection of the analytical with institutional and social determinants of economic phenomena and is much more flexible in terms of the capacity to deal with the international mobility of capital or labour than in the neo-classical or Ricardian traditions.

Whilst there may be disagreement between different strands of thought in the theory of comparative advantage over the nature of the nation state as a unit of analysis, the common *theoretical procedure* requires one to specify price and production relations under autarky *independently* of the determinants of price and production under trade. One of the strongest and most cogent critiques of this approach can be found in Williams (1929), who argues that:

> The Classical (international) trade theory assumes as fixed, for the purposes of reasoning, the very things which, in my view, should be the chief objects of study if what we wish to know is the effects and causes of international trade, so broadly regarded that nothing of importance in the facts shall fail to find its place in the analysis. (Williams (1929) reprinted in Ellis and Metzler (1950) pp.254-5)

A glance at any recent work on the formal theory of international trade will suffice to show that, *for the purposes of reasoning*, many factors which should be determined by the theory of comparative advantage remain fixed. Does this mean that the whole theoretical apparatus of trade theory should be thrown aside?

It is certainly true that, for any analysis of the fundamental causes of the rise of *international* trade, the notion that the nation state is a pre-given entity is a highly artificial construction, if for no other reason than that the historical process of the rise of international trade took place simultaneously with the development of the nation state.[8] There clearly is a place for theoretical analysis of the conditions determining the opening of trade between areas, regions or social formations which were hitherto in relative isolation. However, when it comes to the analysis of international trade at any given time, or over a relatively short historical period, the artificiality of the autarky construct is manifestly obvious if it is defined in relation to the *opening* of trade. Similarly the use of the 'free trade' norm against which one assesses all types of interventionist trade or commercial policies is a product of the free trade ideological bias of both Ricardian and neo-classical trade theory. A more careful usage of trade theory, restricted to the case where trade has already begun, would suggest an approach based on the analysis of alternative trading 'regimes', of which either 'free trade' or 'autarky' are but one of the alternatives which could be considered in relation to an hypothesised pre-given trading regime.[9]

Put in these terms, there seems little incompatibility between the methodology of the theory of comparative advantage and the dependency tradition for the analysis of alternative trading regimes. For both neo-Ricardian trade theory and the dependency tradition, the defining characteristics of the national unit are expressed in distributional terms. In neo-Ricardian trade theory the determinants of income distribution at the national level are crucial. Within the dependency tradition the class character of the national unit is often defined in terms of different configurations of distribution categories. This is most clearly evident in the unequal exchange writers, both in their use of distribution categories[10] and, in some cases, their explicit acceptance of a neo-Ricardian approach to the theory of comparative advantage. The conception of autarky in the dependency tradition in relation to the opening of trade is seldom distinguished from that pertinent to a relative closing of trade, a more 'self-reliant' situation. Furthermore, there is a tendency to play down the place of formal conceptual models because of fears that utilising such modes of thought results in 'ahistorical', 'asocial', 'mechanistic' or 'economistic' analyses. Such fears are certainly well-founded in relation to neo-classical trade theory and the association 'vision', but not necessarily so in relation to the neo-Ricardian approach.[11] Yet the assessment of the viability of a more 'self-reliant' or more 'autarkic' development strategy is often based on some simplified abstract analysis which may be developed without the aid of a formal model, or worse, developed on the basis of a formal model which is internally inconsistent or dependent upon very strong assumptions. This is most evident in the Frank *et al.* unequal exchange tradition of the dependency literature, which has conceptualised centre-periphery relations in terms of chains of surplus extraction assured by the domination of strong states/classes against weak states/classes. It is on the basis of this analysis that the very optimistic prospects for more 'self-reliant' development at the present time are made; a withdrawal from the world market breaks the chain of surplus extraction of 'unequal exchange' and opens the way to successful self-reliant development.

Amin (1973, 1977) and Saigal (1973) have made such an analysis of prospects for more 'self-reliant' or autarkic development in formal terms. I have examined in the Appendix the Amin-Saigal definition of unequal exchange with the aid of a simple neo-Ricardian trade model and have shown the similarity of their views with the Frank *et al.* conception of chains of surplus extraction leading to unequal exchange. It is shown that the model of 'unequal exchange' is in fact internally inconsistent. If one adopts a less rigorous view of the stated model and its assumptions, interpreting it as indicative only of underlying tendencies in the centre-periphery relationship, one is pushed in one of two directions. If the potential for more autarkic or self-reliant development is as strong as is assumed, then the extra-market forces which have prevented national or 'peripheral' capital from also fostering a more autarkic development strategy have not been adequately explained. Alternatively, the assumed potential for more self-reliant development did not exist in the first place.

Whilst this example of the use of formal trade-theoretic analysis is critical, reaching the same conclusion as Brenner (1977, p.92) on Utopian optimism about the potential for semi-autarkic socialist development in the periphery by a less formal analysis, there is no reason why such a formal framework of analysis could not be used in a more positive manner in the process of analysis and assessment of potential gains from a more self-reliant development strategy. Even if such applications were no more than an aid for checking the internal consistency and importance of key assumptions and characterisations of the analysis, the assessment of more self-reliant trade strategies would be greatly enhanced.

Transitions between trading regimes

Clearly there are many issues involved in any discussion of a successful transition to a more self-reliant or autarkic trading pattern, a transition between alternative trading regimes. Yet there is surprisingly little discussion of such questions in the dependency literature. For example, Seers (1979) discusses the *potential* capacity for various nation states or groups of nation states to move towards autarky, without elaboration on how it might be possible to get there. Is there anything pertinent which can usefully be discussed at the high level of abstraction of the theory of comparative advantage?

I would argue that one of the elements often missing in the dependency tradition is an analysis of the nature and function of market processes.[12] Whilst there are strong differences between neo-classical, neo-Ricardian and neo-Marxian views on these matters, they would all imply a common critique on the relative *absence* (in the dependency tradition) of emphasis on the importance of market processes and the powerful social force that they represent. From a neo-Ricardian perspective, the analysis of transitions between trading regimes suggests that, in so far as the market dominated by a competitive drive for profits governs the transition between trading regimes, then unemployed productive capacity and labour will characterise the transition process.[13] This underlines the more general neo-Ricardian (and, for that matter, neo-Marxian) perspective on the inherent tendency towards disequilibrium and crises in the market process.

The implication of these observations for the discussion of more 'self-reliant' trading regimes within the dependency tradition is that, just as there is a Utopian vision of the prospects for semi-autarkic development arising from the unequal exchange tradition, there is a tendency towards a Utopian view of the relative ease with which the market process can be interfered with in order to achieve a transition to the more autarkic or self-reliant trading regime. Even a 'moderate' attempt at delinking by altering relative prices, for example, through tariffs or other protective measures, is unlikely to be achieved without some form of transitional crisis. Whilst it may be apparently possible to achieve a transition without unemployed resources, for example, by tariff and fiscal measures, the form of the transitional crisis in this case will be shifted to the export sector and, more generally, to a balance of payments crisis. If the likelihood of disequilibrium crisis can be established for a 'moderate' price-induced transitional process, there can be little wonder at the capital flight and IMF visitations in more 'radical' attempts at delinking. Thus any attempt to effect major change in trading regimes or delinking requires full consideration of the armoury of market and non-market controls which may be necessary to weather the ensuing crisis in relations with the world market in general. This is not to suggest that such a transition should not be considered or attempted, but that, in so far as the dependency tradition tends to underrate the social force of market relations, it is over-optimistic about the capacity of nation states to effect a transition through more limited intervention in the market process without a far-reaching break with market relations.

Distribution of the gains from trade

The Prebisch/Singer concern with the terms of trade and the distribution of the gains from trade — historically one of the early parts of the dependency tradition and more recently brought to the forefront in Emmanuel's theory of unequal exchange — comes at the end of this paper because of the theoretical structure of the argument. Here the central focus is the relationship between institutional and market forces operating through time on a *given* pattern of international or centre-periphery specialisation which can be analysed, albeit somewhat heuristically, without reference to the trade-theoretic problems of the opening of trade or transition between trading regimes. In this case, the Williams (1929) critique of the theory of comparative advantage does not hold with such force, particularly if the focus is on the international distribution of the incremental gains in social productivity through technical change.

Better terms of trade and enchanced gains from trade might be achieved by either market intervention or more far-reaching social change which influences the institutional determinants of an unequal division of the gains from trade between rich and poor nations, or between the centre and the periphery. Such policies could be implemented in conjunction with the use of the increased resources potentially available for development as a part of a more 'self-reliant' development strategy. It is therefore pertinent to examine under what conditions an improvement of the terms of trade and enhanced gains from trade *could* take place.

There is not much dispute on the potential for any one nation, or group of nations, to improve its gains from trade by exploiting any monopolistic position on the market. Whether such theoretical possibilities for improving the terms of trade can best be achieved via cartelisation or producer associations (the OPEC model), consumer-producer agreements (the UNCTAD model), or export taxes implemented by individual countries is a source of debate. I have argued in Evans (1979) that the producer association route is most likely to achieve improvements in this direction for smaller, weaker, 'dependent' developing countries. More important differences arise, however, from the specification of the institutional determinants of factors governing the distribution of the gains from trade.

The ideas behind the Prebisch/Singer thesis can be expressed in terms of a two-country international trade model in which two nations are replaced by a 'centre' and a 'periphery' producing industrial and primary products respectively.[14] Emmanuel's theory of unequal exchange can be expressed in similar terms, though the particular products exchanged are of no consequence. One aspect of the centre-periphery distinction in Prebisch and Singer, and the defining characteristic in Emmanuel, hinges on the idea that there are institutional differences in the determination of money and real wages in the long run. Thus the greater power of organised labour to strike a money and real wage bargain in the centre leads, it is argued, to a tendency for the 'centre' economies to capture the lion's share of the gains from technical change, provided there is either a tendency towards the equalisation of the international rate of profit or an inability of 'peripheral' capitalists or other producer categories to offset the strong bargaining power of wage workers in the 'centre'. This leads to the thesis about the long-run decline in the barter terms of trade and an unequal international division of the gains from improvements in productivity.

An immediate set of problems with this argument is the classification of the 'centre' and the 'periphery', either on the double criterion of a differential bargaining power of workers and an aggregation of similar commodities called 'agricultural' and 'manufactured' goods, or on the basis of the differential bargaining power of workers alone. For example, should the power of organised labour or the type of commodities produced change over time, how is one to legislate on the movement of particular nations from the 'centre' to the 'periphery'? One only has to think of the differences between nations in the 'centre', say between the United Kingdom and West Germany, to see how problematic this is. Whilst on many criteria organised labour is much more powerful in the United Kingdom than in West Germany, one would hardly want to have the former graduating to a more developed status because of the power of its organised labour to resist restructuring in the current crisis, rather than moving in the other direction. More importantly, the idea that workers can bargain in the long run for higher real wages in the context of a tendency towards the international equalisation of the rate of profit hinges on the position that *within* the 'centre' and 'periphery' national divisions are unimportant, but *between* the 'centre' and 'periphery' the national units are crucially distinct and independent. However, the individual nations in both groups are in a competitive relationship, provided there are no commodities produced only in one nation. Thus it is possible for international capital to abandon any one nation when its workers strike a short-run wage bargain too high in real terms to yield the international rate of profit, provoking a balance of payments crisis and currency devaluation which then effectively slashes the real wage bargain. The competitive power of international capital is further enhanced when the division between the 'centre' producing manufactures and the 'periphery' producing primary products becomes blurred, as is increasingly the case.[15] Thus both the Prebisch/Singer and Emmanuel distribution mechanisms are dependent on the assumption that the individual nation states are independent and competition between them is limited both by the specificity of commodities produced by the 'centre' or the 'periphery' and a lack of international capital mobility. It is one thing to propose a classicial distribution mechanism in which real wages are determined by different institutional, social and historical factors when productive capital is not internationally mobile, as was assumed by Ricardo and Marx, and quite another when this crucial assumption can no longer be held to. (Indeed, a key determinant of the unequal exchange process in Emmanuel is the international mobility of capital and a tendency towards the equalisation of the rate of profit.) In short, the classical distribution mechanism of the Prebisch/Singer and Emmanuel theses is undermined by the rise of interstate relations of competition.

Thus in any assessment of possible improvements in the terms of and gains from trade in a strategy of more self-reliant development depends crucially on the capacity of a 'dependent' country, or groups of countries, to organise collective resistance against the competitive power of internationally mobile capital. Increasingly the question of a solution to uneven distribution of the gains from trade must be posed in terms of the international cooperation of labour, rather than programmes of self-reliant development for single nations or groups of nations. Put in other terms, the limits on national programmes of self-reliant development imposed by international capital are far greater as the international competitive power of capital is increased.

Paradoxically, the nationalism often associated with attempts at programmes of self-reliance acts as an inhibitor to such cooperation. Further, it should be emphasised that this analysis is posed only in distributional terms. The need for collective resistance to capital for distributive justice ignores the fact that, because of its capacity to revolutionise production, capital can not only abandon with contempt those who struggle for distributive justice, but reward those who accept the laws of uneven development with higher wages. Indeed by increasing productivity it can reward *everyone*, in *absolute* terms. In so far as dependency analyses of more self-reliant development strategies also embody a desire to transcend the limits of capitalist development processes, there is clearly a need for analysis at the level of production as well.

Concluding remarks

In this paper I have tried to elaborate on the proposition that, within the dependency tradition, the quest for more self-reliant patterns of trade and production might well be strengthened by a more hard-nosed appraisal of such possibilities in the context of relations of competition in the world market. None of this is to deny the importance of the questions posed in the dependency tradition; indeed, the neo-Ricardian approach to the analysis of trade might well help to give greater content to the analysis of the processes of uneven and unequal development.

The general tendency of the dependency tradition to pose these issues in a 'core-periphery' framework rather than in terms of collective action to limit the competitive power of internationally mobile capital suggests that there is a danger of mis-specifying the fundamental relations of dependence as state-state relations, rather than capital/labour relations. If the latter line is to be pursued, then it should be recognised that this issue has been addressed here in terms of distribution categories without elaboration of the questions of production, or of more detailed examination of class alliances which would be necessary to achieve the desired results.

Appendix

Amin attempts to give content to a definition of surplus extraction via 'unequal exchange'. He assumes a tendency towards equalisation of the rate of profit internationally and the *possibility* of autarkic development. That is, the periphery is able to produce the same use-values as the centre, or non-specific goods. Thus the Amin definition of 'unequal exchange' would apply at most to the last hundred years or so, when it might be argued that there is a tendency towards international equalisation of the rate of profit. In this context Amin (1977, p.211) defines a set of conditions for the transfer of value from the periphery to the core as: 'the exchange of products whose production involves wage differentials greater than those of productivity'.

An explicit core-periphery model in which such a process is analysed is not elaborated, but Amin comments that, within the context of a Sraffa model of the 'centre-periphery' relationship, Saigal (1973) illustrates the Amin definition of unequal exchange. What then is this Sraffa or neo-Ricardian trade model which illustrates the possibility of surplus extraction via 'unequal exchange' in the context of the possibility of autarkic development in the 'periphery'?

Saigal first assumes that there are two countries, A and B (or 'centre' and 'periphery'), and two commodities, 1 and 2, produced with identical techniques of production in each country under constant returns to scale. The organic composition of capital differs between sectors, there are no joint products or externalities, and the balance of trade is assumed to be zero. Then for given, but *different* (up to a scalar multiple), bundles of commodities which enter worker consumption, the level of wages being expressed by the scalars w^A and w^B, it is possible to illustrate the Saigal model by showing the relationship between the long-run steady state rates of profit and terms of trade (p_1/p_2) as in Diagram 1.

It is assumed that country A is the high-wage country, so that $w^A > w^B$. Assuming that sector 1 has the higher organic composition of capital, it follows that under autarky (a) in each country,

$$(p_1/p_2)^{Aa} \quad < \quad (p_1/p_2)^{Ba}$$

and
$$r^{Aa} \quad < \quad r^{Ba}$$

Now if country A specialises in the production of commodity 1, then the relationship between the terms of trade and the rate of profit for given real wages is shown by $\bar{w}^{A1}$; as the terms of trade improve, the rate of profit will rise. The $\bar{w}^{A2}$ curve to the left of $(p_1/p_2)^{Aa}$ is shown with a dashed line to indicate that specialisation is taking place in the 'wrong' direction, with the profit rate less than under autarky. Similarly, the $\bar{w}^{A2}$ curve shows the relationship between the rate of profit and the terms of trade when country A specialises in producing commodity 2. The $\bar{w}^{B1}$ and $\bar{w}^{B2}$ functions are for country B when specialising in commodities 1 and 2 respectively. Given the above assumptions, when the rate of profit

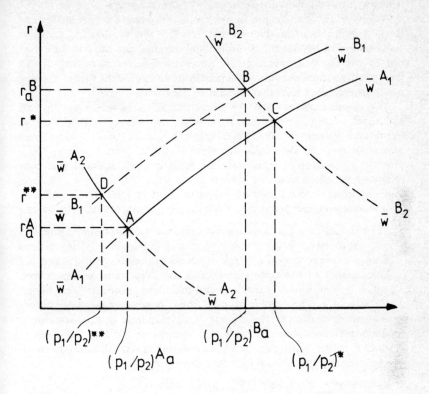

Diagram 5.1. Illustration of Saigal's trade model

is equalised internationally there are two possible equilibrium terms of trade denoted by $(p_1/p_2)^*$ and $(p_1/p_2)^{**}$ with associated rates of profit r^* and r^{**}. In both cases, as noted by Saigal, the equilibrium terms of trade lie outside the Ricardian limbo region, $(p_1/p_2)^{Aa}$ and $(p_1/p_2)^{Ba}$. Further, the equilibrium rate of profit is higher with trade for the high-wage country and lower for the low-wage country in comparison with autarky. It can easily be seen that the point C (D) is not a sustainable equilibrium point under free trade and perfect competition, for it will always pay capitalists in country B to produce commodity 1 (2) domestically rather than to import it. By shifting from C (D) to B, the price of the imported commodity 1 (2) falls, and the rate of profit will rise. Capitalists in country A, given capital mobility, will always try to export capital to country B, but will be unable to export enough (under the given assumptions) to equalise the rate of profit in the two countries.

Thus the 'equilibrium' at C is sustained by a set of ill-defined extra-market forces of 'centre' imperialist domination of the 'periphery'.

Saigal further develops this model for cases in which there are differences in the techniques of production, but in which the 'equilibrium' terms of trade always lie outside the Ricardian limbo region, and can only be enforced by the assumed operation of extra-market forces. Note that, at this level of abstraction, the autarky construct pertinent for the case of opening is not distinguished from that relevant to the closing of trade.

The connections between the Amin and Saigal views on an 'unequal exchange' relationship and those of other dependency writers such as Frank and Wallerstein can be established in a rather general way. These writers develop the twin ideas of chains of surplus extraction from 'peripheral' to 'core' areas in conjunction with unequal national and class relationships which lead to a process of dynamic accumulation and development in the 'centre' and an *enforced* cycle of underdevelopment or backwardness in the periphery. For example, Frank (1969, p.9) writes:

> Thus the metropolis expropriates economic surplus from its satellites and appropriates it for its own economic development. The satellites remain underdeveloped for lack of access to their own surplus and as a consequence of the same polarization and exploitative contradictions which the metropolis introduces and maintains in the satellites' domestic structure. The combination of these contradictions, once firmly implanted, reinforces the process of development in the increasingly dominant metropolis and underdevelopment in the ever more dependent satellites until they are resolved through the abandonment of capitalism by one or both interdependent parts.

In a similar vein, Wallerstein (1974, p.401) argues:

> Once we get a difference in the strength of the state-machineries, we get the operation of 'unequal exchange' which is enforced by strong states on weak ones, by core states on peripheral areas. Thus agricultural capitalism (of the early modern period) involves not only appropriation of surplus-value by an owner from a labourer, but an appropriation of surplus of the whole world economy by core areas.

Frank (1978, pp.103-10) endorses a general perspective on unequal exchange arising out of the debates between Emmanuel, Bettelheim and Palloix without taking a strong position on the different definitions of unequal exchange between, for example, Emmanuel and Amin. At this level of generality there is no distinction made between the requirements for such chains of surplus extraction to operate with or without a tendency towards the international equalisation of the rate of profit, or of the possibility of withdrawal into autarky. However, the spirit of the Frank-Wallerstein argument is well summarised by Brenner (1977, p.92):

The notion of 'development of underdevelopment' opens the way to Third-Worldist ideology. From the conclusion that development occurred only in the absence of links with accumulating capitalism in the metropolis, it can only be a short step to the strategy of semi-autarkic socialist development.

It is therefore not surprising to find Amin commenting favourably on the work of both Wallerstein and Frank.

Thus Amin (1975, p.46) writes:

The second dichotomy in this system which Wallerstein brings out, i.e. center vs. periphery, is equally essential. Wallerstein gives a rigorous definition of it. Since the system is an economic one, it is at the economic level that the new cleavages emerge: the economy of the core-states is self-centred, that of the peripheries is outward-oriented and relegated by the unequal division of labor to producing 'lower-ranking' goods (i.e. goods whose labor is less well rewarded). The early roots of unequal exchange go back to these first centuries of capitalism.

and Amin (1977, p.234) observes in relation to Frank:

Within this framework, we can see that an internal market is formed, but one that is distinguished from that of the center. It is principally a market for products both from industry and submissive precapitalist agriculture, but it is really neither a labor market, since proletarianization is limited, nor a capital market, which remains largely foreign (multinational corporations) and state controlled (since domestic private capital, being spread too thinly, cannot reach modern technology). It is in this sense that the peripheral model remains specific and that Frank's intuition in speaking of 'development of underdevelopment' can be upheld.

Notes

1. In the analysis which follows, I have drawn mainly on the Latin American dependency tradition. However, the main thrust of the argument should not be affected by this bias.
2. For a summary of the original Prebisch/Singer and Emmanuel arguments in terms of a formal model of trade, see Bacha (1978) and Evans (1980a). For a recent reflection on his original ideas, see Singer (1975).
3. For a recent overview of this work, see Sunkel (1979), Sunkel and Fuenzalida (1979) and Palma (1978). See also the papers by Bienefeld, Godfrey and Rodriguez in Godfrey (1980, forthcoming). (The Bienefeld paper is reprinted in this volume, as is a revised version of the Palma paper, Chapters 2 and 1 respectively.)
4. For the latest survey of the Frank tradition in the dependency literature, see Palma (1978). For a recent summary and critique of Frank, and the relationship of his work to writers such as Sweezy and Wallerstein, see Brenner (1977).
5. For an excellent account of the wider issues raised in the dependency tradition, see the paper by Bienefeld in this volume (Chapter 2).
6. The classic article which deals with these issues for development theory in

general is Seers (1963). See also Sideri (1970) for an analysis of power in trading relations.

7. For example, Kindleberger (1962) provides a richer account of the relationships between foreign trade and the national economy. In the second part of his book Kindleberger discusses some of the material and social determinants of the optimal size of different producing and consuming units, the family, factory, plantation, administrative organisation, the nation state, but without any overarching social theory. More recently, Johnson (1968, ch. 1) attempts to develop a rational theory of government in order to examine the role of economic nationalism in the establishment of newly independent nation states.

8. See, for example, Polanyi (1944). For a recent attempt to conceptualise the theoretical problems involved in dealing with the rise of trade and the modern nation state, see Smith (1977).

9. This was the procedure I adopted for the analysis of income distribution and protection in the Australian economy in Evans (1972). This meant that such theoretical constructs as 'effective protection', which is based on the definition of a free trade 'norm' against which the protective effect of a tariff structure might be assessed, must be replaced by measures of the effects of a change in a trading regime from the pre-existing protected situation to some alternative. See Evans (1972, chs. 5 and 8). For a discussion of the use of comparative dynamic analysis in the neo-Ricardian literature, see Steedman (1979b, ch. 2).

10. This is argued cogently in Brenner (1977) in relation to Frank and Wallerstein.

11. For a discussion of some of these issues, see Evans (1980b) and Steedman (1979a, b). It would be a cheap criticism to reject the methodology of comparative advantage as unhelpful because of the static nature of the autarky construct. It is certainly true that the formal representation of two independent structures ('autarky' and 'trade') *is* static, so that any conceptualisation of the transition between these static structures appears to be undialectical. Two issues are of importance here. First, there is a striking difference in the interpretation of transitional regimes between 'autarky' and 'trade' in neo-classical and neo-Ricardian trade theory, as discussed in Mainwaring (1979). Second, the social theory to which one might turn in order to develop a more dynamic, even dialectical, concept of transition is very different for the neo-classical and neo-Ricardian traditions. As argued in Steedman (1977), the compatability of the neo-Ricardian approach to price formation with the Marxian tradition is a source of great potential strength.

12. I have developed this point in relation to UNCTAD and NIEO commodity policy in Evans (1979). Many of these points are pertinent to the dependency literature in general.

13. For a discussion of these issues and a critique of neo-classical perspectives on this issue, see Mainwaring (1979) and Steedman (1979c).

14. Dudley Seers has pointed out to me that Ricardo's famous example of trade between England and Portugal requires only certain institutional assumptions to convert it into a centre-periphery model of exchange of industrial and agricultural products. It could also be added that Ricardo assumed that Portugal is absolutely more productive in both branches than England, though it has no implications for his argument because of a lack of capital mobility. One should be careful not to draw any conclusions from this observation about Ricardo's view of the productive potential of 'peripheries' and the possibility of semi-autarkic development.

15. In re-visiting his earlier work, Singer (1975) recognises the problem of the industrial/agricultural distribution of his earlier work, shifting to a closer examination of the institutional context governing the allocation of expenditure and returns on R&D funds.

Bibliography

Amin, Samir (1973), *L'éxchange inégal et la loi de la valeur: la fin d'un débat, avec une contribution de J.C. Saigal*, Paris, Editions Anthropos-IDEP. English translation, excluding Saigal's contribution, in Section IV of S. Amin, *Imperialism and Unequal Development*, Hassocks, Harvester Press, 1977.

Amin, Samir (1975), 'The Early Roots of Unequal Exchange', *Monthly Review*, 27 (7), Dec., pp. 43-7 (review of I. Wallerstein, *The Modern World System*, New York, Academic Press, 1974).

Bacha, Edmar L. (1978), 'An Interpretation of Unequal Exchange from Prebisch-Singer to Emmanuel', *Journal of Development Economics*, 5 (4), pp. 319-30.

Brenner, R. (1977), 'On Sweezy, Frank and Wallerstein', *New Left Review*, No. 104, pp. 25-93.

Ellis, H.S., and Metzler, L.A. (1950), *Readings in the Theory of International Trade*, Illnois, Irwin.

Evans, H.D. (1972), *A General Equilibrium Analysis of Protection: The Effect of Protection in Australia* (contributions to Economic Analysis No. 76), Amsterdam, North Holland, 1972.

Evans, H.D. (1979), 'International Commodity Policy: UNCTAD and NIEO in Search of a Rationale', *World Development*, 7 (3), pp. 259-80.

Evans, H.D. (1980a), 'Emmanuel's Thoery of Unequal Exchange: Critique, Counter Critique and Theoretical Contribution', *IDS Discussion Paper*, No. 149, Brighton, Sussex, Institute of Development Studies.

Evans, H.D. (1980b), 'Unequal Exchange and Economic Policies: Some Implications of the Neo-Ricardian Critique of the Theory of Comparative Advantage', in I. Livingstone (ed.), *Development Economics and Policy Readings*, London, George Allen & Unwin.

Frank, A.G. (1969), *Capitalism and Underdevelopment in Latin America*, New York, Monthly Review Press.

Frank, A.G. (1978), *Dependent Accumulation and Under-Development*, London, Macmillan.

Godfrey, M. (1980), 'Is Dependency Dead?', *IDS Bulletin*, 10 (1), Special Issue, Brighton, Sussex, Institute of Development Studies.

Johnson, H.G. (ed.) (1968), *Economic Nationalism in New and Old States*, Committee for the Comparative Study of New Nations, University of Chicago; London, George Allen & Unwin.

Kindleberger, C.P. (1962), *Foreign Trade and the National Economy*, New Haven, Yale University Press.

Mainwaring, L. (1979), 'On the Transition from Autarky to Trade', in Steedman (1979a), Essay 12, pp. 131-41.

Ohlin, Bertil (1952), *Interregional and International Trade*, Cambridge, Mass., Harvard University Press.

Palma, G. (1978), 'Dependency: a Formal Theory of Underdevelopment or a Methodology for the Analysis of Concrete Situations of Underdevelopment', *World Development*, 6 (7/8), pp. 881-924.

Polanyi, K. (1944), *The Great Transformation*, New York, Rinehart.

Saigal, J.C. (1973), 'Réflexions sur la théorie de "L'éxchange inégal" ', in S. Amin, *L'éxchange inégal et la loi de la valeur*, Paris, Editions Anthropos-IDEP, Appendix.

Seers, D. (1963), 'The Limitations of the Special Case', *Bulletin of the Oxford Institute of Economics and Statistics*, 25 (2), pp. 77-98.

Seers, D. (1979), 'Patterns of Dependence', in J.J. Villamil (ed.), *Transnational Capitalism and National Development: New Perspectives on Dependence*, Hassocks, Sussex, Harvester Press, ch. 4, pp. 95-114.

Sideri, S. (1970), *Trade and Power*, Rotterdam, Rotterdam University Press.

Singer, H.W. (1975), 'The Distribution of Gains from Trade and Investment –

Revisited', *Journal of Development Studies*, 11 (4), pp. 377-82.

Smith, K. (1977), 'The Mercantilist Economy: Trading Relations and National Space in the History of "Economic" Theory', M.Phil. Dissertation, Institute of Development Studies, University of Sussex.

Steedman, I. (1977), *Marx after Sraffa*, London, New Left Books.

Steedman, I. (ed.) (1979a), *Fundamental Issues in Trade Theory*, London, Macmillan.

Steedman, I. (1979b), *Trade Amongst Growing Economies*, Cambridge, Cambridge University Press.

Steedman, I. (1979c), 'Introduction Essay', in Steedman (1979a).

Sunkel, Osvaldo (1979), 'The Development of Development Thinking', in Villamil (1979).

Sunkel, Osvaldo, and Fuenzalida, Edmundo F. (1979), 'Transnationalization and its National Consequences', in Vaillamil (1979).

Villamil, J.J. (ed.) (1979), *Transnational Capitalism and National Development: New Perspectives on Dependence*, Hassocks, Sussex, Harvester Press.

Wallerstein, I. (1974), 'The Rise and Future Demise of the World Capitalist System: Concepts and Comparative Analysis', *Comparative Studies in Society and History*, 16 (4), pp. 387-415.

Williams, J.H. (1929), 'The Theory of International Trade Re-considered', *Economic Journal*, 1929, reprinted in Ellis and Metzler (1950).

6 DEVELOPMENT OPTIONS: THE STRENGTHS AND WEAKNESSES OF DEPENDENCY THEORIES IN EXPLAINING A GOVERNMENT'S ROOM TO MANOEUVRE *

Dudley Seers

We all assume that, for any particular government, certain policies are 'unthinkable', or at least 'impractical', but we are rarely explicit, even to ourselves, on why we exclude them from consideration. And different people may well make different assumptions about what are data in any situation: bureaucrats, for example, tend to rule out all possible policies outside a narrow range, whereas many academics assume policy to be largely or totally unconstrained. Differences over what governments *should* do are often really about what they *can* do.

Nor surprisingly, discussion of policy options can be quite sterile. Moreover, the failure to recognise the constraints may prevent our seeing the significance of developments that open up new options. On the other hand, it may lead policymakers, especially those who have recently taken power, to adopt policies which are unworkable and sooner or later cost them political office. It seems worthwhile, therefore, to identify and study the factors that shape the boundaries to policy.

To bring out the issues, let us hypothetically suppose that a government wants to radically change the development strategy. I am not thinking of a completely autarkic socialist revolution à la Kampuchea, but of a change involving some 'delinking' of the country from the world economy — by expropriating foreign capital and/or controlling its entry, cutting down imports, etc., with associated internal redistributive measures. What would stop it doing this? In particular, what repercussions would it fear and why?

Some may think this issue trivial. Certainly, it is hardly a central concern of dependency theory. But it is not a trivial issue to many political leaders (or their advisers). As we know from recent experience, those who embark on this strategy with naive optimism may well lose not merely power, and see their policies reversed, but also forfeit their liberties (including the freedom to reside in their own country), perhaps even their lives. And the mere possibility of *coups* and military interventions shapes the policies of governments, even if only subconsciously.

A full treatment of this question would take a good deal of deep theorising about economic and political structures at both international

* I am especially grateful to Manfred Bienefeld, Thomas Biersteker, Robert Borosage, Jose Maria Brandao de Brito, Zofia Dobrska, David Evans, Edmundo Fuenzalida, Norman Girvan, Toma Gudac, Marja-Liisa Kiljunen, Geoff Lamb, Bernard Schaffer, Luigi Spaventa, and Osvaldo Sunkel for comments on earlier drafts. None of them are to be blamed, however, for the contents.

and national levels, the interactions between them, and the dynamics of those interactions. It would have to discuss the important administrative requirements of delinking policies. Since this is a paper, not a treatise, I shall only deal with a few of the economic and cultural determinants of development strategy that are implicit in dependency theory but are largely neglected in the work of neo-classical economists, and then a number of important ones which even dependency theorists ignore — indeed, in a sense, *have to* ignore. I shall try at the end to indicate why these neglected factors are significant if we are to understand the concept of dependence, how much scope they leave political leaders and, finally, what light they throw on the possibilities of generalisation.

External economic constraints on policy ignored by neo-classical economists

Economists have done very little work on external constraints apart from those that are part and parcel of the working of commodity markets. In the case of pure neo-classical economists, this is not surprising. They disapprove of such nationalist concerns. The neo-Marxist wing of the dependency school (Amin, Frank, *et al.*)[1], does not see much to be gained from incremental delinking unless and until there is a world revolution. (However, to study constraints on that course of action certainly raises even sharper questions about the practical feasibility of such highly autarkic policies — another justification for posing the question about repercussions.)

Even in the other sub-schools of dependency, there is not much explicit treatment of the economic consequences of delinking. Yet a good deal can be inferred from their work, because they ask more relevant questions than orthodox neo-classical economists (of either Chicago, Keynesian or Marxist branches). Mainstream economists, for example, would be strictly indifferent to where capital came from: thus when evaluating projects they would concentrate on the rate of return; in macro-economic analysis, e.g. for development plans, they would use an aggregate concept of investment, which added together the capital from foreign and domestic sources indifferently (and even a counterpart aggregate savings)[2] as if the savings of undistributed profits of firms, even foreign firms, were available for any type of investment. (This indeed is precisely what nearly all official statistics do,[3] following the practice recommended in the UN system of National Accounts.) An economist of this type would probably, if pressed, show some preference for foreign capital, because of the technology, management skills, etc. it brings with it.

A dependency theorist would have a very different approach. In many circumstances, he would hardly deny the need for foreign capital, but he would be very concerned about the implications of its entry, especially when it comes via the transnational corporations (TNCs). I shall not review here the whole range of effects (on the balance of payments, employment, income distribution, etc.),[4] merely glance at the role of the TNCs when the 'host government' drastically raises taxes, or adopts pro-labour legislation, or (especially) threatens expropriation.

Both *a priori* and on the basis of experience, the TNCs can be expected to reduce output, employment and perhaps exports; technological imports will almost certainly cease and the inflow of capital be replaced by an out-flow. Some such reaction could, from the viewpoint of the corporation, be just the natural response of a risk-avoiding profit maximiser. It may, how-ever, also be part of a deliberate policy of retaliation, aimed at inducing policy changes – if necessary through changes in government. The corpora-tions may well get support in this aim from local groups which depend on them economically, e.g. the trade unions to which their employees belong and manufacturers or farmers supplying production inputs. (In identifying such allies the work of the dependency school is useful.) The TNCs can also expect help from 'their own' government, which may broaden the campaign by calling on other external and internal allies, and using the additional instruments of retaliation at its disposal, which range from cutting off aid to trade embargoes or even war. Purely economic conflicts rapidly become highly political.[5] Thus, the very existence of TNCs raises the penalties of delinking (one of the usually ignored costs of inviting them in).

We do not need to speculate about the effects of delinking strategies: a number have actually been attempted. Chile (1970-3) provides the *casus classicus* of foreign intervention,[6] not because it is unique, but because, thanks to the openness of the United States political system, especially during the national self-examination as the Watergate scandal unwound, it is so well documented. The programme of the *Unidad Popular* did indeed imply a considerable measure of delinking. ITT made an abortive attempt to stop Allende even taking office, and following the expropriation of the subsidiaries of United States mining corporations, there were United States interventions of various types as part of a deliberate policy of 'destabilisa-tion'. Attempts were made to block exports of copper and hold up supplies of essential imports. Banks (including the World Bank) were pressed not to lend to Chile. Strikes were supported, especially of copper miners and lorry drivers.

These measures aggravated the economic chaos, which was, (it must be said) partly due to the government undertaking very ambitious social and economic development programmes without the backing of the Chilean Congress, and to serious mistakes and weaknesses in administration, especially financial.[7] The Allende government consisted of a coalition of parties which continued to compete for the left-wing vote. Very few mem-bers had ever been in political office before. The government came to power with promises of massive wage increases but that there would be no 'imperialist' devaluation, and actually tried to carry out this combination of policies. It virtually expropriated United States copper mines and foreign policy was rather anti-American. When the stage was set for a military coup, the generals benefited not only from technical advice and equipment provided by the United States government, but they also knew they could count on United States support after taking office.

There are many lessons to be learned from the experience of the Allende government, which evidently strayed outside its room to manoeuvre. Thus one might have expected United States attempts to block copper exports to be crucial. Actually they turned out to have little effect. Copper is a homogeneous product; it does not deteriorate; and it is traded in a well organised world market (where many powers were unenthusiastic about United States intervention in Chile). In these respects it is rather unusual. Embargoes on some other commodities can be much more successful. The origin of bananas, for example, can hardly be concealed; they do not keep long and have to be carried in specially refrigerated ships; they can only be sold in bulk through distribution systems controlled by a few TNCs.

In fact copper exports did decline, but for different reasons, that are also ignored in neo-classical texts. There was a shortage of highly specific spare parts for copper-mining machinery. To depend on a single country (more so, a single company) for technology and associated inputs opens the door to retaliation.

The Cuban government had also faced considerable economic difficulties in the early years of trade embargo — until much of the capital equipment had been replaced by Soviet models. In any case, the growing shortage of foreign exchange in 1972-3 revealed the country's dependence on imports of equipment of various kinds, transport equipment, industrial materials, fertilizers and pesticides for agriculture, etc.

Cutting down imports of consumer goods — by embargo in the case of Cuba, by shortage of foreign exchange in Chile — can also be serious. Colonial links originally encouraged the imitation of foreign life-styles and these are nowadays continuously demonstrated to the middle and upper classes by television programmes and tourism, as well as by the products offered by the TNCs. This helps explain high import propensities (and low savings coefficients).[8] In many countries without the capacity for growing wheat (even in some cases for milling it), the urban masses have acquired a taste for bread.

So government cannot safely let consumption fall below a certain level,[9] either as a whole or in certain key goods and services. This tolerable minimum includes many items that are scarcely *basic* needs in physiological terms but treated as such, especially by the professional and managerial classes, and the cooperation of some of these will be needed, or at least their willingness to stay in the country. Moreover, trade unions, even if they support the delinking strategy, will press for wages sufficient to buy what they consider a 'living wage'. As in the case of Chile (Guyana and Jamaica are among many other examples), militant defence of this may be deliberately encouraged by foreign governments (or regional or international trade union federations). Protecting its internal political base may also lead a government to make big increases in public expenditure.

Attempts to delink a country closely integrated into the world economy may also be thwarted by the mere consequences of loss of 'confidence', especially among financial institutions. A case in point is Portugal[10] where, after the coup of 1974, tourist arrivals dropped sharply, in part because of unbalanced stories in the West European press. Portuguese workers abroad held back their normal remittances, foreign banks insisted on prompt payment of obligations, and the inflow of private capital dropped while capital outflows rose, contributing (together with the effects of the loss of Portuguese colonies in Africa and the concurrent world economic crisis) to serious unemployment and a foreign exchange deficit. At first the gap could be covered from big foreign exchange reserves but in due course the government had to turn to the International Monetary Fund (IMF) for financial help. This was given on terms that in effect reinforced the reversal of the earlier egalitarian policies which was already in train[11] (for example, in the distribution of income) and a steady rightward shift in the composition of the government.

The weight of the IMF in the world is growing, not primarily because it lends much money, but because until it has blessed a government's policies and thus endorsed it as creditworthy, many banks and governments are unwilling to make loans. Its criteria for soundness are not only technical (viz. limits to the money supply); they also include ideological preferences against import, exchange and price controls, etc. — though not against controls on wages — and the Fund asks for policy changes in these directions which become formal in 'letters of intent' and are monitored by the application of performance tests.[12]

These cases illustrate an important general point. Even apart from any policy mistakes as will always occur, or any fluctuations on commodity markets, regimes pursuing radical strategies are especially likely to get into foreign exchange difficulties. They typically promise sweeping egalitarian reforms in order to get power, and they usually at least attempt to carry these out. Moreover, what is perhaps most important, the radical rhetoric continues, even if in fact not much is done. The result, however, is that 'confidence' is lost and the economic basis of the programme undermined, causing standards of living to fall. They are then particularly likely to have to turn to the Fund and be put under pressure to drop the delinking strategy and associated internal policies. Jamaica is another case in point. So are Peru and Tanzania.[13] So is Britain!

Thus the conflict between the internal programme of any government that is even mildly radical and the external constraints on it often leads to the loss of political power, sometimes by a coup.[14] Cuba was an exception but there the government found an alternative external sponsor, a possibility which cannot be general. It seems that highly radical programmes may rarely be implementable in today's integrated world and those who 'arouse consciousness' take on a heavy responsibility, however great the moral need for far-reaching social changes.[15]

There is some tendency, because its 'missions' are so visible, for the Fund itself to be blamed for the economic constraints on policy, even for military coups. But it is, of course, merely the front office of governments (those of the United States, Britain, West Germany, France and Japan) that determine policy under its weighted voting system.[16] What ultimately sets the boundaries on the policies of delinking governments are the political interests of these countries.[17] Powerful and articulate bankers, industrial capitalists, etc. have a direct interest in the development strategies pursued overseas. Workers in them are concerned to protect jobs at high wages, and this requires that other countries (as markets and as sources of food and industrial inputs) are not taken out of the world system.

Reforming the IMF would not in itself be a decisive step in changing the world balance of power. There are many other instruments by which policies of a radical government can be changed (viz. the role of the West German Social Democrats, especially the Friedrich-Ebert-Stiftung, in Portugal, in encouraging adherence to the EEC, long before the Fund came on the scene). Foreign governments or international agencies that want to stop delinking can usually find allies high in the national power structure, among politicians and senior officials.[18]

Cultural constraints on delinking

Even if there are no such special relationships, the values and perceptions of officials who see themselves as loyal patriots, especially those inherited from a previous regime, will have been to some extent shaped by foreign contacts. A course of education in another country, for example at Oxford or Harvard, may lead the student to believe in identities of interest which do not in fact exist. Even if he studied at home, a student's values and perceptions affecting development strategy will inevitably have been to some extent influenced by ideologies originating abroad. Theories and models are usually taught and learned, without consideration of their appropriateness for the local context, including neo-classical economics itself. Such predispositions are reinforced by training courses[19] and conferences and in many cases by the wish to publish in foreign professional journals and to leave open the possibility, at least, of jobs overseas (for example, in the World Bank or the IMF) or directorships of TNC subsidiaries.

Another form of cultural dependence is addiction to foreign technology, especially in manufacturing, but also in agriculture, architecture, civil engineering, etc., which makes the importation of foreign equipment and materials seem essential.

This form of denationalisation, which often reaches high into government may well be a serious obstacle to adopting a thoroughgoing radical strategy. Even these influences, however, are perhaps not so important as the general 'climate of opinion' in the dominant, transnational élite,[20] which includes much of the professional and bureaucratic classes. The cultural currents encouraging the conventional growth-oriented, open-door strategy of 'modernisation' are strong. Even those who recognise and try to swim against them may become disheartened.

So cultural dependence not merely determines in large part the pattern of consumption and the choice of technique in every field and increases the 'brain drain'. It also shapes, in some degree, government development policy, and thus the whole economic structure — a point it would be difficult for conventional Marxists to accept. It is, therefore, of a different, higher, order of importance than economic dependence, just as mental illness is of a higher order of importance than a physical disease: a mental patient may be incapable of recognising his symptoms, of willing himself to recover, or of monitoring his own progress. This raises considerable questions about theories which treat national policymakers as sovereign (in the fields of international relations as well as economics) and the practices of international agencies. It also underlines the significance of strong national cultural traditions, with deep historical roots and widely disseminated among the population.

What dependency theories ignore

Dependency theory has therefore greatly extended the field of policy analysis and introduced significant factors omitted from mainstream economics. It has made us alert to the lack of symmetry in economic and political relations and to the importance of cultural dependence. However, many who belong to this school tend themselves to overlook other important determinants of the room to manoeuvre. I am not only talking about the implications of the internal social structure, which are certainly given insufficient weight in some dependency analyses, but also the failure to take on board demographic characteristics. Theorists from small countries have gone out of their way to argue that the *size* of a country's population is irrelevant.[21] Most tacitly assume all countries to be fairly large.[22]

Is the explanation that a dependency theorist, especially one influenced to some degree by Marxism, would find it inconvenient to admit that a social revolution would not be a sufficient condition for eliminating dependence? Yet size is perhaps the most important determinant of the room to manoeuvre. In a country with a limited population, like Montserrat, even Mauritius, there are not many development options for *any* government. It is likely to be heavily dependent on foreign trade: industrialisation is restricted because, in many industries, there is a minimum official plant capacity.[23] So to follow an independent development strategy of the type indicated above is likely to be catastrophic.[24]

The size of population is, of course, not static, but it has to be taken as datum for quite a long period: indeed if demographic growth is fast, this may well raise a country's dependence on imports, especially of food, long before it relaxes the size constraint at all significantly.

A more plausible way of escaping from the constraints of size (and other constraints as well), at least in the short run, lies in political and economic integration, which can take various forms from free trade associations through common markets and federations to monetary and political unions. Historically it has proved difficult for governments of nations with their own cultural and political histories, and different economic interests, to co-ordinate policy, despite the potential gains from doing so. (Examples are the Latin America Free Trade Area, the European and East African Economic Communities, the United Arab Republic, etc.) 'Collective self-reliance' covering the whole South holds out on paper more promise (especially since the surplus capital in OPEC countries would complement the surplus labour elsewhere), but the basic differences, manifested in political disagreements, seem even greater.

Ideological prejudice may also explain the low weight given in dependence theories to the *ethnic* or *linguistic* composition of the population. To introduce such factors would seem to dependency theorists like going back to the old, discredited, 'modernisation' theories. Yet ethnic heterogeneity, for example, may in a crisis be a source of weakness vis-à-vis foreign governments, particularly if a racial minority is an offshoot of a population of a neighbouring country (viz. the significance of Chinese minorities in Vietnam, Malaysia, etc.).

Dependency writers also tend to deal rather superficially with *natural resources*, treating them generally as reasons for foreign enclaves such as mines and plantations, rather than as determinants of a government's bargaining power. Yet it has become increasingly clear in recent years, as the relative price of oil has risen, that the degree of self-sufficiency in energy profoundly affects a government's room to manoeuvre. The same applies to cereals.[25] This is a corollary of the importance of dependence on specific imports mentioned above.

Many writers in the dependency school also ignore a country's physical *location* in relation to countries which are better endowed in the respects indicated, especially in population size or technology. This can act as a stimulus — the latent threat of China must have influenced the development of Hong Kong, South Korea and Taiwan.[26]

But usually dependency is reinforced. The government of Lesotho, for example, a country technologically dependent and very small, is severely restrained in policy choice by its geographical position as an enclave completely surrounded by South Africa. It is wide open to trade penetration by the Republic and vulnerable to the possible cutting of power supplies, etc. It could not keep out South African television programmes (including news). Constrast (say) an island, similar in other respects, in the Indian Ocean.[27] The Lesotho government also relies heavily on tourist earnings and remittances from its citizens working in its neighbour — as is typical for a small dependent country.[28]

Another consequence of its location is that Lesotho is vulnerable to *military* invasion, the possibility of which always, at least subconsciously, shapes any government's perception of the development options.[29] Some writers in the dependency school certainly emphasise military autonomy; reliance on a single country for military equipment and training, like reliance on a single source for capital or a single market for exports, is seen as a serious constraint on what a government can do. To accept military aid or, especially, to permit foreign troops or bases on one's soil obviously acts as an even greater constriction. But the military vulnerability of a country depends on various geographical factors too, such as the physical nature of the frontier or coastline, and socio-demographic characteristics. Apart from the population's size and ethnic composition, already mentioned, its age structure particularly affects the capacity to wage guerrilla warfare.

A country's dependence on the outside world is also a function of its military preparedness. This is rarely mentioned, perhaps because writers in this school are very conscious of the danger that military capacity will, as so often in Latin America, be deployed against local citizens instead of invaders, reinforcing rather than reducing political dependence. Moreover, it is difficult to arm without increasing the foreign debt and becoming technologically dependent in this sphere too.

Very few social scientists seem willing to tackle the question of the optional level of military expenditure, or appropriate technology in this field. For academics, military expenditure is 'bad' *per se*. In 'development plans', it is always treated as a datum, and economists tend to look on it as a diversion from 'productive' expenditures — thus opting out of a crucial area of economic policy. Yet strictly from the viewpoint of a government pursuing an independent policy, it is just one form of defence, against one form of retaliation, analogous to those in other sectors. An optimal development strategy covers all types of policy.

Conclusions

Adding demographic and geographic factors to those conventionally covered in dependency theory reinforces the point that no government is entirely free to shape its policy without regard to external influences. So there is some substance in the concept of 'global interdependence', though critics of the term are correct to stress the asymmetry in relationships.

These additions carry other, far-reaching, political implications. While most economic and cultural constraints can be described, not implausibly, as features specific to world capitalism, this is obviously untrue of demographic and geographic realities. The latter completely rule out treating dependence as a phenomenon of the capitalist system, (which would imply that it would disappear if the system did), and obviously prevent the exclusion of other economic systems (in particular socialism) from the field of dependency studies, which would obviously be a serious loss.

These additions, however, seem to make the theory even more deterministic. No room to manoeuvre at all seems left for a government with several of the following liabilities: a small population, ethnic divisions, location next to a superpower, few natural resources, a culturally subverted bureaucracy, high consumer expectations and a narrow technological base. If there is any option for government of such a country, it would not be *whether* to be dependent, but *which* external power to be dependent on — just as squires in the Middle Ages had to choose which baron they would serve. And would it be so ideologically dependent that it would not even look for options?

Policy appears in fact overdetermined, increasingly so as the networks of transnational capital and culture proliferate. Incremental change seems doomed: all one can do is to wait for some ill-defined revolution, brought about by unspecified processes. There is a tendency in what one might call the 'vulgar' exponents of dependency (though not in its main theorists, especially Cardoso[30]) to fall into precisely this trap and blame *all* the problems of a country on the 'international division of labour' imposed by hegemonic forces. That may well be emotionally satisfying, and certainly is often politically convenient in the short term, but it is also quite misleading and enervating when policy implications have to be drawn.

Such determination overlooks the role of political leadership. Admittedly economic, cultural, demographic and geographic data set the stage for the political play whoever writes the script. No amount of leadership is going to transform Lesotho or Jamaica (or, say, Kampuchea) into a dominant country or even one capable of much independent action within a few decades — and leaders anyway have finite lives (and much shorter periods in power).

Nevertheless, there are certain possibilities of penetrating the curtain surrounding any country. A capitalist government wanting to diversify commercial links can develop trade with the Soviet Union, Eastern Europe or China (or conversely a socialist one can open up trade with the United States, Japan, etc.). Advantage can be taken of the differences between and within dominant powers. What assets a country does have (for example, access to airfields and harbours, even over-flying rights) can be exploited. Liabilities can be converted into assets: a government heavily in debt may be able to take advantage of the fact that the creditor could not stand default. Where no such possibilities exist, a government still has some scope (for example, in education policy) for establishing conditions in which a future administration, possibly decades later, will have more room to manoeuvre, and this is not a negligible service to the country.

The motivation, willpower, judgement and intelligence of actual or potential political leaders evidently differ significantly.[31] The importance of these personal characteristics follows from the very multiplicity of constraints which have been described. Some are capable of assessing intuitively what can actually be accomplished and of exercising whatever freedom of action they can muster, given these constraints and the interests of dominant powers.[32] On the other hand, some clumsily arouse alarm among these powers, causing them to close their ranks (incidentally, but not importantly, spoiling the prospects of other radical governments). It requires rare skills not merely to frame an optimal set of delinking policies but to mobilise an adequate coalition of diverse political forces to support it; to present it persuasively to the world outside; to explain to the domestic public why it is all that can be achieved; and of course to implement it.[33] (Conventional historians may not have been so wrong in focussing attention on the talents of monarchs and prime ministers!)

It is particularly important for the leadership to be able to sense changes in constraints which open up new options: for example, following disasters (or, from another viewpoint, victories), such as Suez, the Bay of Pigs and Vietnam, when the likelihood of military intervention has receded. A radical government needing loans a quarter of a century ago had little option but to turn to the United States, or to agencies it dominated. Now the governments of Japan and several West European countries can also provide finance and the agencies are more flexible. Since the oil price rises started in 1973, OPEC members have been additional possible sources, though their governments have not in practice been keen so far to make a large portion of their capital available to fellow members of 'the South' (and of course they cannot meet the need for technology). Loans from commercial banks are much more readily available.

Constraints will continue to change. For example, the procedures of the Fund reflect the politico-economic situation when it was established at Bretton Woods in 1944, and are now clearly vulnerable to political attack. One of the functions of political leadership is indeed to help find and promote constructive changes in international institutions. Even some seemingly permanent geographical constraints will be relaxed. The volume of mineral reserves that matters is the amount that could be commercially exploited, and this is a function not only of price but also technological progress — in extraction techniques, ore treatment, etc. On the other hand, with the spread of television, cultural dependence will increase.

Evidently, a condition of political success in such a complex world, full of shifting constraints, is to be pragmatic rather than dogmatic. This may not, however, be easily compatible with the requirement of dedication mentioned above. (Pragmatism can easily be a cover for laziness or even corruption.) The key to the reconciliation of these needs in a leader's mind is patriotism — in addition to intelligence and political skills. This is also needed by the population if it is to tolerate the hardships of retaliation.[34] Unless it is deep and widespread, a government will hardly be able to get various social classes to cooperate in coping with constraints. In fact another requirement of leadership is to develop (and yet control) the public's patriotism. Thus the roots of the capacity to adopt a delinking strategy for a particular country may lie not so much in its productive structure, or even technological capacity (see the chapter by Luc Soete), as in the strength and homogeneity of its culture[35] which can help it and its leadership avoid cultural dependence.

While this approach restores political leadership to its rightful place as a major determinant, especially in the short term, it cuts the social scientist down to size. It implies that there are limited possibility of generalisation. The traditional argument against pure empiricism, that one needs some theoretical structure even to select what to study, put by some writers in this volume, is basically correct. So at least tentative theoretical hypotheses are necessary for research and teaching purposes, let alone policy. Certainly one can theorise to a degree about the international system as a whole, including its linkages — this is precisely what I have been doing — and make some generalisations about national patterns of development (or the lack of it). But can reality be easily reduced to a model with a few variables as some of those on the Marxist end of the spectrum pretend? Such models satisfy both professional elegance and emotional needs, not to speak of the demands of some of those formulating development strategy. But in buttressing faith in some form of autarkic socialism they have (like Chicago-type economics) proved very dangerous for politicians.

Consequently, I come down on the side of Palma (and Cardoso, Sunkel, *et al.*) in favour of tailoring new theory from the material of country studies, rather than trying on the old Marxist clothes handed down from Europe. Such studies do indeed already reveal patterns not merely for individual countries. If framed comparatively they could help the development of theories which cover *types* of country (e.g. small petroleum exporters, or large economies relying on peasant agriculture in particular historical periods) and perhaps a wider range.

But we may have to face the very real possibility that human reality is so constructed that no model can be devised for its analysis (especially a dynamic one) which is both realistic and simple enough to provide a universal development ideology that could be applied with safety in any nation at all, especially if we allow, as we surely must, for demographic and geographical factors, as well as a range of economic and cultural.

Notes

1.   The first group described in Gabriel Palma's paper (Chapter 1 this volume).
2.   Even Raul Prebisch used to work with an aggregate foreign exchange 'gap', which could be considered the *ex ante* residual in the savings-investment account.
3.   See Seers and Dasgupta (eds.), 'Statistical Policy in Less Developed Countries', IDS *Communication* 114, 1975.
4.   Dependency school criticisms of foreign direct investment (and some counter-arguments) are well summarised in Thomas Biersteker, *Distortion or Development? Contending Perspectives on the Multinational Corporation*, MIT, 1978, with empirical material from Nigeria.

5. David Evans focusses attention on the economic and political consequences of interfering with the price mechanism.

6. See, for example, Richard Fagan, 'The United States and Chile: Roots and Branches', *Foreign Affairs*, January 1975.

7. See Stephany Griffith-Jones, 'A Critical Evaluation of Popular Unity's Short-term and Financial Policy', *World Development*, Vol. 6, No. 7/8, 1978. All this, of course, in no way excuses officers who broke their oath of loyalty, let alone their subsequent conduct.

8. The typical 'consumption function' of mainstream economics, in which consumption is treated as a function simply of levels of income, appears to be inadequately specified.

9. The tolerable minimum also depends in part on current political circumstances. When national survival is seen to be at stake, as the experience in a number of countries shows in wartime (Britain or the Soviet Union, for example, in the last World War), consumption can be lowered more drastically than would be compatible with the survival of any peacetime government.

10. See Antonio Rodriguez, *et al.*, 'Portugal: Economic Developments and 18 Months' Intervention by the IMF', unpublished paper of the Institute of Policy Studies presented at the South-North Conference on 'The International Monetary System and the New International Order', Arusha, July 1980. Also Stuart Holland, 'Dependent Development: Portugal as Periphery', in D. Seers, B.B. Schaffer, M.-L. Kiljunen (eds.), *Underdeveloped Europe: Studies in Core-Periphery Relations*, Brighton, Sussex, Harvester Press, 1979.

11. In fact, it would be incorrect to attribute this change in direction to the Fund, which came on to the scene after it had started.

12. Such ideological criteria are not in fact required by the Fund's charter. A critical analysis of its lending procedures can be found in Ismail-Sabry Abdulla, 'The Inadequacy and Loss of Legitimacy of the International Monetary Fund', *Development Dialogue*, 1980:2.

13. See Norman Girvan, 'Swallowing the IMF Medicine in the '70s', *Development Dialogue*, 1980:2. Also, Norman Girvan, Richard Bernal and Wesley Hughes, 'The IMF and the Third World: The Case of Jamaica', *ibid*.

14. Of course, on the other hand, external pressures in favour of a *linking* strategy may push a government along a path that ends in popular uprisings, recent examples being Pakistan and Iran.

15. The potential social costs of such a programme may now be quite widely realised. During the romantic insurrection in Sri Lanka in 1970 led by the JVP on a delinking programme (essentially to use land currently producing exports for food output) there was a striking lack of support from urban workers, despite their nominal adherence to revolutionary parties.

16. These five members between them control 41 per cent of the votes. See Abdulla in *Development Dialogue, op. cit.* Also 'Background Notes on the IMF', in the same issue.

17. More accurately, how they perceive their interests. Thus the German Executive Director of the Fund may have approved of restrictive conditions being imposed on Portuguese government spending, these were hardly consistent with the aim of his government to bring this country into the EEC, which surely implies the need for the country's rapid social and economic reconstruction. Indeed there must now be a big question mark about whether the interests of dominant countries are consistent with the imposition of inflexible and austere policies on many governments in balance-of-payments difficulties (often due in large part to forces which they cannot influence).

18. Some of whom may even be foreign agents. A foreign CIA agent wrote of the Latin American political leaders and senior officials (especially in Ecuador) who were in the pay of the United States government in the 1960s. (Philip Agee,

Inside the Company: CIA Diary, Harmondsworth, Middlesex, Penguin, 1975.) This is not, of course, a phenomenon only of relationships between the governments of the United States and some countries of Latin America.

19. The IMF itself has training courses to which come many with whom it will later negotiate.

20. The mechanisms creating this are summarised in Edmundo Fuenzalida, 'Incorporation into the contemporary stage of the modern world system: conditions, processes and mechanisms', to be published in the *International Studies Quarterly* in 1981.

21. See, for example, Lloyd Best, one of the pioneers of the Caribbean branch of the dependency school, a branch that could not avoid this question ('Size and Survival', *New World Quarterly*, vol 2, no 3, 1966). Cf. however William Demas, 'The Economics of Small Countries with Special Reference to the Caribbean', Montreal, McGill University Press, 1965.

22. The majority of dependence theorists come from at least medium-size countries, as one would expect. (In Latin America, small countries account for a small fraction of the region's population.)

23. These aspects are discussed in John Wyeth, *Development Strategies and Specialisation in Small Countries: A Case Study of Belize*, unpublished doctoral thesis, University of Sussex, 1978. The scope for industrialisation depends also of course on the *per capita* purchasing power.

24. It will be interesting to see if the new government in Grenada succeeds in preserving some independence from governments of *all* types.

25. See D. Seers, 'Patterns of Dependence', J. Villamil (ed.), *Transnational Capitalism and National Development: Studies in the Theory of Dependency*, Brighton, Sussex, Harvester Press, 1979. There it is pointed out that the chronic import requirements of oil in the United States and cereals in the Soviet Union detract considerably from their power, especially now that the Soviet export surplus of oil is apparently dwindling. (If the Soviet government had convertible currency to spare, it could offer delinking governments an alternative source of financial assistance to cope with the resultant foreign exchange problem.) However, most other countries are importers of both oil *and* cereals.

26. The other South East Asian NIC, Singapore, may well also have been stimulated by the proximity of Malaysia.

27. Various relations between distance and dependence are mentioned in my contribution to *Underdeveloped Europe, op. cit.*

28. Location by latitude also determines the country's climate and thus its productive potential in agriculture.

29. There are, of course, many examples of the threat materialising and great powers invading smaller ones, especially neighbours. The United States has often intervened to ensure that the Dominican Republic had an acceptable government.

30. The belief that 'the internal or national socio-political situation is mechanically determined by external dominance' is described as a fallacy in F.H. Cardoso and E. Faletto, *Dependency and Development in Latin America*, University of California Press, 1979). See also Sunkel, e.g. 'Transnational Capitalism and National Disintegration in Latin America', *Social and Economic Studies*, Vol. 22, No. 1 1973.

31. For brevity, I write of individual political leaders: a full analysis would allow for more complex realities — the existence of more than one centre of 'power', for example, the role of party bureaucracies, etc.

32. Dom Mintoff, for example, brilliantly exploited the military advantages of Valetta harbour, and his political base in the dockyard workers, to extract payment from not only Britain and NATO in support of the public finances of Malta, a small country singularly lacking in cultivable land and other natural

resources or in technological capacity, but also (until very recently) Libya. He was noticeably more successful than his predecessor, Borg Olivier, who relied mainly on emigration (to Australia) as a solution for economic problems.

33. 'At any given moment . . . the sudden decision of his will introduced into the course of events a new, unexpected and changeable force, which may alter that course, but which cannot be measured in itself' (Sainte-Beuve, quoted in G.V. Plekanov, *The Role of the Individual in History*, London, Camelot Press, 1940).

34. An example is the Algerian tenacity in the face of French economic warfare a decade ago (over the oil contract).

35. On these points, Japan scores heavily, and has thus not had much difficulty following an autonomous strategy (once it abandoned an outdated militarism) especially vis-à-vis foreign capital.

7 IMPLEMENTING THE NEW INTERNATIONAL ECONOMIC ORDER (NIEO): ATTEMPTS AT REGULATING THE STRUCTURE OF WORLD INDUSTRY*

Zdzisław Fiejka

The redeployment of world industrial production in favour of the developing countries as well as the establishment of a system of information exchange and multilateral negotiation (industrial consultations) are two essential elements of the New International Economic Order (NIEO) in the field of industry. The main objective is that the developing countries should produce at least 25 per cent of world industrial output by the year 2000.

The concepts of redeployment and industrial consultations are new in international economic relations. They represent attempts at modifying the workings of the market in this sphere. They emerged in the mid 1970s when the developing countries called with particular force for rapid and radical revision of international economic relations and the establishment of NIEO.

These ideas have to a large extent lost their original simplicity and universalism. As attempts are being made to apply them, specific theoretical and technical problems have emerged. This paper is concerned with a preliminary evaluation of some of these problems.

They are particularly relevant since current attempts at modifying the workings of the market in international economic relations to bring about more equity, justice and global rationality via information exchange and harmonisation of national policies actually tend to create uneven opportunities and benefits. New channels of dependence are also being created that affect weaker and smaller partners and thus additional sources of inequality are emerging. They call for a further refining of the concepts and methods of implementation of the new order.

The origin of the concept of redeployment of industry and consultation in the UN system

In the basic documents of the VIth Special Session of the United Nations General Assembly (May 1974) which defined the New International Economic Order, 'redeployment' was not mentioned. The aim of building up a 'new international economic structure' with the help of 'reallocation' of world industrial potential was summarised and broadly developed in the

* This is an abbreviated version of the article published in *Sprawy Miedzynarodowe* No. 7-8 (1979) and later presented at the joint seminar at Ojrzanow (8-14 October 1979).

Lima Declaration and Plan of Action at the UNIDO General Conference in March 1975. The developed countries were to 'encourage industries which are less competitive internationally to move progressively into more viable lines of production or into other sectors of economy, thus leading to structural adjustments within the developed countries and redeployment of the productive capacities of such industries to developing countries'.[1] For detailed specification of which industries should be reallocated to the developing countries, the Plan of Action called into being a 'system of industrial consultation', endorsed at the VIIth Special Session of the UN General Assembly (1975).[2]

A superficial view of the debate for the new allocation of industry could easily lead to seeing the developing countries as the sole promotors and beneficiaries of this concept, with the highly developed countries as their opponents. The reality is, however, more complex.

There are three broad reasons for structural change in world industry: new factors of technological progress; contradictions of technological and educational development; and new terms of raw materials and energy supply. In conjunction, these developments have caused many branches of industrial production in highly developed countries to be no longer economically viable. They may still, however, be profitable for the proprietors due to subsidies and tax concessions and to the strong tariff and non-tariff barriers protecting them from international competition. The increasing costs of running these unprofitable branches of production have become one of the main causes of inflationary pressure.

Changes in the structure of industrial production in the highly developed countries are required in their own interest. Not all of them are yet prepared to make such changes. Long-term structural policy raises complex problems of social and professional mobility. It requires a harmonious regional development, and reconciling the interests of entrepreneurs, trade unions and consumers. Various forms of protection provide a way of evading these problems in attempting to preserve the monopolistic position of industries in these countries.

These developments open up new opportunities for the activity of transnational corporations (TNCs), which escape national control and operate with global strategies, making use of new possibilities of a division of labour on an international scale among their own (or affiliated) branches situated in various countries. Thus, behind the aim of redeployment, there appear complexes of national interests in highly developed capitalist countries, as well as the interests of the TNCs and those of developing countries at the periphery of the capitalist system scrambling for a place in the new international division of labour.

The need for structural changes in the developed economies does not arise simply from redeployment objectives. It would arise anyway out of the structural crisis in capitalism. Although the importance of the developing countries has increased, their commercial and industrial needs do not influence significantly the trends and patterns of development of the highly developed countries.

The Lima target is also a political act recognising the limitations to the world's natural resources and the necessity to make use of these resources in a more rational way, granted limits on future world industrial development, in order to protect the interests of the developing countries.

Finally, it is worth remembering here that the target is not an international industrial plan or even an attempt at indicative planning in this field; it is only a broad estimate of what industry is desired by the developing countries and approved by the majority of the UN members.

The criteria of redeployment

As the world economy develops there are continuous changes in the structure of production, due to technological progress, changes in demand, etc. Until recently the highly developed capitalist countries enjoyed a near monopoly in industrial production. This monopoly was broken by the Soviet Union, the European socialist countries and Japan after World War II (see Table 7.1).

TABLE 7.1. *The distribution of world manufacturing output, 1960-75*

	Europe (excluding socialist countries)	North America	Japan	The USSR and European socialist countries	Total
1960	31.6	37.8	3.9	18.1	94.4
1975	27.8	27.0	7.1	27.7	89.6

Source: UNIDO International Development Survey. Special Issue for III General Conference.

Recently a new group, the newly industrialising countries (NICs), with opportunities for rapid industrialisation has emerged, rich in oil or other natural resources, and/or with cheap manpower at their disposal, as well as a selective access to technology and markets. With the support of other developing countries, they use the slogans of the NIEO for achieving their aims, and demand the adjustment of the world economy of capitalist countries to 'two, three or more Japans'.[3]

So far, the pattern of industrial deployment on the global scale has been spontaneous, whereas the redeployment of industry postulated in the Lima Plan of Action is to be stimulated and organised. This requires a programme and a set of rules. What criteria should be applied to select branches of industry for redeployment? How are decisions on the direction of reallocation to be made? What is the role of international cooperation? Answers to these questions are supposed to be generated by research and international debates at UNIDO.

The report of the Lima Conference is general and ambiguous. Apart from those branches of industry in developing countries which are 'less competititve internationally', the reallocation is also to apply to the 'primary processing of raw materials' — the first phase of industrialisation. This would lead to radical changes in the structure of the world economy. Although the developing countries do not possess the monopoly or even a decisive share in the world supply of raw materials, some of them are big producers and exporters of minerals or agricultural products.[4] Industrial processing on the spot would increase their economic power.

It would also lead to further differentiation between developing countries. Countries which are poor in natural resources (of which there are many, inhabited by the majority of the world's population) would not profit much.[5] So other solutions are needed. To shift the 'internationally less competitive industries' seems to benefit a wide range of countries. In practice, however, it is difficult to define it operationally.

There has been little interest in following the conventional criteria, i.e. labour and capital intensity, but recently it has been proposed that the product cycle could provide a guide.[6] In the developing countries, the labour-intensive and raw-material-intensive industries will keep on developing, followed by the reallocation of those which are mature and capital-intensive branches of industry. In the developed countries, the present trend of development, including starting technologically new lines of production, will be maintained, especially branches of industry requiring high-level skills (using highly specialised services and research).

It is unlikely, however, that the product cycle can provide a complete answer. The multiplicity of social objectives and economic conditions, as well as a strong desire by many countries to increase their technological capability, thwart the universal functioning of such a principle on the global scale. The same applies to a theoretical criterion which assumes that the national objectives of industrialising should be a derivative of 'optimum global development'.[7] In the debates, the principle of respecting each country's sovereignty in the choice of industrialisation policies has been pressed. It means that international objectives can be reached only through first fixing national industrial goals, and subsequently by finding ways of co-ordinating them.

In conclusion, it seems futile to look for a general principle of redeployment to the developing countries in the international deliberations.

The standpoint of the advanced capitalist countries

The attitudes of governments of the developed capitalist countries differ considerably.

The first group of countries decisively rejects the usefulness of the concept of planned or negotiated redeployment, holding that this should be a part of the evolutionary process of restructuring national industries under the influence of market forces. Special programmes for adjustment assistance to their own industries can often be found in these countries, but they are, according to the supporters of this view, meant to help individual firms or persons, and do not aim at structural changes of whole branches of industry. The extreme representative of this group is the United States, a country characterised by a large domestic market, net exports of technology and a relatively small involvement in the world trade in manufactures. A similar attitude is taken by Switzerland.

The second group covers countries where the state respects the market mechanism and the decisions of entrepreneurs concerning the choice of industrial lines and the location of production, but tries to carry out a policy of structural changes and indirectly influences these decisions. Governments of these countries are concerned with prospective structural changes, not so much because of an economic philosophy in favour of planning, as because of the limitations in the availability of natural resources; great dependence on foreign sources of energy, markets, sources of technological progress; and the need for identifying areas which will in future call for state intervention. In this group one can put Great Britain, West Germany, most other EEC countries and Japan. France may also be considered a member, though she is characterised by a more activist attitude towards redeployment and support for the creation of a system of international industrial consultations. Only Japan is visibly involved in redeployment. The industries concerned here are metallurgy, chemicals, refining, paper and food. The share of these branches in Japanese foreign investments has, however, already fallen in the 1970s.[8] It has also been noticed that fear for the pollution of the environment in Japan has decreased recently and damage caused by a great concentration of industry has been brought under control.[9]

The third group covers the so-called 'like-minded' countries, which actively support redeployment and are involved in the development of international institutions which can facilitate it. They are all small countries dependent on exports from a few efficient manufacturing sectors: Netherlands, Norway, Sweden, Austria, New Zealand. The policy of these countries is against protecting firms which are competitively weak. They are not, however, in favour of fully autonomous decisions of entrepreneurs, either for social reasons (employment) or because they want to preserve neutrality or a national capacity for defence supplies. Only the Netherlands has introduced a programme of adjustment assistance specially meant to help those firms which will reallocate their activities to the developing countries.[10] Both the small investments involved in the project and their limited applicability indicate that Dutch activity in this field does not go beyond the sphere of experiment and an act of good will.[11]

The attitude of the socialist countries

The reallocation aim is not directly addressed to the European socialist countries. However, the high level of industrial development achieved by them as well as the emergence of certain limitations in sustaining the rates of growth and trends of development followed so far (the decrease in the growth of labour resources, difficulties in satisfying the needs of highly energy- and raw-material-intensive industries, foreign debts, etc.), as well as the quest for ways of increasing the overall effectiveness of production, have made these countries interested in the question.

In the pronouncements of the representatives of the socialist countries concerning an international programme of redeployment, two problems come to the fore.

Firstly, decisions concerning production patterns in the developing countries should be the result of the social objectives of those countries and should emerge from their national economic plans and strategies of industrialisation.

Secondly, they question the concept of redeployment of industry as a form of assistance in the industrialisation of the developing countries and doubt whether it can be consistent with the latter's goals of strengthening their economic independence; helping solve the question of food supplies; increasing their potential for skill development; developing their own technology capability; increasing the investment potential of the country and/or helping satisfy the basic needs of the population.

Socialist countries try to support the industrialisation of the developing countries within their capacities, in a way which differs from that of the capitalist countries, corresponding to institutional differences. They argue that bilateral intergovernmental agreements on cooperation and exchange could be used more widely. International cooperation of this type assumes, however, mutual readiness as well as the willingness and capacity on both sides for the long-term planning of national and industrial development. Few developing countries fulfil these requirements either because of the limitation of state power or the lack of political stability. Also the socialist countries do not have much access to the markets of these developing countries which are closely linked with the interests of transnational corporations. Potential reallocation of certain industries raises other problems, e.g. the need for long-term, low-interest credits for the recipients of the redeployed industrial capacities. Yet other developing countries are certainly interested in reallocation of certain industries from the developed socialist countries, and it seems that the latter do not yet make full use of the opportunities available, e.g. in reallocation of the labour-intensive traditional industries such as cotton, or raw-material-intensive and energy-consuming branches such as iron metallurgy.

There has, however, been some progress in the international division of labour affecting the socialist countries. The share of industrial products from the developing countries increased significantly; the share of finished manufactured products in Polish imports amounted to 10 per cent in 1975, and the share of semi-finished manufactures to 20 per cent.[12] These figures suggest a considerable opening of markets to the processing industries of the developing countries (during the first half of the 1970s, when foreign trade exchanges grew fast). It is expected that the reduced growth of labour resources will stimulate Polish interest in reallocation of some labour-intensive branches of industry, and also the redeployment of some of the raw-material-intensive branches. In exchange, Poland could possibly increase industrial production in fields in which she has a comparative advantage in relation to partners among the developing countries, e.g. certain branches of mechanical engineering, chemicals, etc. A promising field of mutual cooperation, production and trade is that of semi-finished products and industrial materials.

The socialist countries have common interests with the developing countries in changing an inequitable international division of labour which was imposed by the old industrial centres. Their initiatives in favour of stabilising the conditions of exchange and establishing long-term economic links and a new international specialisation of production may prove a key form of assistance for the industrialisation of developing countries.

Consultations versus reallocation

In the Lima Declaration the ideas of redeployment and consultation were linked, but in practice, during the last five years they have been developing independently. The very establishment of the consultation system was controversial. All groups of countries approved of the principle of industrial consultations, but they differed over its practical application.

The socialist countries apparently see the proposed system as a new form of international organisation of industrial cooperation, which is to modify market mechanisms, and increase the flow of information, eventually bringing about a more rational development of industrial production on a global scale. The capitalist countries regard the consultations as simply an exchange of information about market conditions between producers and other groups, e.g. trade unions, associations of consumers, etc. They aim at lowering the level of these meetings and making them less official. The developing countries regard themselves as the only beneficiaries of the system of consultations proposed: they are not unanimous about practical solutions and have divergent aims in relation to the scope of consultations and the ways of dealing with specific problems of particular regions.

So far, 'sectoral' consultations have been taking place, covering tendencies in the development of particular branches on the global scale and their resultant problems.[13] These industrial consultations have become part of the regular programme of UNIDO, though the meetings are still experimental. They aim at finding out what benefits could be achieved for the developing countries and for international cooperation in general.

Generally speaking, the meetings of experts and the investigations preceding them are considered beneficial by the officials concerned. The main results are the so-called 'broad agreements on the global context' in which a particular branch of industry will develop in the developed and the developing countries. Against this background, the meetings attempt to work out at the sectoral level the Lima target, as well as defining the main obstacles faced in the branches under discussion.

Some fundamental questions arise. Can the 'broad agreements on the global context' of a particular branch of industry provide the basis for international specialisation of production and for reallocating productive capacities from the highly developed to the developing countries? It will still be some time before these aims are fulfilled. The main reason for this is not just that the decisions taken in the UN system are only recommendations to national governments, but that they reflect the opinions and expectations of experts rather than national goals for development of particular branches of industry. Many countries, in particular the developing countries, are not capable of planning the *current* development of their industries, let alone the long-term development. This is done for them by international experts and international organisations — a useful and well-meaning activity but one which reflects an escape from reality. The future is projected not on the basis of the output potentials and socially-defined needs of the developing countries, but from abstract assumptions, often deduced from purely arbitrary numbers (for instance, the 25 per cent target); then detailed studies are made to support these assumptions. The international mechanism of debate is set in motion not so much for the exchange of information concerning future trends in supply, demand, costs of production or required investments, as for 'pseudo-multilateral negotiations' with the international bureaucracy.

It is too early to evaluate fully the functioning of these mechanisms, but many of the activities seem to support not so much the legitimate aspirations of the developing countries as illusions about their development.

Differentiation among the developing countries has grown. As has already been mentioned, the NICs have gained chances of catching up in industrialisation and economic and social development. Ambitious projections of global reallocation of industry favour the group and the international formulation of new perspectives for market growth and new fields of investment increase international confidence in them.

Will reallocation embrace the move of 'the less competitive internationally' branches of industry? On the basis of preliminary analysis, it seems that the new industries of the NICs are relatively modern and rather competitive internationally. Will these countries succeed in ensuring steady modernisation of their productive capacities and technology?

Much depends on the future pattern of international cooperation in the field of technology and science. Scientific research and new technological innovations are now an integral part of productive forces. In the developing countries, backwardness in R and D and dependence on the industrial centres is serious and most difficult to overcome.

More generally, it is hard to identify whose preferences are reflected in the assessments of development trends during the consultations. The small developing countries find it difficult to utilise and translate them into opportunities for industrial growth in their own countries. Regional consultations might be an improvement. The global estimates made so far are really only useful for the big TNCs.

A few broader conclusions are suggested:

— The aim of reallocating involves discussing the industrialisation of the developing countries against the background of the structural crises in the developed market economies and the limitations of global development; the common interests of the countries concerned are considered rather than theoretical criteria, fixed *a priori* or imposed from outside.

— Consultations and negotiations aim at providing an alternative for the activity of the market mechanism in the sphere of international division of labour. They require international programming and regulating the development of industry on a global scale. It is too early to evaluate fully the path chosen. So far, however, numerous contradictions between national interests and the interests of various groups have emerged and no operational formulae for solving them have yet been found.

— Organising this process through governments, with the principles of sovereignty and consensus in decision, leads to ambiguous directives for the international authorities appointed to regulate it. Against this background, there is an increasing role for factors which are relatively autonomous and outside the control of the governments (or trying to evade such control), that is the secretariats and experts of international organisations. The significance of big TNCs carrying out their own global strategies increases as well. How can these social forces be controlled in order to satisfy contemporary human needs? No answer has yet been found to this question.

Notes

1. Second General Conference of the United Nations Industrial Development Organisation, Lima, Peru, 12-16 March 1975, *Lima Declaration and Plan of Action on Industrial Development and Cooperation*, para 59 (c).

2. The reallocation of industry to the developing countries and the establishment of new institutions for international cooperation in industry are also broadly dealt with in the 1976 Report to the Club of Rome (RIO) and in the subsequent discussion in Algiers. RIO, *Reshaping the International Order*. A Report to the Club of Rome, Jan Tinbergen, Co-ordinator, New York, 1976, and *Towards a New International Order*. Report on the Joint Meeting of the Club of Rome and the International Ocean Institute, Algiers, October 1976.

3. Carlos F. Diaz-Alejandro, 'International Markets for LDCs: the Old and the New', *American Economic Review*, May 1978, p. 268.

4. See Chapter 10 this volume.

5. Such an industrial shift might, however, suit some of the highly developed capitalist countries which suffer from high concentration of industries which pollute the environment, or with limited sources of energy. This part (Section III) of the Programme of Action was approved, unlike many other issues, without serious dissent at the VIth Special Session of the General Assembly of the UN.

6. *Redeployment of Industries from Developed to Developing Countries*. Studies undertaken by UNIDO — document ID/B/222, 28 February 1979, p. 9.

7. B. Herman and J. Tinbergen, 'Planning of International Development', in *Progress and Planning in Industry, Proceedings of the International Conference on Industrial Economics, Budapest, 1970*, Budapest, Akademiaj Kiado, 1970.

8. *Industrial Development Survey, Special Issue for the Second General Conference of UNIDO*, New York, UN, 1974.

9. *The Economist*, 4 January 1975.

10. Memorandum on the restructuring of the Netherlands economy and development cooperation presented in Parliament of Holland on 9 December 1974. In 1974, a special programme was formulated for this purpose and a fund was established (35 million guilders). It covers the costs of the abandoned production or its modification so that the developing countries may profit from it.

11. Norway alone is said to have undertaken certain preliminary studies. New Zealand has established an organisation for the allocation of certain branches of processing industry to islands in the South Pacific.

12. Z. Fiejka, *Zmiany w wewnatrz przemyslowym podziale pracy miedzy Polska a krajami rozwijajacymi sie* (Changes in the intra-industry division of labour between Poland and developing countries), Gospodarka Planowa, No. 12 (1978).

13. The first stage of consultations dealing with iron and steel, artificial fertilizers, leather goods, oils and fat, and petrochemicals, has already been completed. Further consultations for agricultural machinery, capital goods, food and pharmaceuticals are in preparation.

8 SPECIALISED INFORMATION AND GLOBAL INTERDEPENDENCE: PROBLEMS OF CONCENTRATION AND ACCESS

Rita Cruise O'Brien

The inequality of access to specialised information (technical and non-technical) in North-South relations has a major effect on the outcome of negotiations vital to developing countries. Economic and political leverage among industrialised countries is partly based on the concentration of information and knowledge in those countries, and in the principal transnational firms. Information is a product which can be acquired at a cost, and a resource which affects both the capacity for decision-making at the national level and for bargaining in the international context. Differential access to information can be a central element in the world's income determination, among other things. Research on present stocks and flows, including new technological capacity, will reveal features of concentration and problems of access globally. Until now, information dependence and problems of information access have been considered, if at all, in a 'separate box' in dependence theory. What is required is the analytical integration of the 'information factor' into basic theory, especially given its centrality to the productive base of the advanced capitalist system.

The locus of economic activity in 'post-industrial' societies is shifting from manufacturing objects to handling information and symbols. The sharpest aspect of competition may in future be as much based on information and knowledge as on capital and production. Although the information and knowledge sector in industrialised countries has in recent years become an important scholarly concern,[1] there has been to date no systematic consideration of problems of access and scarcity as they affect the international bargaining process.[2] It has often been said that world politics is changing very rapidly but conceptual paradigms have not kept pace. Information concentration in the capitals of the North, and in sectors such as finance, commodities and marketing of manufactured goods, places negotiators from developing countries at a serious disadvantage. They face great difficulties not only over scarcity and access in one-off situations but also in relation to the build-up of expertise and infrastructure at national or intergovernmental level which will affect their interests on a continual basis.

What is known or can be readily obtained in industrialised countries about resources, weather, technology or market conditions, or indeed about information itself, enhances leverage in negotiation. Much of this information which is gathered and systematised for retrieval is not available outside its storage point. In the industrialised countries, universities and

160

research institutions as well as privately financed research and development give public and private decision-makers considerable advantage in their capacity to bargain, and may even dictate the parameters of the negotiating environment.

The manpower and expertise marshalled by industrialised countries in preparation for GATT negotiations or the WARC 1979, for example, far outweighs that available to developing countries.[3] In bargaining terms, there is considerable concern that the lack of information resources in the South in intergovernmental negotiations makes the bargaining process untenable, leads to the formulation of 'political positions' in the absence of technical preparedness, or jeopardises the advantages previously achieved by the incapacity to sustain and specify negotiating positions in meetings which take place at certain intervals. There is an analogy here (as yet unexplored) with the early years of labour/management collective bargaining.

The international economic and political system has emerged in recent decades from a series of closed systems to contractual relations. Political independence and even partial delinking from the transnational economic system through nationalisation has changed the environment of information need and access. Newly independent countries, pursuing economic policies based on their own interests, have new information requirements, which imply the development of new information systems and means of interaction.

Yet part of the weakness of developing countries is often the lack of knowledge of where to look for the required information, some of which is publicly available.[4] In firm to government negotiation, timing is often crucial and expertise is brought in to advise on specific negotiation. Although an expert adviser may provide more information than is on his specific brief,[5] the national government may not be able to retain or build further on the information required. Thus, even if the information were made available, it is possible that its maximal use would be further inhibited by the lack of need articulation at the national level and of infrastructural supports. The problem is, therefore, not only of international imbalance and inequality but also of the national assessment of requirements, expertise and institutional arrangements. The lack of adequate assessment of present needs and capacity or of future needs puts a particularly dramatic twist on certain intergovernmental negotiations in which future disadvantage may be negotiated now, especially with regard to scarce resources. Energy, space and the electro-magnetic spectrum (required for broadcast and telecommunications) are good examples of these.

At the same time as the international negotiating environment has altered from closed to open/contractual systems, one of the most major changes in 'post-industrial' societies has been the shift in investment to information-related industries. This has increased the power of those countries which possess the expertise, knowledge and information capacity. European countries, for example, are concerned about their access both to technology and channels of telecommunications in the face of United States hegemony. Some of the issues considered by the OECD are also relevant to developing countries, including transborder data flows, investment, planning, intergovernmental cooperation, training and the assessment of future requirements.[6]

The information society: national and international issues

There is a growing literature which explores the economic and social implications of the centrality of information to advanced industrial societies. Statements on the information base of the economy,[7] some of which are controversial, and the changes it is likely to entail in terms of resources and power focus attention usually on the domestic environment. Daniel Bell's concept of 'post-industrial' society[8] is based partly on the growing importance of the tertiary sector and adaptation of the hitherto dominant mix of resources of capital, labour and energy to the new use of information and organisation of the flow of knowledge. As early as 1970, concern was expressed about its unique dependence upon the compilation of theoretical knowledge (Bell), the potential paralysis of societies over a plethora of facts without obvious paradigms for understanding it (McGeorge Bundy), or the value systems of a former era which cannot keep pace with technological change (Herman Kahn).[9] The development of computer technology has intensified this trend: there is concern about future patterns of employment, given the potential for off-loading onto automated control large areas of production and services. In relation to management systems based on information, it has been underlined that the scarce resource is not information but human attention.[10] There is also a growing literature on the control of privacy and personal vulnerability or the loss of security through the uncontrolled concentration of information in certain institutions.[11] In political terms, it is felt that to raise the possibilities of the formation of new constituencies around changing issues and priorities will present a challenge of governance in older institutions and power centres.[12] Many of these tensions in society have global reverberations and in a certain sense the changing model of the domestic political environment is directly analogous to changes internationally. But much more attention is paid to the political implications of information access and policies at the national level.

In recent years, a number of studies have examined imperfections in technology markets and the dependence of developing countries on imported technology, much of which is inappropriate. Rather less attention has been devoted to the more general question of market information and the basis on which new types of arms-length systems of exchange depend.[13] While the centrality of information to the functioning of economic systems ought to be given more prominence, reviews of the concepts and assumptions used in the literature of economic theory, particularly in relation to risk, uncertainty and the economics of search, do not address themselves to some of the complex qualitative issues involved in differential access and use of information in international negotiation.[14]

The structure of the modern transnational corporation is information dependent,[15] its 'appropriability' of information[16] being perhaps as important as its research and development capacity and the control it exercises over markets and technology. These corporations are dependent on multinational computer systems to increase their manoeuvreability in their relations with governments, suppliers and customers. It is acknowledged in the business literature that these systems will enhance their power and influence in relation to governments and will widen the gap between rich and poor nations.[17]

Modern telecommunications systems have evolved under United States leadership, and specifically in response to the needs of transnational corporations and defense surveillance. United States defense and enterprise depends on a system of 'free flow' of information and open borders.[18] The reduction of non-technical barriers like tariffs on 'alternative voice-data circuits' has led to the immense growth of private carriers since the end of the 1960s upon which many forms of transnational enterprise (and business consortia) are dependent. These tendencies have led certain specialists to ask whether the information policy-making process at the international level has been able to deal adequately with technological breakthroughs which promote interdependence.[19] Few have asked the basic question: in whose interests and at what cost?

Recent research and writing on international relations has been trying to improve on the 'realist' school which dominated thinking in the 1950s and 1960s by developing models of complex interdependence[20] which give new prominence to interaction based on 'low politics' rather than pre-eminent attention to military security and force. Scholars who favour this approach have been careful to point out the difference between their positive use of the term 'interdependence' and its use by some policy makers to buttress particular prescriptions through resort to a symbolism which suggests that conflicts of interest are *passé*.[21] The concept of 'asymmetric interdependence' allows for reciprocal interaction which is not based exclusively on mutual interest but nevertheless results in a mutually acceptable resolution of conflict. 'Less dependent actors', we are told, 'can often use the interdependent relationship as a source of power in bargaining over an issue and perhaps to affect other issues'.[22] This can be formulated as a simpler proposition: that the *more powerful* can use the interdependent relationship as a further source of power. New forms of interdependence (whether asymmetric or not) in areas of 'low politics' may be seen as justifying the present systems of interaction in which the 'rules of the game' or the parameters of negotiation are effectively determined by the more powerful actors.

It may, therefore, be essential to rethink the model: the new agenda item of information in world politics suggests the necessity of analytical distinction according to the *capacity* of the actors in an interdependent situation. That is, the inequality of access to information adds a new dimension to asymmetry which may be originally based on political and economic divergence: it is a divergence in the capacity of the parties involved. Having better access to and control of information in a negotiating situation is an important factor of power. Differential capacity in a situation of asymmetric interdependence gives prominence to the value of information as an independent variable affecting the outcome of negotiations.

Information access and international negotiation: problems for developing countries

The importance of information access to the realisation of the principal aims of the New International Economic Order has already been recognised. The locus of debate on this issue and the political or technical form it is likely to take are still in doubt. Discussions on reform of the international monetary system, or on the allocation of resources of the sea and space are often pre-empted by the more powerful nations, leaving the developing countries with only a 'Yes, but . . .' role or encouraging them to politicise issues as a substitute for the technical arguments which they may not possess. Such responses have been regarded as 'obstructionist' by the more powerful actors in international bargaining but may, with the hindsight of nearly a decade of North-South interaction, be seen instead as having been quite astute. Might they now not be considered as (variably effective) delaying tactics which gave much-needed time for the preparation of better informed and more effective positions?

Mutual lack of confidence in the present global negotiating environment may be in part explained by differing access to specialised information. It is in the interests of both the North and the South that serious consideration be given to this issue in the coming years. The limitations of the market model of free flow of information have already been recognised with reference to the structure of ownership and control, problems of access and the vastly different resources of the data rich and data poor. Two principal implications are the need for rapid technological change in the information sector and for institutional alternatives to the current negotiating environment.

Will these new developments *increase* the already substantial potential for centralisation and control of information in traditional world centres, thus enhancing power and leverage? Can these developments be marshalled by developing countries (individually or in regional or sectoral groups) in order to *decrease* their present information disadvantage?

Answers to these questions can only be related to the time factor involved and the capacity to relate information systems to specific negotiating requirements. In the short run, the power of information exchange among consortia of large private banks[23] vastly outweighs the access to information of even frequent borrowers from the South. The general trends of technological changes in information are: microprocessors reduce cost; improved information systems enhance volume and specificity; telecommunications systems, including satellites, facilitate transmission. In the longer run, technological change and its effect of cost reduction may be able to reduce the data dependency of developing countries and facilitate the marshalling of information resources to their interests. As in the case of information generally, the greatest problem in the improvement of information access through electronic means may lie in the knowledge and organisational supports required to make use of the information given.

There is a growing literature on the uses of information technology and development,[24] but little of it is related to international negotiation. With the substantial reduction of hardware cost, will expertise or electronically produced software, whether bought in or developed locally, be the greatest cost? Are there enough incentives for it to be made commercially? Can it be adapted from other systems? Can it be obtained from non-commercial sources?

A powerful impetus to the rapid accumulation of information systems in developing countries may come from the moves to promote self-sufficiency in computer technology and to add informatics to the agenda of the New International Economic Order.[25] The potential danger of such general initiatives is the mistaken assumption drawn from other economic sectors that telecommunications and information systems will in themselves promote growth and development, the only problem being their rapid acquisition.[26] The use of high technology in other sectors has frequently produced new forms of dependence rather than enlarging independent capacity. It has even generated new dimensions of inequality and poverty, when weighed against the opportunity cost of alternative investment. Developing countries cannot ignore changes in information production, but will they enter this field with wisdom derived from what has preceded it?

Informatics cannot in itself reverse the traditional concentration of knowledge and expertise in capitals of the North and in major transnational firms. As the cost of hardware production is reduced through technological change, there is already evidence for concern that information systems will be 'unloaded' on developing countries in return for lucrative software contracts. Among the questions raised in industrialised countries are those regarding the planning and professional capacities required for electronic processing and storage of information. Sometimes these are 'teething problems', sometimes much more fundamental ones involving large financial loss or a weakening of decision-making capacity. Such problems are even more costly for countries of limited income.

Informatics may not at all aid the integration of technological change at national or international levels. It may create a new form of dualism in developing economies generated by professional engineers and systems analysts who define their own professional development in terms of new gadgetry and new prestige expenditure. There is a risk of producing codifying and storing false information if the data base of national statistics remains as poor as it is in many developing countries. There is also a risk of reducing employment potential by promoting electronic information processing in service sectors or in banking or municipal government. And it is not at all apparent that the new forms of information will be any more reliable.

There is a host of intergovernmental issues raised by changes in information production and transmission, not least that of transborder data flows. An awareness of these issues has been created among developing countries which as yet lack the organisational capacity for long-term consideration. For the present the Intergovernmental Bureau of Informatics (IBI) has provided a surrogate forum for discussion of some of these issues.

Conclusion

Suggestions for strengthening information sharing and expertise are timely, especially in view of the call for the establishment of new organisational capacity for countries of the South based on economic and technical cooperation.[27] In the immediate future the bargaining capacity of countries will be weakened by the lack of political initiative for information sharing on a bilateral or multilateral basis and also of a Secretariat (like the OECD) to serve their information needs in a systematic way. At both national and intergovernmental levels an enlargement of information capacity in an organisation for the South may turn this situation around. But serious consideration is required concerning where and how electronic resources can be most effectively deployed. The present enthusiasm for informatics claims too much, both in terms of national planning and intergovernmental cooperation. Information systems themselves will not promote growth and development, nor will they strengthen the South in bargaining terms. Scepticism and critical reflection now may direct resources where they will be best served and thus forestall the creation of new forms of disadvantage.

Notes

1. Marc Uri Porat, *The Information Economy: Definition and Measurement*, U.S. Dept. of Commerce, Office of Telecommunications, May 1977, estimated that in 1967 46 per cent of United States GNP was in information-related activities, which accounted for more than 40 per cent of the work force (1970) and earned 53 per cent of all labour income (1970). John McHale, *The Changing Informa-*

tion Environment, London, Paul Elek, 1976, assesses the information impact in qualitative terms in various sectors.

2. A.G. Oettinger, *et al.*, *High and Low Politics of Information Resources for the 80s*, New York, Ballinger, 1977, discusses global strategies of interdependence based on technical facility without much consideration of the asymmetries of information and power contained in that interdependence. A three-year research project, 'The Political Economy of Information in the North-South Negotiating Process', based on three sectors of negotiation (minerals, finance and telecommunications) has recently been launched at the Institute of Development Studies. (Information can be obtained from the author.)

3. The team preparing the United States position for the GATT negotiations has been estimated at 160, and for the WARC a conservative estimate of 930 (including only government employees) was made by the F.C.C. Chairman in 1977, U.S. Senate Foreign Relations Committee, 'The New World Information Order', November 1977.

4. Library support in specialised fields is poor in most developing countries and use of international information and data resources is often not effective. UNIDO, for example, produces guides to information resources on subjects like industrial quality control and the machine tool and fertilizer industries, but it is not clear how many of these are available in the libraries of countries concerned.

5. Some advantages and limitations of the outside adviser are explored in C.J. Lipton, 'Government Negotiating Techniques and Strategies', Paper 8, New York, United Nations Centre for Transnational Corporations.

6. OECD, Information, Computer and Communications Policy Unit, Symposium on Transborder Data Flows and the Protection of Privacy, Vienna, September 1977, *Information for a Changing Society: Some Policy Considerations*, 1971; *Education and Training of Information Specialists for the 1970s*, 1973; *Information in 1985: a Forecasting Study of Information Needs and Resources*, 1973.

7. Following the work done by Porat on the United States, the Information, Computer and Communications Policy Unit of the OECD has done similar calculations for other OECD countries. The inclusion of the educational sector in the calculation of the 'information economy' is, along with others, a subject for discussion.

8. *The Coming of Post-Industrial Society*, London, Heinemann, 1974. A recent critical review of Bell, Dahrendorf and other 'modern improvement theorists' may be found in J. Gershuny, *After Industrial Society? The Emerging Self-Service Economy*, London, Macmillan, 1978.

9. From the U.S. House of Representatives, Committee on Science and Astronautics, *The Management of Information and Knowledge*, 1970.

10. Herbert A. Simon, *Administrative Behaviour*, 1976 edition, p. 294. This could be applied to the problems of the utility of most data banks.

11. Noted more than a decade ago in M. Shubink, 'Information, Rationality and Free Choice in a Future Democratic Society', *Daedalus*, Vol. 96, 1967.

12. McHale, *op. cit.*, pp. 78-87.

13. G.K. Helleiner, *World Market Imperfections and the Developing Countries*, Overseas Development Council, Washington D.C., Occasional Paper No. 11, May 1978, pp. 11, 12.

14. R. Cruise O'Brien and G.K. Helleiner, 'The Political Economy of Information in a Changing International Economic Order', forthcoming.

15. Productive knowledge, rather than capital, has become perhaps a more important element in the operations of such firms. Constantine Vaitsos, 'Corporate Integration in World Production and Trade', in Dudley Seers and Constantine Vaitsos (eds.), *Integration and Unequal Development: The Experience of the*

EEC, London, Macmillan, forthcoming.

16. Stephen P. Magee, 'Information and the Multinational Corporation: An Appropriability Theory of Direct Foreign Investment', in J.N. Bhagwati, *The New International Economic Order: the North-South Debate*, Boston, MIT Press, 1976, pp. 318-19.

17. B. Nanus, 'Business, Government and the Multinational Computer', *Colombia Journal of World Business*, Spring 1978, pp. 20, 24.

18. Johnathan F. Gunther, *The United States and the Debate on the World Information Order*, Academy for Educational Development, Inc., Washington, 1978, and William H. Read, 'Foreign Policy: the High and Low Politics of Telecommunications', in Oettinger, et al., *op. cit.*, pp. 197-200.

19. Oettinger, *ibid.*, Introduction.

20. Robert O. Keohane and Joseph S. Nye, *Power and Interdependence: World Politics in Transition*, Boston, Little Brown, 1977, esp. Chapter 2.

21. Fred G. Bergsten, et al., 'International Economics and International Politics: A Framework for Analysis', *International Organisation*, Vol. 29, No. 1, Winter, 1975, pp. 20-1.

22. Keohane and Nye, *op. cit.*, p. 11.

23. SWIFT, the Society for Worldwide Financial Telecommunications, serving 500 European and North American banks for the purpose of improving the transmittal of international payments messages became operational in 1977. By 1978, it was expected to transmit 300,000 messages per day. William H. Read, *op. cit.*, p. 225. For a succinct and informative elaboration on the importance of private data networks, see H.P. Gassman, 'Data Networks: New Information Infrastructure', *The OECD Observed*, Paris, No. 95, November 1978.

24. Ithiel de Sola Pool, et al., MIT Research Programme on Communications Policy, *Low-Cost Data and Text Communication for Less Developed Countries*, 1976; G. Russell Pipe and A.A.M. Veehuis, *National Planning for Informatics in Developing Countries*, Mouton, 1976.

25. Intergovernmental Bureau of Informatics, *Informatics in the Service of the New International Economic Order*, July 1978.

26. 'Serving the Information Needs of Developing Countries', in a Background Paper by Ithiel de Sola Pool, OECD Informatics Studies 11, *Conference on Computer and Telecommunications Policy*, Paris, 1976, pp. 290-1.

27. Shridath S. Ramphal, 'Not by Unity Alone: The Case For Third World Organisations', *Third World Quarterly*, London, Vol. 1, No. 3, July 1979.

9   THE PROBLEM OF TECHNOLOGICAL CHOICE

Zofia Dobrska

In the late 1940s when the theory of economic development started to emerge from general economic theory, the choice of techniques of production in the so-called underdeveloped countries was not a debatable issue. The classic principle, according to which production technique is determined by the relative scarcity of productive factors, was functioning in economic doctrine[1] even though policies of big companies and colonial administrations were already eroding it.[2]

When, however, the governments and élites of the newly independent countries took it upon themselves to formulate national development programmes with no external, even well-intentioned, advice, the orientation radically changed. The causal link between modern technology and the affluence of Western societies seemed convincingly simple and attractive for them to disregard the complex nature of this interrelationship. Thus an uncritical belief in the wonderful effects of modern technology plus prestige reasons (keeping up with the Joneses) determined the views of the governments and the élites of developing countries.

The fascination with modern technology is easy to understand. It was mainly theoreticians who raised doubts as to its usefulness for developing countries, while its benefits were propagated in unison by two such powerful forces as transnational corporations and almost all the socialist Left.

This concurrence of views between two antagonistic forces is an interesting paradox. While the viewpoint of transnational corporations may easily be explained, the analysis of the roots of the leftist conceptions deserves a more profound approach. Research is needed on the extent to which this fascination, which arose in the USSR in the 1920s, was the outcome of traditional inferiority complexes towards the West, the fear of external threat, the particular needs of a great country, or simply ignorance. Anyway, socialist countries came to be the main spokesmen of the development of modern technology *per fas et nefas*, both in their own societies and in developing countries.

It is true that social costs of the implementation of such a policy were reduced in socialist economies by a simultaneous implementation of another fundamental principle of socialist thinking, full employment. As a result, although wrong technological choices leading to too capital-intensive techniques in manufacturing and too labour-intensive techniques in other sectors of the economy hampered the growth of social welfare, they did not deprive the majority of the population of the chance to satisfy their basic material needs. Yet to recommend similar solutions for developing countries — whatever their institutional conditions — was certainly erroneous from a Marxist viewpoint. In the 1970s, academic analysts in the socialist countries began to abandon this position and appreciate the significance of appropriate technology.[3] Unfortunately, this reorientation has not been observed so far among most of the spiritual disciples of these theoreticians, i.e. the ultra-leftists in developing countries.

In the late 1950s and early 1960s a number of Western scholars also took up the defence of the most modern technologies. They argued that it was advisable to abandon technologies which reflected the scarcity of productive factors and ensured maximisation of the immediate increase in income in favour of those maximising the surplus, which was said to ensure automatically a higher long-term rate of growth of national income. It was not the first case in the history of economic thought that theoretical substantiation of practical solutions was offered at a time when the adverse effects of such solutions were becoming evident. The gap between modern technology and the socio-economic realities of the developing countries became increasingly conspicuous. This was evidenced both by the failure of a number of large-scale investment projects carried out in developing countries in the preceding years and the one-sided and unequal development of countries where such projects were successful.[4] At the same time, the technological dependence of the developing countries grew, with all its economic and political consequences.

As a result, in the mid-1960s the process began of the revaluation of both global and specific development strategies, particularly the problem of choice of production techniques. The process, initiated by academic circles and spread by international organisations (particularly UN agencies), can be observed today — although to a very small extent — in the government circles of the countries involved. Its effects, that are more intellectual than practical at the moment but should not be underestimated, include better understanding of the essence and types of technical progress, of the differences in micro- and macro-economic effectiveness of particular techniques, of the socio-political implications of technological choices (both in domestic and international aspects) of the mechanisms that determine transfer of technologies from more to less developed countries, as well as the role of transnational corporations in this domain. In all these fields theoretical thinking and analytical research have considerably enriched our knowledge of reality.

One of the achievements of this period was an increasingly critical attitude to technological solutions from the highly developed countries. The evolution in this field may be evidenced by changes in terminology: from the term 'traditional' or 'village' technology, which was controversial due to its static approach and the dissociation from modern science, through 'intermediate' technology, which suggests attempts at creating an artificial mixture of old and new techniques or following an outdated technique, and 'low-cost' technology, where attention was focussed on the volume of global expenditure rather than its effectiveness, to 'appropriate' technology, which is the best term not only for presentational reasons but also because it is sufficiently broad to cover various technological choices. Besides, the term introduces the element of relativity (the requirement of verification of the effectiveness of any technological choice in concrete economic and social realities) in place of an absolutist approach to the criteria of choice (traditional, modern, labour-intensive or surplus maximisation techniques).

At present, literature concerning the choice of production techniques in developing countries is much richer than what was being written on economic development thirty years ago. Looking through that literature one notices that all the most important aspects of the choice of production techniques were discussed by particular scholars on various occasions and their economic and socio-political implications were taken into consideration. At the same time, even the latest literature includes recurring erroneous hypotheses and simplifications that were characteristic of the level of our knowledge some twenty years ago.[5] Since it would be boring and useless to repeat correct hypotheses that were put forward previously, or to question errors stemming not from shortcomings of our general knowledge but from the lack of erudition of their authors, I intend to focus – without trying to be original – on three problems relating to appropriate technology, which not only might be helpful for systematising our knowledge in this field, but also have some practical implications.

First, I would like to answer the question why such a large part of the Left from less developed countries denies the concept of appropriate technology and follows the pattern implemented in developed countries. Second, I shall attempt a comparison of objective impediments to the implementation of appropriate technology. Third, I would like to point to certain new elements of the world economic and social situation which appeared in the 1970s but which, in my opinion, will be rather long-lasting. These elements create more real chances for the spread of appropriate technology than in the past.

Some comments on the Left and appropriate technology

The analysis of the causes of the reluctance of many leftist intellectuals of Third World countries to accept the concept of appropriate technology is interesting not only for practical reasons, that is to say, the increasing role of these circles in shaping public opinion, but also because the concept seems logically the closest one to socialist visions of the world, and one could expect that it should have arisen in socialist countries. At any rate, it should have been accepted as theirs by leftist social thinkers, since appropriate technology envisages: (1) the possibility of a rapid increase in employment and labour productivity, and thereby of raising the living standards of the majority of population which have so far been most unprivileged; (2) safeguarding social equality not only through more equal distribution of the ownership of means of production but also through ensuring for all social groups more equal distribution of knowledge — the third factor of social differentiation (after ownership and status);[6] (3) humanisation of the working process through the adjustment of production techniques to the perception capacities of the social groups that handle them (reducing alienation); (4) weakening of the monopolistic position of big business, both indigenous and foreign; (5) weakening of technological dependence on the highly developed countries.

Last but not least, one of the main arguments of the advocates of modern, capital-intensive technologies, that is the beneficial long-term effect of surplus maximisation is, from a socialist point of view, completely meaningless.

By definition, surplus maximising technique creates less jobs and leads to a smaller immediate increase in production than income maximising technique. Its only merit is that, under the capitalist mode of production, it produces higher profits, that is a higher surplus, which can be invested, thus allowing for a higher future rate of growth of the economy.

It is, however, evident that the above holds true only in a capitalist enterprise, where the part of the value added devoted to the wage fund is treated as a cost to be minimised and not as a desirable component of the national income. In a family enterprise the only rational technique from the point of view of the future rate of growth is whatever maximises production, as the higher is the family income/value added, the greater are the possibilities of devoting some part of it to investment.

One could argue that in a socialist economy where wage labour prevails the government, wanting to obtain a high investible surplus, has to make a choice similar to that of a capitalist entrepreneur. In reality, however, the situation is radically different. A socialist government does not need to choose techniques characterised by high capital-output ratios in order to obtain the necessary surplus. It can implement those maximising production and employment and at the same time secure the desired investment fund through an appropriate division of the increased income between consumption and accumulation.

For a capitalist entrepreneur the level of wage in the economy is an external datum. In consequence he should choose a technique which, at a given wage level, maximises his profits. This aim will be attained in a situation where both the volume of production and the level of employment are lower than would be possible with other techniques. In the socialist economy the situation is reversed. It is the increase in the volume of production and of employment which is the goal and this implies the utilisation of income maximisation techniques. The wage level will be manipulated in such a way as to provide the necessary investment surplus. In consequence — in identical starting conditions — the average wage will be lower than in a capitalist economy, but as the level of employment will be much higher, the overall wage fund — that is, the consumption level of the population — will be noticeably greater than under capitalism. The size of the surplus can be the same as under capitalist rules of the game, but, as it will be utilised to develop production goods characterised by a lower capital/output ratio, the rate of growth of national income will be higher.[7]

What then is the source of such a denial of the concept of appropriate technology? One may risk a statement that the general psychological predispositions of radical social activists make them easily succumb to fascination with the most modern technology as such. They are particularly sensitive to differences in the level of development of productive forces between the less developed and highly developed economies and they are inclined to identify these productive forces with the level of technological development. They are thus fascinated with a certain ideal pattern of a new world, which under no circumstances (including technological) should be inferior to the most modern achievements.

Their emotional attitude towards the problems often misleads them and makes them identify technological independence with economic independence, although the two phenomena do not have to go hand in hand.[8] Besides, the slogan of technological independence may be propagated from various points of view, since the advocates of appropriate technology put forward as serious arguments as the advocates of modern technology.

However, one of the most important causes of the hostility of the ultra-leftist thinkers towards appropriate technology seems to be the incompatibility of this concept with the model of social changes which they advocate. There should be no illusions: appropriate technology is the concept of evolutionary, slow and long-lasting change, which may come to be 'opium for the masses' and may involve replacing revolutionary movements by the so-called 'grass-roots' development effort. In socialist-oriented countries it implies, according to leaders of the ultra-left, a much slower pace of change and socio-economic transformations than the implementation of shock-programmes based on the most modern technology. If the number of leftist advocates of appropriate technology is increasing, it does not mean that leftist intellectuals do not recognise the theoretical importance of that argument; it means that practical experiences have deprived them of belief in the feasibility of such solutions and convinced them that a good bicycle will take you farther than a jet you cannot manage.

Appropriate technology must seem dangerous to ultra-leftists who believe it is possible to construct immediately a highly advanced socialist society, since, while increasing social equality, it at the same time strengthens the private ownership of means of production instead of putting an end to it. Moreover, one of the assumptions of appropriate technology is its partial adjustment to the existing cultural and social framework, whereas revolution attempts, among other things, a radical change of social mentality. Large and modern industry, which employs armies of workers, was analysed already in the classics of Marxism not only from the economic but also from the social point of view. The big industrial working class in a capitalist system was said to represent the force stimulating revolution, while in the socialist system it is the leading class in the construction of a better world.

Appropriate technology is incompatible with an autocratic conception of socialism since its implementation involves considerable decentralisation of both ownership and the control of investment and production, and this limits the direct intervention of central planning authorities. This does not have to lead to the abandonment of the basic social goals of socialism, or a decline in the general economic efficiency of the system. It does, however, lead to the weakening of control exercised by the highest administrative bodies over the economic and social life of the country and limitation of the power of the state itself. For those followers of socialism in developing countries who assume the primacy of politics over economics, the economic and social advantages of appropriate technology do not compensate for such adverse political consequences. The primacy of the state apparatus, explained by the necessity to defend socialist achievements against home and foreign enemies, then comes to be the purpose in itself, irrespective of its repercussions on the well-being of the population.

The choice between the power of the state or welfare of its population is evidently pointless in the long run, as there can be no efficient state organism unless its citizens enjoy at least a moderate level of well-being and culture. Unfortunately, in the short run the dilemma can and does arise.

Impediments to implementation of appropriate technology

When the concept of appropriate technology was becoming fashionable its advocates were inclined to think that difficulties in its implementation stemmed almost exclusively from subjective obstacles, that is to say, investment decisions that did not take into account the economic calculus (the 'prestige projects'), or were based on a wrong calculus due to improper definition of economic goals (profit, investment surplus) or on erroneous evaluation of the cost of their implementation (the problems of shadow prices, non-renewable resources, and the like). The only objective barriers to the extension of appropriate technology they took into consideration were the policies of transnational corporations and the organisational shortcomings of foreign aid.

It was only when theory was put into practice — either in the form of field studies or attempts at implementing technologies that were regarded as appropriate — that the theoreticians realised that there were numerous objective factors hampering the process which had to be taken into account if programmes of action were to be realistic.

Even the so-called subjective investment choices, though wrong in economics, could often be rationally defended, at least from the viewpoint of decision-making centres. Thus those criticising big investment projects for their frequently low economic returns might forget that there were also non-economic goals, e.g. demonstrating the efficiency of the government concerned or helping mobilise the population. The latter factor was particularly significant in countries where the sense of national community was just arising and needed visible symbols. By their very nature, solutions based on appropriate technology do not fulfil these non-economic tasks effectively, which will always weaken their attractiveness in the eyes of local politicians — and donors of foreign aid.

One of the objective barriers to the adoption of appropriate technologies is their relatively narrow range. It is true that there are examples of successful improvement of traditional production methods or completely new solutions,[9] but they cover, rather fragmentarily, sectors of production (agriculture, building, energy, food and textile manufacturing) which are limited (though important). So far, however, researchers have focussed almost exclusively on technology that is appropriate for individual producers or small industrial works. From the viewpoint of the employment and earnings of the poorest people, this is evidently the right priority. At the same time, however, it should be borne in mind that to function properly every national economy also needs highly concentrated and very capital-intensive production sectors.

One of the weaknesses of the opponents of the blind imitation of the technological solutions of the highly industrialised countries was a categorical denial of such solutions. While they rightly criticised the implementation of capital-absorptive technologies or technologies which could not be effective in developing countries, due to the scale of production or the weaknesses of the economic infrastructure, they attached too little importance to other modern solutions. Many of these solutions embody 'pure' technological progress, that is to say *in any conditions* they are more effective than methods applied previously, or are specially well adapted to the conditions in some developing countries.[10]

However, the reasoning in the categories of appropriate technology must be global, i.e. it should cover the entire national economy, not only some sectors. From this viewpoint some of the most modern, large-scale enterprises may prove to be as appropriate as small-scale undertakings based on simple technological solutions. 'Appropriateness' does not exclude 'modernity'; it means only that 'modernity' should not be a goal in itself.

Lack of technical staff is one of the barriers to a rapid extension of appropriate technology. In the literature on the subject there are two points of view. One is illustrated by the following quotations. 'If all the best and most generous scientists in the Third World', writes I. Sachs,[11] 'trap themselves in the self-imposed ghetto of village technology providers, who will take care of the remaining part of the technology spectrum?' A. Parthasarathi[12] stresses that a considerable part of public opinion in the Third World regards any alternative technologies as a diversionary tactic on the part of the North 'in the sense that it seeks to redirect a significant part of the scientific and technological capacity of Third World countries towards the development of these new "rural oriented" "appropriate" technologies, *leaving the main muscle of industrial power* — the petro-chemical complexes, the steel plants, the railways, the power plants — *in the hands of transnational companies'*.

The reasoning underlying this point of view seems incorrect but it is worthwhile discussing, since it clearly depicts, in my opinion, the lack of a full consensus as to the meaning of the term 'appropriate technology'. The two authors identify it with the traditional technique and suggest that concentrating on this will lead to the deepening of technological dependence of the Third World. The assumption that control of the entire modern sector of industry may be taken over by Third World specialists within a short time is only an illusion, the more so as aspirations for ambitious and many-sided development are growing. In this situation a strict selection as to key sectors of the economy should be made: first, with respect to sectors which are really necessary at the given stage of the country's economic development; and second, with respect to those which are most vulnerable either from the viewpoint of their role in the economy or from especially damaging policies in foreign technological centres. It is in these specialities that engineers and researchers should be trained on a large scale, sufficiently acquainted with the latest technological achievements and at the same time sufficiently aware of the realities of their own countries to ensure the most appropriate functioning of modern industries and modern technologies in the existing economic and social conditions.

As for the staff specialising in problems of small-scale rural or artisanal technology, an increase in their number need not seriously weaken the cadres of specialists dealing with modern technologies. Conceptual work in this field can be a by-product of more fundamental research, whereas adjustment and initiation work will require people with different predispositions and skills than those who would be selected by modern research centres.

There is no need to fear that there will be a lack of staff stemming from wrong distribution of existing resources. It is the lack of such staff in relation to total needs that constitutes one of the major barriers to the spread of appropriate technologies. What is involved is not so much the lack of creative staff, as of people talented and willing to implement appropriate technology in rural areas. Their role is crucial for two reasons: first, they are responsible for the ultimate adjustment of new technologies to the conditions of the environment; second, their personal contact and example are the only ways to make potential users adopt such technologies. Thus, on the one hand, appropriate technology creates smaller needs for capital but, on the other hand, greater demand for semi-skilled and skilled staff, and particularly for organisational skills (the latter being specially scarce in pre-industrial society). The more backward the country, that is the more appropriate technology it needs, the more difficult is the problem of staff. This is why appropriate technology is more likely to be adopted in countries with higher levels of development, particularly those with an artisanal tradition, in other words, Asia rather than Africa south of the Sahara.

Researchers also point to another problem. Implementation of new technologies always brings additional risk, at least from the viewpoint of the producer. The lower the income of the producer and the larger the part of income involved, the greater his unwillingness to face the risk. For example, researchers are of the opinion that the green revolution spread more slowly among small farmers than among wealthier Indian farmers not only because of the difference in the capital resources which can be devoted to implementing modern technologies, but also because wealthy farmers could introduce new varieties on only parts of their plots, thus minimising the risk of failure. Small farmers, on the other hand, who did not have such possibilities, stuck to the old methods which yielded income which was low but more or less steady. The elaboration of methods which would reduce this risk, or 'socialise' it, with the aid of the state, is one of the pre-conditions for a successful implementation of appropriate technology.

The need for the extension of the conceptual work on appropriate technology, and on organisational requirements connnected with its implementation, as well as the necessity to socialise the risk, mean that the future of these techniques is heavily dependent on the attitude of the governments of developing countries. There are several reasons why this attitude is often — either officially or in practice — unfavourable. They stem not only from ignorance of the problem, but also from very concrete and objective factors.

First, changes in the pattern of technological development would endanger directly the interests of the ruling élites. Big private capital has to take into account that its privileges will be limited (in availability of public credits, tax reductions, custom protection, etc.) and the state bureaucracy will have fewer opportunities for well-paid jobs in large public enterprises or illegal income (bribes with large foreign orders).[13]

Second, as has already been mentioned, big modern investment projects are of greater propaganda importance. Besides, they facilitate central government control of the country's economy and the life of its citizens. It would, however, be a simplification to think that overcentralisation is motivated only by political reasons. The planning of economic development, the organisation of production and its control are easier with a small number of big enterprises than with a large number of small, more autonomous enterprises. In the latter case, more subtle and flexible tools of state intervention would have to be worked out. Thus it is easy to understand why a number of developing countries chose, particularly in the early years of independence, centralism as the only acceptable form of control of the development process. (This, however, is not to say that the effects justified this choice.) Moreover, many governments regard decentralisation as a threat to national unity, since it may give rise to separatist tendencies. This aspect should be taken into account by anyone elaborating technology policy for countries with powerful national minorities or strong tribal antagonisms.

The large-scale implementation of appropriate technology has another important aspect which is not fully realised by either theoreticians or practitioners. It would involve the co-existence of two different systems of management, functioning on the basis of different rules. It is true that this might seem to happen already where there is economic 'dualism'. But the latter is characterised by the domination of the modern over the traditional system, which is partly isolated from the national economy and partly subordinated to it (not only because of the nature of the links between the two systems but also because of resulting deformation of each of them). Even when the traditional system is protected by the state (for example, in India) this is regarded as a transitional and exceptional phenomenon.

The extension of appropriate technology requires 'equal rights' in the rules of the game for the different systems, varying not only from inappropriate to appropriate technology but even within the latter, according to the degree of its modernity and capital-intensiveness. How is this to be achieved in a way that would ensure a harmonious development of the economy as a whole? As A. Parthasarathi rightly asks,[14] 'How do you manage the overall process? What kind of objectives, policies and institutional structures are appropriate and feasible for managing in the same sector, in the same region, in similar product categories, the co-existence of these [techniques]?' According to the author, in order to reach the desired objective 'one will need differential levels of credit pricing, technical complexity and so on'. The question is whether this is really indispensable and, if so, to what extent and by what mechanisms can one avoid illegal 'areas of contact' between the two systems that would give rise to corrupt practices?

The answer to this question cannot be unequivocal, since 'managing the overall process' cannot be identical for different types of economy. What is needed is more comprehensive research and discussion on the most appropriate forms of co-existence between the different techno-economic entities constituting the national economy.

Prospects for appropriate technology

Despite serious obstacles to the extension of appropriate technology, there are grounds for saying that it has greater chances today than in the past to play an important part in the development process of the Third World.

It has already left the preliminary stage of the crystalisation of views and conceptual and research work, and a network of specialised centres has been created. This stage is called by N. Jequier 'the first generation in appropriate technology'.[15] As a result its advocates are better prepared theoretically and more experienced today than a dozen years ago, not to mention the fact that their number has considerably increased.

Also, the very logic of the process of industrialisation of developing countries has created conditions for easier acceptance of appropriate technology. Some spectacular technological solutions have been shown to be ineffective, emphasising the need for greater economic rationality. Even in these fields where alien industrialisation patterns have turned out to be viable, there is a growing need for the establishment of the whole network of small-scale industries, repair shops, sub-contractors and so on, related to the big projects and ensuring their proper functioning.

The process of revaluation of concepts and conclusions from painful experiences was accelerated by the changing economic situation of the whole world, caused by the oil crisis and long-lasting economic stagnation in the highly-industrialised countries. Although there was a rapid flow of capital to the Third World at the beginning of this period, the majority of petroleum importing countries have found themselves in an extremely difficult economic position. This will limit the possibilities of implementing big capital-intensive projects. The necessity to scrutinise the effectiveness of each investment expenditure will increase the chances for the choice of a more appropriate technology. Besides, it may be expected that since it is a human tendency to make a virtue out of necessity, the governments of many developing countries will suddenly find virtues in appropriate technology they would never have noticed under more favourable circumstances, and they will be able to explain to their publics why the pace of North-style industrialisation has slackened.

There is another factor which, in my opinion, will contribute to the adoption of appropriate technology in the near future. Unlike 'traditional' or 'intermediate' technology, which are always regarded as solutions appropriate only for less developed countries, appropriate technology attempts to solve problems that are significant both for developing and for highly developed countries. It is true that the need to change existing technological patterns in the developed countries stems from social and environmental reasons and not so much from the economic ones that weigh most in developing countries. But it is important that this has come to be a universal need.

The fact that out of approximately 600 specialised groups working in the field of appropriate technology only around 200 are in developing countries and 400 in industrialised capitalist countries,[16] and that more than a half of the latter are dealing exclusively with internal problems, is the best proof that the conceptions of appropriate technology are not just a diversionary tactic on the part of the North, but reflect certain general needs shared by all countries. This increases the prospects for appropriate technology being adopted by developing countries which are so vulnerable to unequal treatment. It broadens the basis for cooperation and dialogue between the representatives of the North and South on the basis of a full partnership.

Notes

1. ArthurLewis, 'Economic Development with Unlimited Supplies of Labour', Manchester School of Economic and Social Studies, May 1954.
2. For example, the Groundnuts Scheme in Tanganyika.
3. See Razvivayusciyesia Strany, *Zakonomemosti, Tendencii, Perspektivy*, Moscow, 1974; Y. Nyilas, 'Marxist Approach to the Problems of Appropriate Technology', *Trends in World Economy*, No. 26, Budapest, 1978.
4. Integration links among developing countries that were so fashionable in the early 1960s, were, among other things, an attempt at eliminating or at least lessening the gap between the possibilities of modern techniques (economies of scale) and the absorptive capacities of the developing countries. The fact that they were a failure not so much for economic as political reasons showed how technological choices depend on the institutional framework.
5. Such basic errors may be found in the thinking of both sides, that is to say both conservatives, who identify economic goals with profit maximisation, referred to as investment surplus (see David Lim, 'Scale and Technology . . .', *Weltwirtschaftliches Archiv*, Heft 1 (1979)), and leftist scholars, who still maintain that industrialisation based on the most modern technology, if implemented on a sufficient scale, may soon solve problems of employment in the Third World (see M.B. Bhagavan, 'A Critique of Appropriate Technology . . .', Paper presented at the International Seminar on Technology Transfer . . ., Turku, Finland, November 1977).
6. How this factor is neglected by many leftists is evidenced by the statement by Bhagavan (*op. cit.*, p. 47) who, stating that the alternatives are 'either training numerous people in basic industrial and managerial skills to start and run any number of small-scale labour-intensive units, or having crash programmes to train small numbers of managers', supports, from a socialist standpoint, the latter alternative without taking into account its social effects.
7. Zofia Dobrska, *Wybor Technik Produkcji w Krajach Gospodarczo Zacofanych*, Warsaw, 1963.
8. See also the 1975 Dag Hammarskjöld Centre Report which on this issue is equally firm and sweeping: 'who controls technology controls development' (p. 17).
9. See N. Jequier (ed.), *Appropriate Technology: Problems and Promises*, Paris, OECD, 1976; I. McRobie, 'Intermediate Technology: Small is Successful', *Third World Quarterly*, April 1979.
10. Examples of such solutions are the replacing of petroleum as a fuel by alcohol produced from sugar cane or manioc, or some highly modern and efficient technologies implemented in steel or the paper industry, the scale of production being much smaller than for traditional technologies.
11. Ignacy Sachs, 'Controlling Technology for Development', *Development Dialogue*, No. 1 (1979), p. 29.
12. Ashok Parthasarathi, *ibid.*, p. 35.
13. One example of this is a large hospital in one African country, equipped with the most sophisticated foreign diagnostic devices but at the same time lacking sheets for its patients, since it 'does not pay' for the administration to order them!
14. Parthasarathi, *op. cit.*, p. 37.
15. *Hearings before . . . the Committee on Science and Technology US House of Representatives, Ninety-fifth Congresss, Second Session*, No. 110, Washington, 1978, p. 83.
16. *Ibid.*, p. 82.

10 TECHNOLOGICAL DEPENDENCY: A CRITICAL VIEW*

Luc Soete

Technological dependence is generally considered a crucial element in overall dependence. Yet despite its importance, it has, with a few exceptions (Merhav (1969), Sercovitch (1970) and an excellent article by Monza (1972)), rarely been analysed in a formal general dependency framework.[1] Most of the discussion has either developed into debates on rather specific issues such as transfer pricing,[2] private technology appropriation,[3] technology market imperfections,[4] etc., or led to a set of descriptive statements about the 'marginalisation' of science and technology in backward countries.[5] These contributions undoubtedly have been important in emphasising the existence of technological dependence even in situations of effective import substitution policies, but they have, in retrospect, added little to our understanding of the *economic* implications of being technologically dependent and more generally of the possibility of change.

Yet it is precisely these *economic* implications, primarily in terms of economic exploitation, which are crucial when assessing dependency levels. Political domination, like cultural domination, if not expressed in economic exploitation, is essentially of little relevance to the dependency debate. Moreover, the question of the 'self-reinforcing permanency' of technological dependency has to be analysed and established very carefully. When discussing technological dependency not only is one confronted with essentially *dynamic* concepts, such as technical change; one is also dealing with a set of relations/transactions/flows, of which the costs might be easily measurable but the benefits can never be taken fully into account.

There are good reasons to presume that, just as in the advanced countries, the dynamic and positive effects of technical change have been underestimated in less developed countries (LDCs). First, there is the 'major innovation syndrome', described by Rosenberg (1976) as a typical economist disease, but found to be also a typical technological dependency disease (Vitelli, 1979). Second, there exists growing evidence that local technological capabilities in LDCs have been underestimated, which 'is partly a result of the influence of "marginalisation" arguments, which lead to the *a priori* conclusion that innovation, technological adaptations and the skills required for them are absent in Third World economies' (Cooper and Hoffman, 1978, p. 34). And, finally, there are what we would call the specific technological dependency fallacies, which, by reducing

*I am grateful to M. Bell, S. Cole, C. Cooper, M. Godfrey, K. Hoffman, S. Jacobson, R. Kaplinsky, M. Lipton, M. Naur, K. Pavitt, D. Scott-Kemis, D. Seers, G. Vickery and, last but not least, G. Vitelli for critical comments. None of them would however fully agree with the views expressed in this paper.

most of the discussion of technological dependency to the specific exchange value aspect of technology and focussing on the way the latter is used for 'the international redistribution of the economic surplus', ignore completely the crucial dynamic aspects of technology.

In this paper we will only pay attention to the last critique. The first two are by now well documented and need not be discussed again here. We have limited the analysis to international aspects of dependency, ignoring most of the intra-national issues. The latter are no doubt of crucial importance, yet as Bienefeld points out in his paper: 'The common denominator of dependency analysis is . . . its central concern with the potential difficulties which may arise as a consequence of an economy's integration into the international market'.[6] It is that central concern which is also the focus here.

This paper consists of two main parts, with four sub-sections. In the first two sections we argue strongly for an economic analysis of international dependency aspects. In section I, we suggest that from a simple economic point of view the terms of trade concept is probably the 'best' international dependency concept. In section II, we develop what could be called an 'industrial organisation' classification scheme for some of the most obvious dependency elements. In the last two sections we move to a more detailed discussion of technological dependency. Section III presents the technological dependency argument, while section IV puts forward some critical comments.

Compared to other papers in this volume, this presents undoubtedly the most sceptical and least 'sympathetic' view of dependency. This should come as no surprise. As mentioned before, to the extent that technology is essentially a dynamic concept, dependency does not seem to be the appropriate framework to analyse technological dependencies. At the same time, however, the discussion on technological dependency illustrates most clearly one of the fundamental weaknesses of dependency analysis, i.e. its primarily static nature and its failure to cope with dynamic phenomena such as technical change.

I   The Economics of Dependency

'Dependency is defined as a peripheral insertion in the world system through which former colonies and other underdeveloped countries are exploited economically, and their backwardness is maintained over time' (Oteiza and Sercovitch, 1976, p. 666). No doubt this economic exploitation requires and involves not only economic domination; 'the whole question of power, and therefore the political dimension' (*ibid.*) is intrinsically linked with the notion of dependency. Why then talk about the 'economics' of dependency? While political domination is required to create or maintain dependency, it is the degree of *economic* exploitation, and the extent to which this can be maintained over time, which determines the level of dependency. If political domination does not lead to economic exploitation (in relations between advanced countries, e.g. the United States vis-à-vis West Germany or Japan), it is difficult to say much about dependency.

Economic exploitation remains the crucial element in any dependency debate. The most useful concept of dependency focusses precisely on the creation and maintenance of that sort of exploitation, i.e. on the existence of a set of structural mechanisms which obstruct the growth of the economy and prevent its filtering down to the masses in 'dependent' economies, while creating exactly the opposite conditions in 'dominant' economies. In dos Santos' words, dependency relates to

> a situation in which the economy of certain countries is conditioned by the development and expansion of another economy to which the former is subjected. The relation of interdependence between two or more economies, and between these and the world trade, assumes the form of dependence when some countries (the dominant ones) can expand and can be self-sustaining, while other countries (the dependent ones) can do this only as a reflection of that expansion, which can have either a positive or a negative effect on their immediate development (dos Santos, 1970, p. 231).

One of the interesting features of this definition is that it leaves room for further interpretations (in dependency terms) of global interdependence.

First, global interdependence arguments are by definition based on more complicated and less clearly identifiable dependency relationships than the simple North/South-dominant/dependent relationship. Most dominant countries are very dependent on imports of raw materials, energy or minerals. Speaking more generally, one might even argue that because of their greater integration in the world economy, the advanced countries are more dependent than most backward countries. The latter will very often be less affected by world market crises. It is interesting to note that the more advanced 'backward' countries (e.g. NICs) very often become, because of the nature of their advance, more dependent, in terms of exposure to world market shocks and crises. Levels of dependence, therefore, do not necessarily correlate with levels of development, but are also linked with other, at first sight, totally external factors, such as geographical factors, including country size.[7]

Second, and more important, global interdependence in the form of, for example, further international specialisation along the lines of an international division of labour, will lead to increased dominant/dependence relationships, if increased trade between North and South worsens the terms of trade for the South. Most free trade and new international division of labour proponents strongly deny that this could happen. One can, however, demonstrate formally, and within a basic neo-classical framework, that increased trade between North and South will lead to worse terms of trade, when the export supply-curve of the South has a negative slope (Chichilnisky, 1978).[8] The latter depends primarily on so-called 'income' effects, due to abundant labour supply and a dualistic production structure,[9] typical of most LDCs.

In other words, deteriorating terms of trade for developing countries are a clear indication of increased dependency vis-à-vis dominant countries. At first sight this might seem a very narrow 'trade-economistic' dependence indicator. One might, however, consider it as the most useful empirical dependency concept, as well as being closest to what the early dependency writers had in mind. Prebisch's point (1950, 1959) that, due to the existing elastic labour supply, LDCs will be unable to retain the benefits of their productivity rises, but will pass them to developed countries' consumers in the form of lower prices, while a similar inelastic labour supply curve (labour scarcity and trade union wage pressure) will lead to higher prices for developed countries' exports, is consistent with dos Santos' definition and is most clearly expressed in falling net barter terms of trade for LDCs. The main contribution of dependency ideas is, in this view, not so much the analysis of exploitation of backward countries and the mechanisms of that exploitation — something that the theory of imperialism had already discovered fifty years before —[10] but the way in which, through existing international trade patterns, a set of dominance/dependence relationships could be developed and maintained (even when political domination became more limited with decolonisation and with the growing political importance of the Third World in international fora), largely because of a set of, no doubt politically influenced, but in the final analysis, *economic* factors (the price elasticity of primary products, labour supply in backward countries, material substitution, etc.). The major dependency critique is, in this view, primarily related to those more radical versions which do not allow for any 'autonomous' change in any of these economic factors, but assume that they are completely determined and given by cultural, political and military domination. How wrong they were can be readily observed from the evolution of the terms of trade in the seventies. Since 1974 world dependency relations have resembled far more an OPEC-NOPEC (non-oil exporting countries) structure than a North-South structure. As illustrated in Table 10.1, this radical change in the terms of trade for the North and the South, which cannot be explained by any of the usual statistics, indicates a change in economic dependency relationships, which can only be described in OPEC-NOPEC terms. This might raise doubts about the meaning of terms of trade as a dependency measure. Surely the Western world, by controlling most financial markets, possessing the most advanced technology and exporting more than 80 per cent of all capital goods, keeps OPEC very dependent in investing oil money and importing new technology and capital goods. Nonetheless, the crucial point about dependence is not so much absolute levels but *relative* levels of dependency, i.e. as expressed in *relative* prices. To be dependent on the import of capital goods, when the latter have fallen in price to a fourth of that obtained for a unit of

TABLE 10.1.   *Terms of trade index number by country group, 1954-6, 1960, 1965, 1970-6*

Regions, countries and territories	Average 1954-6	1960	1965	(1970 = 100) 1970	1971	1972	1973	1974	1975	1976
Developed market economy countries	90	96	98	100	99	100	99	87	90	89
Developing countries and territories	108	100	94	100	100	97	105	163	159	165
Major petroleum exporters	97	113	103	100	111	106	117	290	286	303
Other developing countries and territories	112	95	91	100	95	92	97	96	88	89
of which:										
Fast growing exporters of manufactures	106	85	86	100	100	95	95	84	85	87
All other countries	113	97	92	100	96	94	101	94	90	94

Source: UNCTAD, 1978.

exports, is not very worrying in terms of dependence. What is worrying is how in the long run, with oil running dry, import capital goods dependency can be reduced. But once again, at that time, this is something which will express itself in the evolution of the terms of trade.

This 'economic' approach does not ignore the political dimension of dependency thinking. No doubt the above-mentioned economic 'external' factors are and were the result of political and military domination; domination which can and could express itself either very directly (military) or indirectly (TNCs). But there remains the crucial point about the *limits* of political or military domination, which both theories of imperialism and the more radical versions of dependency theory seem to ignore. Foreign military domination, if not based on local popular support, has clearly defined limits, as illustrated by so many catastrophic guerrilla wars; political domination, if not based on military domination, has even stricter limits, as illustrated by the oil crises in 1974 and 1979. It is only *economic* domination, as empirically observable in worsening terms of trade, which will give some indication of how effective and damaging domination was.

No doubt United States political domination vis-à-vis Saudi Arabia (or is it the latter's increased integration/dependence in/on the world economy?) has limited higher oil prices (by pressing for increased production to over 9 million barrels a day) but the United States nevertheless had to accept oil price increases of more than 700 per cent over the period 1973-9. The change in the terms of trade summarises the combined effect of all these interrelated dependency relationships.

II   A Classification of Dependence Elements

This leads us to consider in a somewhat more formal framework the various elements of dependence. One should really relate each dependence element to two sets of criteria: the degree of scarcity as opposed to its availability, and the number of sellers compared to the number of buyers.

A product can be relatively scarce[11] and therefore create conditions of dependency (e.g. oil). These can be further exacerbated (or reduced) depending on the number of sellers. Similarly a product which is not fundamentally scarce (though it might be exhaustible, there are large world reserves), or for which there are many substitution possibilities, will rarely create similar conditions of (buyer) dependency. Even if there is only one seller, it will be practically impossible to create strong dependency. What might happen is that temporary scarcity might occur, because of insufficient production, and the time-lag necessary to increase it. On the other hand, short-term market-fluctuation *seller* dependency might exist, and be further exacerbated by the extent to which export earnings are primarily derived from such a product (e.g. copper and copper export dependency of Zambia, Zaire, Chile, etc.). This is the traditional export dependency discussed in UN fora and for which various stabilisation schemes have been developed. It is important however to bear in mind that this sort of export dependency will only be of importance when the product is not fundamentally scarce (e.g. copper and all agricultural raw materials). No OPEC country complains about its total export dependency on oil, nor does South Africa complain about its export dependency on gold and platinum. Total dependency can only exist if there is just one seller (or one buyer) and if the product is relatively scarce.

These concepts and notions, similar to those of industrial organisation theory, allow us to identify several international relationships, corresponding to various levels of dependency, which are a function, on the one hand, of the degree of seller and buyer concentration (assuming that the extent of collusion is inversely related to the number of sellers or buyers), and on the other, of the scarcity and substitutability of the product. The concept of scarcity raises the question of information and information costs, which cannot be dealt with here. Suffice it to say that scarcity might be defined as a function of known or estimated economically extractable reserves, in static reserves production years or in reserves as a ratio of future projected demand. Let us briefly, and without pretending to be exhaustive, apply these scarcity and number of sellers/buyers notions to some of the elements of dependency which might exist between countries. (See Table 10.2.)

It is obvious from this very incomplete list of dependency elements that *total* dependence is more the exception than the rule. There is practically always more than one seller, and even when there is some agreement between sellers, there is always an alternative seller outside the agreement or else a black market. At the highest level of dependency, the lack of total dependency can be explained by the fact that the world is (fortunately) composed of more than one political or military 'superpower'. This does not imply however that dependency costs might not be extremely and excessively high. To repeat the process of developing an A-bomb is to pay a high price for becoming somewhat more politically independent.

The other obvious fact from Table 10.2 is that the South is, with the exception of oil, more dependent than the North. Within this dependency, technology (including nuclear technology) (elements 1, 5, 8 and 9) plays a crucial role. Not only because of the well-known concentration of inventive activity in the North, but also and mainly because of the specific nature of technology as a commodity and the way in which it is being appropriated and priced. This is the main topic to be discussed next.

TABLE 10.2.   A classification of dependence elements

Level of scarcity/ degree of substitutability	Product/element	Number of sellers	Dependence created	Comments
Scarce.	1. *Military nuclear power*	A few sellers; with some level of agreement to limit selling. Large number of 'interested' buyers.	Political, military, and economic.	To the extent that information is not totally scarce and that there are independent sellers or black market or stealing, *dependence is not total* (e.g. Pakistan, Israel, South Africa, India).
Scarce, but with some degree of substitutability at a higher cost level.	2. *Oil*	Several sellers; cartel OPEC, with outside followers. Large number of buyers.	Economic, political (e.g. EEC-Arab diplomacy).	Dependence mainly in terms of worsened terms of trade/balance of payments problems for non-oil producers. Price mechanism should allow for substitution possibilities. Political dependence remains limited (e.g. the Netherlands and the oil boycott).
Scarce, with a large black market.	3. *Military power*	Several sellers, grouped in blocks, competing against each other with a large black market. Relatively limited number of buyers. Buyers' market.	Economic (spare parts) and as a consequence political. Very costly to change.	Far more limited dependence than 1. There is always a seller from another block and a black market. Cost is however very high (Egypt).

Level of scarcity/ degree of substitutability	Product/element	Number of sellers	Dependence created	Comments
Kept scarce because of the possibility to develop 1.	4. *Nuclear energy*	Several sellers, some selling control agreement, but competing against each other. Several number of buyers.	Economic (spare parts, repair and servicing). Political (uranium supply) to avoid 1.	At the time of buying, dependence is limited, but total economic dependence afterwards in terms of spare parts, repairs and servicing. Political dependence remains limited however.
Scarcity is a function of the necessary imitation lag.	5. *New technology*	A few sellers, who will try to protect themselves from imitation through patenting or secrecy.	Economic (high price to be paid for buying unknown technology, restrictions in use, licence agreements, etc.).	The economic dependence is limited in time because of imitation possibilities, which will increase the number of sources of technology, decreasing its 'price'.
	6. *Non-fuel minerals*		*High buyer 'import' dependence.*	
(a) *Scarce and geographically concentrated*	– Gold (30 years)*	South Africa (58% of world production, 49% of world reserves).	) Economic (prices),) political.	Prices are influenced by political and monetary factors, and Russian sales. The fact that racism can be openly practised is full proof of the North's and South's political dependence.
	– Platinum (122 years for the group)*	South Africa (> 80% of world production and reserves).		

Level of scarcity/ degree of substitutability	Product/element	Number of sellers	Dependence created	Comments
	– Industrial diamonds (28 years)*	Zaire (74% of world reserves, 37% of world production).	Economic (prices), but De Beers Central Selling Organisation is the market controller. Political.	Zaire remains crucial to the Western World. Any 'unrest' (May 1978, Shaba) causes major price rises.
	– Cobalt (45 years)*	Zaire (> 80% of world production and reserves).	Economic (prices from $ 3/lb. in 1974 to $ 25/ lb. in 1979), but deep sea mining is an alternative. Political.	Idem.
	– Silver (18 years)*	Several sellers; Mexico (14%), Peru (11%), USA (11%) and Canada (12% of world production).	Low economic (prices extremely volatile, in 6 months from £4/troy ounce to £21 and back to £6 (1979-80) due to speculation).	Less geographic concentration and thus less possibility for keeping prices up.
	– Tungsten (47 years)*	China (47% of world reserves, 21% of world production).	Low economic (prices very volatile).	Chinese sales are destabilising.
	– Tantalum (66 years)*	Zaire (57% of world reserves, but only 4% of world production), Thailand (20%), Malaysia (13%), Canada (11%).	Low economic.	Less geographic concentration. International Association of Tantalum Ore Producers but with no influence on prices.

Level of scarcity/ degree of substitutability	Product/element	Number of sellers	Dependence created	Comments
(b) *Low level of scarcity or high substitutability, production geographically concentrated.*			*Low buyer 'import' dependence.*	
in South Africa	Chromium (340 years)*	South Africa (68% of world reserves, 34% of world production).	⎫	Developed countries (DCs) dependence remains low despite 100% import dependence for most DCs in these products. This is mainly because of the low level of scarcity and substitution possibilities.
	Manganese (190 years)*	South Africa (42% of world reserves, 24% of world production).	⎬ Low economic	
in LDCs	Niobium (952 years)* (columbium)	Brazil (70% of world production and reserves).	Low economic.	
	Tin (44 years)*	Large number of sellers, with Indonesia (12%), Malaysia (26%), Bolivia (14%), Thailand (12% of world production).	Low economic, because of substitution (aluminium) and US buffer stocks.	Despite the scarcity of the product and an International Tin Agreement since 1965, DC dependence remains low, because of US buffer stock influence on price.
in centrally planned economies	Vanadium (340 years)*	USSR (73% of world reserves, 31% of world production).	Low economic.	

Level of scarcity/ degree of substitutability	Product/element	Number of sellers	Dependence created	Comments
in developed countries	Cadmium (38 years)*			Substitution possibilities, low prices with oversupply.
	Lead (35 years)*			
	Potash (462 years)*	Primarily US, Canada and Australia.	Low economic.	
	Titanium (ilmenite) (131 years)*			
	Zinc (24 years)*			
	Zirconium (63 years)*		*Very low buyer import dependence some export dependence.*	
(c) *Low level of scarcity and no geographic concentration of production.*	Bauxite (311 years)*	Guinea has 31% of world reserves, but Australia has 30% of world production.	Low economic.	International Bauxite Association (1974) unsuccessful because of Australian opposition.
	Lithium (n.a.)*	Chile has 59% of world reserves, but US have 73% of world production.	Low economic.	

Level of scarcity/ degree of substitutability	Product/element	Number of sellers	Dependence created	Comments
	Phosphate (229 years)*	Morocco has 67% of world reserves, but US have 41% of world production.	Low economic.	US export cartel (Phosrock) controls 80% of world exports, despite LDCs World Phosphate Rock Institute.
	Titanium: rutile (350 years)*	Brazil has 74% of world reserves, but Australia has 85% of world production.	Low economic.	Substitution.
			High seller export dependence.	
(d) *Low level of scarcity, no geographical concentration and many sellers.*	Copper (63 years)*	Representing more than 50% of total export earnings: Zambia (96%), Zaire (67%), Chile (73%).	Economic (incidence of the price of copper on export earnings).	Though relatively scarce, no import dependence is created because of oversupply, and substitution possibilities. Prices fluctuate heavily. CIPEC a government organisation grouping. Most LDC producers aim at co-ordinating measures to raise copper earnings, but largely ineffective.
Scarce but not basic necessity products.	7. *Agricultural products*	*Many sellers* with no export diversification. (Sellers, with more than 50% of total export earnings).	*Sellers export dependency.*	*Typical oligopsony situations.*

Level of scarcity/ degree of substitutability	Product/element	Number of sellers	Dependence created	Comments
	Coffee	Burundi (88%) Uganda (73%) Rwanda (62%) Colombia (51%)	Buyer's market, with buyers having most of the commercialisation in hand.	Despite some similarity with mineral raw materials in terms of advanced countries' import dependence (very often 100%), only sellers export dependence is created, because of the 'oligopsony' market, and the nature of the products. Most of these products, including hard fibres, jute, rubber, and tea (and the two minerals tin and copper), are now covered by the Common Fund agreement (March 1979). International commodity agreements exist for some (sugar, cocoa, coffee) without much success however. Others which might be covered by UNCTAD's Integrated Programme for Commodities include bananas, meat, tropical timber, vegetable oils and oilseeds.
	Cocoa	Ghana (51%)	Economic dependence (very high price fluctuations, with important effects on export earnings).	
	Cotton	Chad (58%) Sudan (56%)		
	Sugar	Mauritius (88%) Reunion (86%) Fiji (76%) Cuba (75%)		
Scarce 'package' of capital, technology and entrepreneurship.	8. *Transnational corporations*	Large number of 'buyers'. Sellers interested in stable regimes (see e.g. their readiness to	Host-country dependence – economic (transfer-pricing, profit repatriation, etc.).	Nationalisation is possible when the mineral is scarce (e.g. oil). However, it offers no solution to technological dependence.

Level of scarcity/ degree of substitutability	Product/element	Number of sellers	Dependence created	Comments
		collaborate with socialist countries).	— political (stability of the regime). — cultural.	
Scarce 'package'.	9. *Technology transactions* a) 'packaged' technology (e.g. turnkey projects)	Small number of sellers and buyers.	Economic information dependence; lack of information might not lead to the best choice, or the lowest price. Less economic information dependence.	Bargaining.
Relatively scarce pieces of knowledge.	b) 'simple direct sales' technology transactions.	Many sellers.		
Scarce capital.	10 *Financial capital*	Large number of sellers.	Host-country dependence, in terms of future 'management' of the economy (IMF intervention, etc.).	If the world financial system breaks down, because of too high debts of LDCs, it will be mainly at the expense of Western banks and probably oil-rich nations. Financial dependency is therefore generally considered as less important.
	11 *Aid* — food aid — tied aid	Many 'donors', but far more needs.	Political dependence. — very often disruptive economically. — also economic dependence.	There are many examples of the importance of political dependency (Vietnam and Kampuchea, Bangladesh, Biafra, etc.).

* static reserves/production ratio

III   Technological Dependency: The Argument

The notion of technological dependency is intrinsically linked with the specific nature of technology as a 'public good' (the social cost resulting from the 'consumption' by an additional user is zero), which only acquires commercial value (exchange value) through appropriation. In a market economy, the latter is crucial in terms of the supply of technology. 'A firm will only invest in technology if it is assured of some degree of appropriation of the knowledge', furthermore, 'the less perfect the appropriation of the technology by the innovator, . . . the less the innovator will be prepared to invest in a new technology in comparison with the optimal level' (Cooper and Hoffman, 1978, p. 7).

This supply requirement has important restrictive consequences in terms of the demand for technology, its utilisation, and pricing; 'the very existence of a market for technology is a source of suboptimality' (*ibid.*, p. 8).

This suboptimality is at the basis of technological dependency which, in LDCs, is linked with the *private appropriation* aspect of technology.

> Certainly there is a use-value aspect of technological dependence. It is involved in the very little differentiation of technical skills in backward countries. But this is not the dominant one. The mechanisms of technological − and with it, commercial and financial − dependence are, in the last resort, means for the international redistribution of the economic surplus. And this redistribution depends upon the monopoly power conveyed by technological assets, that is, the exchange-value aspect of technology (Sercovitch, 1976, p. 2-3).

Given that most technology is developed and appropriate in the advanced countries, technology monopoly power is primarily *foreign* in LDCs. In addition,

> Those who control the generation and the mechanisms for appropriation of technological advantages have also the capacity to control their exploitation, wherever it may take place, either directly or through associates, or licensees, with or without ownership links. The control of foreign technology suppliers on decision-making concerning investment, production, management, and marketing in the context of concentrated and non-price patterns of rivalry make technological dependence a self-reinforcing phenomenon (*ibid.*, p. 5).

From there it is not difficult to put forward the 'permanent nature' of the technological dependency argument despite the possible dynamic externalities of imported technology.

> Foreign technology suppliers supply, together with their proprietary know-how, a protective umbrella against risk and uncertainties as well as education, under the form of certain types of skill formation. Though local entrepreneurs and personnel go through a learning process which

enhances their technical skills, in so far as this is not translated into a legal appropriation of what they learn and create and a change in business behaviour patterns, those gains are found to be recurrently lost in the long-run. So the process is characterized by a permanent dis-appropriation of externalities (*ibid.*, p. 6).

In other words, it is the lack of domestic private appropriation of the dynamic externalities of the imported technology, such as learning by doing, which leads to the permanence of technological dependency and closes the vicious circle.

It is rather difficult to understand some of the logic of the technological dependency argument, especially the last part. If some technical change cannot be appropriated, such as (by definition) learning by doing, that will only be to the advantage of society, the technology diffusing rapidly and being used in an optimal way. In other words, one can as well argue that the very nature of some of the externalities of imported technology — by not allowing private appropriation — will actually reduce technological dependency.

IV Technological Dependency: A Critique

Let us take a more systematic look at the major shortcomings of the technological dependency argument.

First, as for overall dependence, it is worth pointing out that technological dependency consists of a set of relationships far more complicated than simple dominance dependency. Inventive activity is no doubt extremely concentrated in the North, but one has to bear in mind that that concentration is primarily in six countries; the United States, the USSR, Japan, West Germany, France and the United Kingdom, which account for more than 80 per cent of total world R & D expenditures (Annerstedt, 1979a). In addition, it can be shown that, correctly measured (on the basis of inventive activity *manpower* data), the backward countries' world share is more or less in line with other socio-economic world inequality indicators (see Table 10.3).

Figures on higher education, which illustrate in a certain way the future potential[12] of LDCs in assimilating imported technology or developing indigenous technological capabilities, indicate that the world share of backward countries has been rising rapidly over the last fifteen years. Obviously one should not make much of these figures; quality variations, definitional problems, etc. make them highly unreliable. Nevertheless, the fact that a country like Sri Lanka has more scientists and engineers per million population than a number of advanced OECD countries (Soete, 1979) points to an underlying *scientific capability* in some backward countries which cannot be analysed in simple North-South dominance/ dependence terms. At the same time, in a large number of Northern countries, inventive activity is very peripheral, with some government

TABLE 10.3.   *Science and technology and socio-economic indicators for various regions, 1973*

	World total		OECD	Centrally planned economies	All other
Territory (000 km²)	135,830	100	23.6	18.7	57.7
Population (million)	3,860	100	19.1	10.0	70.9
Economic active population (million)	1,480	100	21.4	12.6	66.0
World exports (bn. US $)	576,710	100	70.8	10.0	19.2*
World manufacturing value added	n.a.	100	59.4	32.0	8.6*
GNP (at market prices, US $ bn.)	4,894	100	67.2	15.9	16.9
R & D expenditures (US $ bn.)	100.2	100	63.9	33.0	3.1
Researchers (000)	2,700	100	46.5	42.2	11.3
Higher education graduates (000)	4,740	100	53.7	21.8	24.5

* LDCs only

Source: OECD, 1979a, Annerstedt 1979b, UNIDO, 1979, UN Trade Yearbook, 1977.

supported research in a few areas. Industrial innovation is small and very often controlled by foreign firms, most new technology is imported. Not only is technological dependency something which cannot just be analysed along North/South dominance/dependency lines; it also does not seem closely related to economic dependency and economic exploitation. We would even like to put forward a more controversial argument: to be technologically dependent is not something to be particularly worried about; on the contrary, past experience suggests that technological *in*dependence is more worrying.

First, the fact that most Northern countries, from Spain to Japan, Sweden or West Germany, are technologically dependent is rarely emphasised. Part of the problem is how one measures or even defines technological dependency. Some Latin American *dependencia* writers have put forward the idea that 'total autarky would be the only state of the economy where technological dependence would not arise' (Cardettini, 1976, p. 3). That might seem a useful definition if one can throw the baby out with the bathwater and forget all about technological dependency, but unfortunately, it is incorrect. Even in an autarkic society technological dependency will be a major concern, to the extent that more sophisticated inventive neighbours might well decide one day to use their technological superiority in an expansive mood. History is filled with examples of what happens to technologically autarkic societies. China's recent swing is a case in point.

The most useful measure or definition starts from the notion that independence is linked with self-sufficiency, i.e. that there is a broad balance between imports and exports. Various balance measures have been used in empirical technological dependence-transfer of technology studies: net exports of machinery and transport equipment (SITC7); net exports of capital goods (SITC 7 − (consumer goods and electrical components) + SITC 69 and SITC 861); and more meaningful measures such as net exports of technology-intensive products (various definitions). However, none of these separates out payments (receipts) made for the technology component of the imports (exports) and none of them includes technology payments or receipts for investment transactions or other technology transfers.

Undoubtedly, the best measure of international technology flows consists of the balance of *technological* payments,[13] including payments and receipts for the use of patents, licences, knowhow, trademarks, copyrights, technical assistance, etc.. Technological independence might then be identified in terms of a positive balance of technological payments. This is still a long way from what one really needs − the export/import unit price for technology − but might nevertheless help us to arrive at some general observations in relation to international technology flows. In Table 10.4, technological balance-of-payments figures are given for the most important OECD countries. Of these countries only two, the United States and the United Kingdom, can more or less be considered as techno-

TABLE 10.4.   *Technological balance of payments for some OECD countries, 1975-9* (US $ millions)

		1975	1976	1977	1978	1979
Austria :	Receipts	13	20	22	28	
	Expenditure	84	86	103	118	
	Balance	-71	-66	-90	-90	
Belgium/Luxembourg (1) :						
	Receipts	97	105	131	145	
	Expenditure	180	195	246	288	
	Balance	-83	-90	-115	-142	
France (2) :						
	Receipts	192	194	277	346	
	Expenditure	514	585	546	679	
	Balance	-322	-389	-268	-333	
West Germany (3) :						
	Receipts	308	289	335	430	492
	Expenditure	720	693	816	964	1065
	Balance	-421	-404	-481	-534	-573
Italy (4) :	Receipts	72	80	122	103	
	Expenditure	384	321	422	498	
	Balance	-315	-241	-300	-396	
Netherlands :						
	Receipts	186	209	224	277	
	Expenditure	282	354	358	446	
	Balance	-96	-145	-134	-169	
Sweden :	Receipts	41	58	75	70	
	Expenditure	116	137	132	137	
	Balance	-75	-80	-57	-67	
United Kingdom (4) :						
	Receipts	491	602	632	744	
	Expenditure	483	478	518	625	
	Balance	+9	+124	+115	+119	

TABLE 10.4 *(continued)*

		1975	1976	1977	1978	1979
United States (5) :						
	Receipts	4008	4084	4474	5429	5804*
	Expenditure	473	482	434	607	706
	Balance	+3535	+3602	+4040	+4822	+5098
Japan (4) :	Receipts	142	175	204	281	321
	Expenditure	697	800	986	1169	1274
	Balance	-556	-625	-782	-888	-953

(1) Including film business. (2) Not including technical cooperation and studies. (3) Excluding copyrights, trademarks. (4) Excluding film business and copyrights. (5) Excluding film rentals but including management fees.

* estimated
Source: Vickery, 1980.

logically independent. Countries such as West Germany and Japan, often viewed as major innovators, run large deficits in terms of technological payments and receipts, and cannot be considered technologically independent.

Second, from the figures in Table 10.4, it also appears that to be technologically independent does not seem to be particularly beneficial for the countries concerned. Is it not paradoxical that precisely the two OECD countries which have enjoyed technological independence have the worst performance in terms of labour productivity, GNP and GDP growth rates in the whole OECD area over the last fifteen to twenty years? These countries were also the biggest R & D spenders, in terms of their R & D/GDP ratio (respectively 2.3 and 2.1 per cent in 1975), and were further characterised by a strong emphasis in government R & D spending on defence (practically 50 per cent of total government R & D expenditure), as such more directed towards basic science and research (OECD, 1979b). Thus there seems to be something fundamentally wrong about the economic advantages/disadvantages of being technologically independent/dependent.

That is the starting point for our second critique of the technology dependency argument: the serious underestimation of the benefits and dynamic spillover effects of imported technology or of so-called 'transfer' of technology. At a more theoretical level, it raises the question of the relevance of technology-public good considerations in an international environment with distinct macro-economic national interests and micro-economic private firm interests.

Our main point here is that within *international* boundaries there does not exist any reason for a high degree of conformity between the two.

Macro-economic national interests in the field of technology can best be defined in terms of creating and keeping a technological lead over rival nations. Similar to Schumpeter's view of *entrepreneurial* competition, one can identify international competition amongst *nations* as a continuous search for temporary monopoly positions, of which technology monopolies are not the only ones, but certainly the most clearly definable. Within such a Schumpeterian framework, it is obvious that these monopoly positions are the basis of higher wages of more generally higher incomes in the monopolist country. The monopoly position will however be continuously eroded by technology transfers. These are primarily to the advantage of the private firm, in terms of maximising *internationally* some of the technology monopoly rents. These will already be eroded at home by new entrants, and induce the firm to pay more attention to costs, by setting up production facilities near potential export markets (tariff-jump considerations) or investing in low-wage countries, or simply cashing in on the technology component (licensing, knowhow, etc.). However, behind this 'product life cycle' rationale lies the crucial fact that this international profit maximisation pattern may not necessarily be to the advantage of the innovative nation. As we have indicated elsewhere (Soete, 1978), within such a Schumpeterian product life cycle framework, the innovative country will be condemned to perpetual, continuous and rapid innovation if it wants to maintain its technological lead. More recently, Krugman (1979) has demonstrated formally how in an innovative North/non-innovative South world, where innovation takes the form of new products produced immediately in the North, but only after a lag in the South, new industries have to emerge continually in the North in order to maintain its living standard; the new industries will be declining and disappearing sooner or later in the face of low-wage competition from the South. This is because the North's higher wages reflect the rent on the North's monopoly of new technology. 'This monopoly is continually eroded by technological borrowing and must be maintained by constant innovation of new products. Like Alice and the Red Queen, the developed region must keep running to stay in the same place' (Krugman, 1979, p. 262). The conclusion of Krugman's analysis is obvious, but fascinating. While the North will be able to achieve some 'moving equilibrium' through a large enough rate of innovation in order to *maintain* its living standards, not just to grow, any slowing of innovation or acceleration of technology transfer will narrow the wage differential between North and South and might even lead to an absolute decline in living standards in the North. Perhaps the most interesting aspect of this model is, paradoxically, its set of simplistic and, from a traditional trade point of view, totally unrealistic assumptions.[14] Yet despite these simplifications, the conclusions which emerge are extremely powerful and very appealing, not least because, as Krugman observes, 'The picture of trade seems in some ways more like that of businessmen or economic historians than that of trade theorists' (Krugman, 1979, p. 265).

Turning back to Table 10.4, it might well be possible to explain the relative decline in economic performance of the United States and United Kingdom not only in terms of a decline in inventive and innovative activity, but also, and maybe primarily, in terms of increased international diffusion of their technology, and its increased transfer abroad. Kitti and Schiffel's (1978) data on foreign patenting in the United States and United States patenting abroad strongly support the idea of a rapidly increased international diffusion of technology, while Vernon and Davidson's (1979) evidence on transfer of technology by United States based multinationals points out 'that for individual new products, the interval between US introduction and first overseas production has rapidly been shrinking, a shrinkage which continued into the 1970's' (Vernon and Davidson, 1979, p. 4).

More generally, and in relation to our North/South discussion, two additional points have to be emphasised: that the costs of innovation have increased rapidly, and that firms will consequently be less willing to innovate at full costs; and that the sharply decreasing cost of information, in addition to increased diffusion (e.g. the South African A-bomb and United States satellite control) will make exclusion far more difficult. As we have shown elsewhere (Soete, 1978), this trend has led a number of firms to prefer to keep some of their innovations secret, instead of applying for a patent. This might well have aggravated the decline in industrial innovation, to the extent that *total* exclusion will obviously limit very drastically the use of and investment in technology.

It is not difficult to see where this argument leads. Instead of focussing on the limits, costs, and problems generally associated with international technology transactions, one should really emphasise far more than before the enormous benefits and advantages of a continuous and massive import of technology. While the latter increases technological dependency, it also illustrates the very limited usefulness of the concept.

Continuous and massive technological dependency is indeed the most direct (and least costly) way for backward countries to 'catch up' with the North. Why would a country like China, enjoying all the advantages of technological *independency* (as defined by Cardettini), suddenly opt for technological *dependency*, unless it were convinced of the crucial 'short-cut' value of technology imports on its long march to industrialisation? Why is it that within the rich industrialised countries (OECD) there are already some voices in favour of 'joint steps to restrain technology exports to the South' (Usui, 1979), if not that some Northern countries are worried about the combined effect of declining industrial innovation in the North and increased international diffusion to the South for the preservation of their living standards? Why then is most of the technological dependence literature only concerned with problems which might arise from technology transfer (from contractual restrictions to transfer pricing and inappropriateness), ignoring or even denying (see Sercovitch, quoted above), most of the beneficial aspects?

In our view this can be explained in terms of the micro-economic focus of much of the technology debate. Discussions on the 'free good' aspect, its appropriation and the implied market imperfections are no doubt very useful when discussing technology market issues, even at an international level, and might eventually lead to some macro-economic considerations about the international distribution of 'gains from technological advance' (see e.g. Cooper and Hoffman, 1978, p. 23). These remain however very vague and are limited to discussions about the direct 'transaction' gains, 'the sharing of the profit stream resulting from monopolisation between the seller and the buyer' (*ibid.*, p. 22). Not much is said about all the other, far more crucial, macro-economic aspects of technology transfer, including all sorts of dynamic spill-over and diffusion effects as well as improved terms of trade, etc.

No doubt these benefits are difficult to measure and it will take time and much empirical research to assess some of them. Research on technology is however not a very scarce good, if one is to believe the various bibliographies on transfer of technology and technological dependency. Let us hope that — even within *dependencia* thinking — more attention will be paid to the crucial role for developing countries of the international diffusion of technology on development 'shortcuts'.

Notes

1. Thus it is not touched on in the review of dependency by Gabriel Palma (Chapter 1 this volume).
2. Vaitsos, 1974, as the major contribution; for more recent work, see Murray, 1980.
3. On patents, see Vaitsos, 1973, Patel (ed.), 1974, and for the most recent UNCTAD proposals in relation to the revision of the Convention of Paris, UNCTAD, 1979. On trademarks, see O'Brien, 1976, and for recent contributions, Patel (ed.), 1979.
4. For a good summary, see Cooper and Hoffman, 1978.
5. Well summarised in the following:

   The result is that the scientific institutions are alienated from production activities or 'marginalised' because there is no demand for locally-developed technologies from the productive sectors. Consequently science in underdeveloped countries is largely a consumption item, whereas in industrialized countries it is an investment item. Furthermore, the lack of pressures on science from the local economy means that the main determinants of research orientation are the individual decisions of research workers; and these research workers take their lead from the international orientations of research. The scientific communities in the underdeveloped countries are outposts of advanced country science, with very limited links with the economic and social realities which surround them. There is no conspiracy or individual bad faith about this: it is simply the way the system works. (Cooper, 1973, p. 5-6).

6. See Chapter 2 this volume.
7. See Chapter 6 this volume.

8. As shown in Chichilnisky and Cole (1978), this analysis can be further extended to a proof that increased growth in the North with increased exports of the South will lead to lower growth in the South.
9. It is interesting to note that the importance of these income effects has been known for a long time and accepted by neo-classical trade writers such as Johnson, 1959.
10. See Chapter 1 this volume.
11. By scarce we mean that the price elasticity of demand is low in the medium term, and that at current prices there are few substitutes and/or limited supplies that can be economically extracted.
12. Despite possible shortcomings, see R. Dore's (1976) 'diploma disease' analysis.
13. There are various problems in comparing technological balance-of-payment figures across countries. For more detail, see OECD, 1977 and Vickery, 1980.
14. There are no differences in factor endowments because there is only one factor of production (labour); and all goods, old and new, are produced with the same cost function, leaving no room for differences in labour productivity. Neither neo-classical nor Ricardian trade explanations are relevant; there is no fixed pattern of trade, but trade is determined by a continuing process of innovation in the North and technology transfer to the South.

Bibliography

Annerstedt, J. (1979a), 'Indigenous R & D Capacities and International Diplomacy', in D. Ernst (ed.), *The New International Division of Labour, Technology and Underdevelopment*, Oxford, Pergamon Press.

Annerstedt, J. (1979b) and OECD (1979a), *A Survey of World Research and Development Effort*, Draft.

Cardettini, O. (1976), *Technological Dependency and Self-Reliance in Underdeveloped Countries*, Lima, STPI, mimeo.

Chichilnisky, G. (1978), *Terms of Trade and Domestic Distribution: Export-Led Growth with Abundant Labor*, Development Discussion Paper, No. 41, Harvard Institute for International Development, mimeo.

Chichilnisky, G. and Cole, H.S.D. (1978), *Growth of the North and Growth of the South: Some Results on Export Led Policies*, Development Discussion Paper, No. 42, Harvard Institute for International Development, mimeo.

Cooper, C. (1973), *Science, Technology and Development*, London, Frank Cass.

Cooper, C. and Hoffman, H.K. (1978), *Transactions in Technology and Implications for Developing Countries*, Science Policy Research Unit, University of Sussex, Brighton, mimeo.

Dore, R.P. (1976), *The Diploma Disease*, London, Allen and Unwin.

Johnson, H.G. (1959), *International Trade, Income Distribution and the Offer Curve*, Manchester School of Economic and Social Studies, Vol. 27.

Kitti, C. and Schiffel, D. (1978), 'Rates of Invention: International Patent Comparisons', *Research Policy*, Vol. 7, No. 4, pp. 324-41.

Krugman, P. (1979), 'A Model of Innovation, Technology Transfer and the World Distribution of Income', *The Journal of Political Economy*, Vol. 87, No. 2, pp. 253-66.

Merhav, M. (1969), *Technological Dependence, Monopoly and Growth*, London, Pergamon Press.

Monza, A. (1972), 'La teoria del cambio tecnologico y las economias dependientes', *Desarrolo Economico*, Vol. 12, No. 46, pp. 253-78.

Murray, R. (1980), *Intra-firm Trade and the Control of Transfer Pricing: Issues for the Third World*, Brighton, Harvester Press, forthcoming.

O'Brien, P. (1976), 'Trademarks in Developing Countries', *The Journal of Modern*

African Studies, Vol. 14, No. 2, pp. 297-310.

OECD (1977), *Data Concerning the Balance of Technological Payments in Certain OECD Member Countries: Statistical Data and Methodological Analysis*, DSTI/SPR/77.2, mimeo.

OECD (1979a), (See Annerstedt (1979b).)

OECD (1979b), *Science and Technology in the New Socio-Economic Conte t,* Committee for Scientific and Technological Policy, SPT(79), published OECD, 1980.

Oteiza, E. and Sercovitch, F. (1976), 'Collective Self-reliance:' Selected Issues', *International Social Science Journal*, Vol. 28, No. 4, pp. 664-71.

Patel, S.J. (1974), 'The Patent System and the Third World', *World Development*, Vol. 2, No. 9.

Patel, S.J. (1979), 'Trademarks in Developing Contries', *World Development*, Vol. 7, No. 7.

Prebisch, R. (1950), *The Economic Development of Latin America and its Principal Problems*, ECLA.

Prebisch, R. (1959), 'Commercial Policy in the Underdeveloped Countries', *American Economic Review, Papers and Proceedings*, Vol. 49, No. 2, pp. 251-73.

Rosenberg, N. (1976), *Perspectives on Technology*, Cambridge, Cambridge University Press.

dos Santos, T. (1970), 'The Structure of Dependence', *American Economic Review, Papers and Proceedings*, Vol. 60, No. 2, pp. 231-36.

Sercovitch, F. (1970), *Foreign Technology and Control in the Argentinian Industry*, University of Sussex, D.Phil. Thesis.

Sercovitch, F. (1976), 'Technological Dependence/Self-Reliance: Some General Remarks', Annex A to O. Cardettini, *op. cit.*

Soete, L. (1978), *Inventive Activity, Industrial Organisation and International Trade*, University of Sussex, D.Phil. Thesis.

Soete, L. (1979), *Technologie-Overdracht en Multi-nationale Ondernemingen, Tijdschrift voor Ontwikkelingssamenwerking*, Vol. 4, No. 2, pp. 18-34.

UNCTAD (1978), *Handbook of International Trade and Development Statistics*, Supplement 1977, New York.

UNCTAD (1979), *The International Patent System: The Revision of the Paris Convention for the Protection of Industrial Property*, TD/B/C.6/AC.3/2, Geneva, mimeo.

UNIDO (1979), *International Flows of Technology*, Document ID/Conf./3 for the Third General Conference of Unido.

Usui, M. (1979), *Development of the Third World and the Future of Advanced Industrial Countries*, SERC, University of Sussex, mimeo.

Vaitsos, C.V. (1973), 'Patents Revisited: Their function in Developing Countries', in C. Cooper (ed.), *Science, Technology and Development*, London, Frank Cass.

Vaitsos, C.V. (1974), *Inter-Country Income Distribution*, Oxford, Clarendon Press.

Vernon, R. and Davidson, W.H. (1979), *Foreign Production of Technology-Intensive Products by U.S.-Based Multinational Enterprises*, Graduate School of Business Administration, Harvard University Working Paper, mimeo.

Vickery, G. (1980), *Technological Payments in International Transactions: A Satisfactory Measure of the Output of R & D and of Technological Competitivity?* OECD Science and Technology Indicators Conference, Paris, mimeo.

Vitelli, G. (1979), *Imported Technology and Development of Local Skills*, Institute of Development Studies, University of Sussex, mimeo.

INDEX

141, 142-3, 144, 154, 156, 183-4,
205 n.14;
embargo, 138;
free, 21, 40, 79, 101, 122, 129;
terms of, 14, 52-6, 58, 63, 124-5,
128-30, 182-6;
theory of international, 20, 51, 56
See also exports; imports
trade unions, 14, 52, 54, 102, 106,
137, 138, 151, 156, 184
transnational corporations (TCNs),
14, 15, 17, 18, 47, 48, 60, 62, 63,
99, 101, 103, 119, 131, 136-7,
138, 140, 151, 155, 158, 160, 163,
165, 169, 170, 174, 176, 186, 194,
203
transnationalism, 59, 60, 98
transport:
in Nigeria, 114
Trinidad, 17, 100-8
Trotsky, Leon, 35, 66 n.22
Turkey, 15

underdevelopment, 14, 41, 42-50, 54,
59, 64, 81, 86, 97, 130-1
unemployment. *See* employment
unequal exchange:
theory of, 119-31
Union of Soviet Socialist Republics,
144, 148 n.25, 152, 197
unionisation. *See* trade unions
United Nations Industrial Development
Organisation (UNIDO), 151, 153, 156
United Nations Conference on Trade
and Development (UNCTAD), 125
United States, 14, 15, 16, 39, 60, 91,
93, 101, 104, 106, 137-8, 144, 148
n.25 and 29, 154, 162, 166 n.1,
186, 197, 199-201, 203
See also North America

Vaitsos, Constantine, 59
Vietnam, 91, 142
Villamil, José, 59
Vuscovic, Pedro, 58-9

wages, 23, 27, 34-5, 52, 54, 57, 80,
84, 87, 88, 93, 102, 125-9, 137,
138, 139, 140, 172, 173, 184, 202
wallerstein, Immanuel, 44, 45, 46, 119,
130-1
Weisskopf, Thomas E., 48
West Africa, 115, 116
West Germany, 18, 126, 154, 197, 201
Western Europe, 18, 22, 23, 24, 25,

26, 29, 31, 32, 33, 35, 36, 39, 145
Williams, J.R., 121, 125
working class, 17, 28, 34-5, 62, 99, 102,
106, 174
World War I, 28
World War II, 47, 60, 112, 114

Yugoslavia, 15

Zaire, 186
Zambia, 186